P9-DMV-277

HOW THE POLICE GENERATE FALSE CONFESSIONS

HOW THE POLICE GENERATE FALSE CONFESSIONS

An Inside Look at the Interrogation Room

James L. Trainum

ROWMAN & LITTLEFIELD
Lanham • Boulder • New York • London

BUNCOMBE COUNTY PUBLIC LIBRARIES

Published by Rowman & Littlefield
A wholly owned subsidiary of The Rowman & Littlefield Publishing Group, Inc.
4501 Forbes Boulevard, Suite 200, Lanham, Maryland 20706
www.rowman.com

Unit A, Whitacre Mews, 26-34 Stannary Street, London SE11 4AB

Copyright © 2016 by Rowman & Littlefield

All rights reserved. No part of this book may be reproduced in any form or by
any electronic or mechanical means, including information storage and retrieval
systems, without written permission from the publisher, except by a reviewer
who may quote passages in a review.

British Library Cataloguing in Publication Information Available

Library of Congress Cataloging-in-Publication Data

Name: Trainum, James L.
Title: How the police generate false confessions : An inside look at the interrogation room / James L.
    Trainum.
Description: Lanham : Rowman & Littlefield, 2016. | Includes bibliographical references and index.
ISBN 9781442244641 (cloth : alk. paper) | ISBN 9781442244658 (electronic)

™ The paper used in this publication meets the minimum requirements of
American National Standard for Information Sciences Permanence of Paper for
Printed Library Materials, ANSI/NISO Z39.48-1992.

Printed in the United States of America

Dedicated to the Norfolk Four, whose story I have used throughout this book and is, unfortunately, way too common an occurrence in the criminal justice system.

CONTENTS

ACKNOWLEDGMENTS

Having been a cop for twenty-seven years, I know that some of my colleagues will look upon this book as a betrayal of the thin blue line. It isn't. Every day there are more and more stories coming to light about wrongful convictions, many of which are the result of false confessions obtained during police interrogations. To prevent false confessions and other types of false statement evidence, you first have to understand how they happen. That is what I have hoped to shed light upon, and more importantly, to identify solutions that would help eliminate the problem, leading to better police work and more criminals in jail, which is what we all want.

Little if any of the material presented here is mine alone. I have taken full advantage of decades of past research, as well as the ongoing work of those in academia and all fields of the criminal justice system. I wish to express my deepest appreciation to the many persons who have taken the time and energy to advise me not only regarding this book but also in my evolution regarding the topic. I hope that through this book I have done justice to their work. All of us have the same goal as even the most critical of my law enforcement colleagues—ensuring that we get the right guy, but do it the right way.

I would especially like to thank Shawn Armbrust, Esq., Mid-Atlantic Innocence Project; Todd Barron, Royal Newfoundland Constabulary; Marissa Bluestone, Esq., Pennsylvania Innocence Project; Anita L. Boss, PsyD, Clinical & Forensic Consulting; Prof. Robert Cialdini, Arizona State University; Leah Colao, Marymount University Forensic Psychology student; Prof. Gary David, Bentley University; Gregory DeClue, PhD; Constance DeFranco, Marymount University; Ashley DeMarch, Marymount University Forensic Psychology student; Prof. Steve Drizin, Northwestern University School of Law; James Doyle, Esq., Bassil, Klovee & Budreau; Kelsey Foss, Marymount University Forensic Psychology student; Prof. Brandon Garrett, University of Virginia School of Law; Michael Garvey, director, Philadelphia Police Department, Office of Forensic Services; Andy Griffiths, PhD, IKAT Consulting; Honorable W. Louis Hennessy, District Court of Maryland; E. Desmond Hogan, Esq., Hogan, Lovells; John Holloway, Executive Director of the Quattrone Center for the Fair Administration of Justice; Pennsylvania Law School Prof. Saul Kassin, Williams College, Department of Psychology; George H. Kendall, Esq., Squire, Patton, Boggs; Mollie Kennedy, Marymount University Forensic Psychology student; Prof. Richard Leo, University of San Francisco School of Law; Sandra Levick, Esq., Public Defender Service for the District of Columbia; Prof. Mary Lindahl, Marymount University; Tom Lowenstein, Policy Director, Innocence Project New Orleans; Gregg McCrary, Behavioral Criminology International; Prof. Christian Meissner, Iowa State University, Department of Psychology; Peter Neufeld, Esq, Neufeld, Sheck & Brustin, LLP; Prof. Laura Nirider, Northwestern University School of Law; Marilyn B. Peterson, Marymount University Forensic Psychology student; Prof. Kim Rossmo, Texas State University; Donald P. Salzman, Esq., Skadden, Arps, Slate, Meagher & Flom, LLP; Barry Scheck, Esq., Neufeld, Scheck & Brustin, LLP; Jon Shapiro, Esq., Greenspun Shapiro, PC; Prof. Brent Snook, Memorial University in Newfoundland; and Deja Vishney, Esq., Wisconsin State Public Defenders.

I would like to thank the editors and staff at Rowman & Littlefield, whose edits and suggestions make me sound a lot smarter than I really am. And a special thanks to Associate Editor Kathryn Knigge. Not only did she propose the process, she offered encouragement and occasional hand holding.

Among many of the unnamed that I would like to thank are my critics and the attorneys who have subjected me to often brilliant cross-examination when testifying as an expert on interrogations and false confessions. Their arguments have helped me sharpen mine, or in some cases modify them.

And finally, thanks to my long-suffering wife, Diana Havlin. After warning me about how all consuming this project would be, she never once said "I told you so" as I rose very early, very often to try to meet deadlines. She did the initial edits for me, correcting my tenses and finishing my thoughts. I could not have done it without her.

INTRODUCTION

The day begins as always with the alarm going off at 6:00 am. Hit snooze twice, and avoid thinking about what will be facing you at work that Monday morning. No time for breakfast. Just some coffee in a travel mug and out the door.

But this Monday is a bit different. Two doors down, you see police cars in the driveway, police tape strung around the house. Something must have happened to the old man who lived there. You stand briefly on your front lawn, then walk over to speak to a neighbor standing on her front porch. "What happened?" you naturally ask. She is not sure. Just heard that the old man's daughter had not heard from him so she went over late last night to check on his welfare. Then the police came. Someone said there was a lot of blood.

"Would not surprise me if somebody had enough of the old man's crap and offed him," you comment. The old man was the neighborhood's pain in the ass. Always complaining, threating to file lawsuits, leaving obnoxious letters under car windshield wipers. You had had your share of run-ins with him, the latest being just last week. The old guy came out of his house, screaming like a maniac, only because your dog pissed on the curb in front of his house. It had already been a bad day for you, so you screamed back. Caused a bit of a ruckus; some of the neighbors came out to watch, but you walked away after you had your say and thought nothing more of it.

The commute to work was no worse than usual. Nor was the day. Arriving home, you let out the dog in the back yard and popped open a beer. The police cars and tape were gone, and the neighborhood looked normal again. Then, there is a knock on your door.

Two guys stand on the porch. Dressed in sport coats and ties, notebooks in hand. They identify themselves as detectives, explain they are investigating the "incident" that happened a couple of doors down. When you ask what happened, they say that an old man got hurt, and they are not quite sure how it happened. You comment that you had heard that there was a lot of blood. The detectives exchange glances, then say that they were talking to everyone in the neighborhood, taking statements, and would like your help in finding out what might have happened. "Sure," you say, "always glad to help the police." They ask you if you would come "downtown" with them. You pause, wondering why they could not talk to you at your home. But you want to be cooperative, so you say "yeah." And off you go.

What you didn't know is that there was no "incident"; the detectives knew exactly what had happened. The old man had been murdered, beaten to death in his living room by his front door. They thought it looked as if it probably happened when he opened the door in response to a visitor. And the detectives had been doing their job. Talking to neighbors. One had told them about your screaming match with the old guy. Another said they saw you out walking late last night . . . or was it the night before? A third neighbor never liked you anyway. For the detectives, a picture was beginning to form.

Then there was that comment you made about all that blood. How did you know about that? And you were just being so cooperative. Didn't even ask why they wanted you to come downtown. Maybe you are being too cooperative?

At the police station, the detectives escort you in a small, windowless room, with three chairs and a table. They ask you if you wouldn't mind waiting for them for a few minutes while they get some stuff together. "No problem," you say. "Take your time."

You wait a lot longer than a few minutes, but you don't mind. This is actually kind of exciting, being in the middle of a police investigation. The room you are in looks just like those on TV. This will be something to talk about in the office tomorrow.

The two detectives return, shutting the door behind them. You don't know it, but a nightmare is about to begin. Never in your wildest dreams would you ever have thought you would become what you now are—the primary suspect in a murder investigation.

This is not as far-fetched as it sounds. Innocent people get caught up in police investigations all the time. It's a normal part of the process. Criminal investigations can be messy. Clues don't come in all at the same time. Investigators must sort the wheat from the chaff, determine what is relevant and what is not, and then try to make sense of it all. In the meantime, new information is coming in, the bosses want the case closed, and the lab just said it will take at least six weeks for the DNA results to come back. Working under pressure, with incomplete information, mistakes are made.

Mistakes can be identified and corrected, and in criminal investigations they usually are. But way too often, tunnel vision, that mindset that causes one to focus on what they believe to be the truth and ignore any evidence to the contrary, prevents the correction. Mistake plus tunnel vision begets more mistakes, which can have terrible consequences.

The first step to obtaining a false confession is mistakenly identifying an innocent person as a suspect. The second is interrogating them. "Bull," you are probably saying to yourself right now. Short of actual torture, something that went out of use with the abolishment of the "third degree," you would never confess to something you did not do, much less a murder.

When sitting in judgment of others, we tend to project what we think we would do in a given situation. Because most people believe that they would never confess to a crime they did not do, they don't see how that is possible in others. Because of this, law enforcement considers confessions to be the "queen of proofs."[1] For a prosecutor, it represents a "slam dunk," probably leading to a guilty plea. For the cops, it is the end of the investigation. For the jury, it is all they need to hear. Even when overwhelming exculpatory evidence, including DNA evidence, exists, a confession often trumps everything else. Yet as we see more and more in the media, false confessions do happen.

But again, getting back to you. Is it possible that you would admit to something you didn't do? Have you ever taken responsibility for something, even though it wasn't your fault, just to deescalate a situation? Maybe some minor situation at work, where the boss just wanted an "admission" so the company could just "put this behind them." Or have you paid a speeding or parking ticket, knowing that you are innocent of the offense but not able to afford to take the time off work to go to court to fight it? Both are false confessions, and as you will see, both are the result of some of the same dynamics that can lead to someone falsely confessing to a more serious crime.

That is exactly what happened to Danial Williams, who, in 1997, confessed to a brutal gang rape and murder for which he was convicted and sentenced to life in prison. In 2007, I was asked by Williams and his codefendant's attorneys to review the case. His unfortunate odyssey is also chronicled in Tom Well's and Richard Leo's book *The Wrong Guys*,[2] and on the website that documents the investigation.[3]

When the murder occurred, Danial was a twenty-five-year old six-year veteran of the US Navy who had enlisted upon graduation from high school. His supervisors respected him. He never made trouble in school and had been raised by his parents to respect law enforcement personnel. At the time of the murder, Danial was a newlywed caring for his wife who had terminal ovarian cancer. He was not your stereotypical murder suspect, and definitely not someone you would think would be insane enough to confess to a crime of such magnitude unless he was guilty.

But confess he did. Danial admitted to the police that he knew that his neighbor, nineteen-year-old Michelle Bosko, was alone in her house. Her husband, also a sailor, was deployed out to sea. On the night of the murder, according to Danial's confession, he left his sleeping wife and knocked on Michelle's door. When she refused to open it, he broke it down with a hammer. Danial stated that he attacked Michelle, dragged her back to her bedroom, raped her, and beat her to death with a shoe, afterward returning to his still sleeping wife.

With Danial's confession and subsequent arrest, the police were able to close a particularly horrific crime in less than forty-eight hours. Except, there were more than a few discrepancies between Danial's confession and the crime scene. Contrary to his statement, there were no signs of forced entry into the apartment, and Michelle had been stabbed to death, not beaten. But the police knew from experience that suspects often provide incorrect details in their confessions, usually in an effort to minimize their own involvement or to protect someone else. And since Danial provided many correct details (those that "only the true killer could have known"), the police overlooked the contradictions.

Soon after Danial confessed and was subsequently charged with the crime, the police discovered they had a slight problem. The DNA in the semen found on Michelle's body did not belong to Danial! The police took that in stride, alleging that Danial was simply trying to protect someone else. And, the police said, that someone was Joseph Dick, a sailor who shared the apartment with Danial and his wife. Upon questioning, Joseph confessed his involvement to the police, saying that he and Danial raped and killed Michelle together. All was good until the laboratory reported that the DNA from the crime scene did not match Joseph either. So the police amended their theory once again: Joseph must have been protecting someone as well.

In the end, the police ended up charging seven sailors with the gang rape and murder of Michelle Bosko. A total of four confessed, with the details of each confession wildly different from not only the others but also from the crime scene evidence. Two of those who confessed agreed to plead guilty and testify against the others. All of those who had confessed to the crime were convicted—the three who did not had the charges dismissed, although the police continued to consider them guilty participants in the murder.

But the DNA from the crime scene matched none of the seven. So obviously the police were missing someone. That someone turned out to be Omar Ballard.

Omar's DNA matched the semen found on Michelle's body. The police had come across Omar's name early in the murder investigation. He was a friend of Michelle and her husband, had been to their apartment on several occasions, and was the suspect in a sexual assault on another woman in the same apartment complex. Omar was forgotten once Danial confessed, but his name surfaced again when he bragged in a letter to a girlfriend that he was the one who had killed Michelle. When questioned by the police, Omar admitted to the rape/murder, and, unlike the four sailors, was able to provide numerous details that were consistent with what the police knew about the crime scene. When asked if he knew the others who had been charged with the crime, Omar said that he did not, calling Danial and the three others who confessed "fools."

The case of the Norfolk Four is not an anomaly. With the advent of DNA technology, more and more false confessions are coming to light— many of which were given by ordinary people who would never have thought that they were capable of such a thing.

So how could this happen, especially in a society that many say coddles the criminal element rather than pursues too harshly? Suspected criminals have rights: All must be read their Miranda rights and agree to talk to the police without an attorney present before any questioning can begin. Confessions that a judge determines were obtained through coercion, even nonphysical coercion, are thrown out of court. There are numerous checks and balances in place to prevent the innocent from being wrongfully convicted. Surely, some people say, false confessions must be an extremely rare phenomena.

In the following chapters, we will explore these questions and more. We will look at the past and see what drove the advent of modern police interrogation tactics. Do these tactics, as some claim, eliminate false confessions, or are these confessions more widespread than we currently believe? Does current police training actually contribute to innocent people being identified as suspects and being subjected to police interrogations? What is it that the police do that convinces a guilty suspect that it is a good idea to confess, and could those tactics work on innocent suspects? And why do most confirmed false confessions contain numerous details that should have only been known to the real perpetrator?

We will examine the claims that modern police training may not only induce an innocent person to confess but may also adversely impact the reliability of information that the police obtain from victims, witnesses, and even informants. And are the police the only ones responsible for false confessions? What role might the prosecutor, judges, and even defense attorneys play in convincing the innocent to confess?

Finally, we will examine what is being done today in the law enforcement industry to prevent not only false confessions but also false or unreliable statements from witnesses, victims, and informants. We will see not only the safeguards that are being recommended and often implemented but also how some law enforcement agencies are using totally new ways to interrogate suspects.

Throughout this book, we will be using what happened to Danial Williams and his codefendants, along with other case studies, to highlight the issues surrounding police interrogations and false confessions. Some of the cases that we will discuss have ended in the exoneration of the suspect. Others have not but are used as examples of problematic tactics and confessions. The Norfolk Four case is what many consider to be the "perfect storm." It encompasses just about everything that can go wrong with a police interrogation and investigation—including the final outcome. In spite of the overwhelming evidence of their innocence, including Omar Ballard's admission that he acted alone, his DNA being the only DNA found on the crime scene, and the lead interrogator's history of obtaining false confessions and own conviction of corruption, the four sailors have not been exonerated. One has been released from prison, having served his full term. The others are out, granted conditional parole by a governor who, though admitting the existence of the evidence pointing to their innocence, does not feel that he can grant a full exoneration because they "confessed." It is true—the power of a confession can trump all reason.

I

HISTORY

It was the fall of 1666 in London, England. An uncontrollable inferno had left untold numbers dead and thousands more homeless after it raged through the town. The fire burned out of control for days on end. Rumors of arson or a terrorist-inspired attack spread. The authorities were hard-pressed to solve the arson, but solve it they did when a suspect confessed. Robert Hubert admitted that he, along with twenty-three other conspirators, started the fire by firebombing a local bakery. Hubert was tried, convicted, and executed based on his confession.[1]

Seems simple enough, right? Open and shut case. The problem is that Hubert's confession to the arson that resulted in the burning of London in 1666 was false. Not only did Hubert's physical condition render him incapable of the actions he said he took to start the fire and that it was later proven that he was not even in the country at the time, the fire was also determined to have been an accident. And like Danial Williams's confession to the murder of Michelle Bosko, Hubert's confession was rife with details that did not match the facts.

Thus, we know that the phenomenon of false confessions is not new. The Salem Witch Trials is an often-pointed-to example of a historic incident of this type. We tend to think that false confessions were probably much more common in the past than today, mostly because we believe that torture was the go-to investigative tool of our ancestors. In our minds, the current criminal justice and courts system have progressed over time from trial by ordeal to the use of court-sanctioned torture (i.e., the Inquisition) to the not-so-secret "third degree" applied by the police and finally to the "scientific" methods we use today.

In this chapter, we are going to briefly explore what turns out to be some misconceptions about how our distant (and not so distant) ancestors attempted to ascertain the truth in criminal investigations. And since the American criminal justice system is based primarily on a combination of Judeo-Christian and Western cultures, this general history will focus on those two lenses. We will examine the framework under which torture was used and safeguards that were sometimes put in place to prevent false confessions. We will see that those living in historical times did not always have the same view as to the value of confession evidence that we do today. And we will learn that our new scientific methods are not that new, nor all that scientific.

DIFFERENT TYPES OF TORTURE

Before we get too far in, we need to understand the difference between common, ordinary torture and judicial torture. John H. Langbein, in his book *Torture and the Law of Proof*, defines *judicial torture* as "the physical coercion by the state to gather information, usually a confession, to further an investigation or for a judicial proceeding." There were rules as to its application.[2] Torture as a form of punishment or execution, such as burning at the stake or crucifixion, is a totally separate matter that is beyond the scope of this book.

BIBLICAL TIMES

As eras of history go, the period covered by the Old Testament was a pretty rough-and-tumble time. But from all of the wars, murders, plagues, and forced enslavement came laws that were remarkably enlightened when it came to confessions and the rights of the accused. Aaron Kirschenbaum says in his book *Self-Incrimination in Jewish Law* that "torture as a method of investigation is virtually unheard of in Jewish history." This is because, under Jewish Talmudic law, any confession, even one given voluntarily, was not admissible as evidence in a criminal case. This not only removed the incentive to torture but also the stigma that naturally attaches to a defendant if they choose not to make a statement on their own behalf.[3]

ROMAN TIMES

Early in Rome's history, judicial officials had no problems torturing witnesses or suspects to obtain information or confessions as long as those subjects were slaves. Free men and women were exempt from torture. Even so, Romans were aware of its dangers when it came to inducing false witness statements and confessions. Caesar Augustus, Rome's emperor from 27 BC to AD 14, warned against using torture too soon in an investigation, saying that its use should be used only in cases in which the suspect is "so close to being proved [guilty] by other evidence" that the confession "appears to be the only thing lacking."[4] Later emperors acknowledged that some "have so little endurance that they would rather tell any kind of lie than suffer torture."[5]

Later, Rome expanded the use of torture to extract information and confessions to include its use on freemen. In their book *Confessions of Guilt: From Torture to Miranda and Beyond*, George Thomas and Richard Leo theorize that historically, the increased reliance on torture by governments often coincides with an increase in what the government perceives are threats from outside or within. During the second century, the same time that Rome not only increased its use of torture in general but also began applying it to persons other than slaves, the empire was expanding "and [had] accumulated more enemies, which made it more vulnerable."[6] This is a pattern that is often repeated in history to this day.

THE REST OF THE WESTERN WORLD

For most of the rest of the Western world, judicial torture was unnecessary because one did not have to rely solely on witness statements or torture-induced confessions to get to the truth. God would reveal the truth for them by personally intervening through trial by combat or trial by ordeal. In trial by combat, the accuser and the accused would literally battle it out (or hire others in their place), allowing God to grant victory to the innocent. In trial by ordeal, the suspect was forced to perform some task, such as grabbing hold of a hot iron, plunging their hand into boiling water, or being thrown into a body of water. The interpretation of what the outcome of the ordeal revealed varied. Sometimes if the suspect sustained no injuries, or floated, they were innocent. Other times, if the suspect's injuries healed properly within a set period of time, or they sank, they were innocent. The clergy were an important part of the trials, especially the trials by ordeal, as they were the ones responsible for the correct interpretation of the outcome. [7]

The trials, especially trials by ordeal, were usually ordered in cases in which there was doubt about the suspect's guilt, such as if there were no witnesses to the crime, there were multiple possible suspects, or the suspect did not wish to confess. Even in cases in which there was little doubt as to the suspect's guilt, a trial may have been ordered, as that would put the responsibility for passing judgment onto God's shoulders and not man's. [8]

The mere threat of an ordeal, a form of judicial torture, was sometimes enough to resolve the issue. If the suspect confessed to avoid the ordeal, then they were considered to have brought judgment upon themselves. [9]

If the suspect was someone of high social status, they could be given the opportunity to clear themselves of any suspicion of wrongdoing by taking an oath during which they swore to their innocence. Such oaths were required to be taken on a holy relic to increase their reliability. [10]

Around the turn of the thirteenth century, scholars and others in the church began to question the validity of the trials. Some pointed out that there was nothing in the Scriptures or other church documents that supported the trials. Others questioned why, if trial by combat was supposed to be infallible, often both combatants would hire seasoned warriors to take their place. There were also cases in which suspects had been hanged based on trial by ordeal and it was later discovered that the crime of which they had been accused had not even occurred. [11] Some authorities were frustrated with the fact that God showed mercy to obviously guilty suspects, allowing some through their ordeal unscathed. [12] These frustrations contributed to the Church withdrawing support for the trials. So without the required participation of the clergy, a new system was needed.

Two such systems were devised: an inquisitorial system and an accusatorial system. The inquisitorial system took root in Continental Europe and the accusatorial system in England. The accusatorial system has had the most impact on the criminal justice system in the United States, but the inquisitorial system has some points of interest, especially when it comes to dealing with confessions and the use of judicial torture, something that never really caught on in Europe to the same extent as in England.

INQUISITORIAL SYSTEM

In general, with the inquisitorial system, the judge is actively involved in the investigation of the crime. In the search for the truth, it was the judge who could summon and interrogate witnesses as well as suspects in order to determine guilt or innocence. However, when it came to convicting someone of a crime that called for a "blood punishment" (execution or mutilation), the judge faced two huge hurdles, one personal and one procedural.

The personal hurdle was the judge's everlasting salvation. If the judge who sentenced someone to death and/or mutilation had any doubt as to their guilt, they had committed a mortal sin. [13] The level of proof had to make the suspect's guilt "as clear as the light of the midday sun." [14] The procedural hurdle, which helped to alleviate the personal one, required that in order to convict someone who would be subjected to blood punishment two "unimpeachably trustworthy eyewitnesses" [15] must testify to the suspect's guilt. If such "full proof" was lacking, such as only one eyewitness was available, then both hurdles could be conquered if the suspect confessed. This opened the way for the suspect to be subjected to judicial torture.

The decision to subject someone to judicial torture was not one that was made lightly. It was only to be used as a last resort, and only after the investigation had determined that a crime had actually been committed. And as mentioned above, the judges first had to determine that sufficient evidence (via the two trustworthy eyewitnesses) existed to lead a reasonable person to believe that the suspect committed that crime.

Judges faced several restrictions in carrying out their duties. Some people, such as those of "high status," may be exempt from the torture procedures. Other who were exemptions included pregnant women, young children, and the old or sick if it was determined that torture might lead to their death. The actual torture had to be supervised by the judge who ordered it, and it was forbidden to take place on Sundays.[16]

The suspect was given several chances to confess before they actually underwent torture. They were first threatened with torture as an inevitable consequence if they failed to confess. If that did not work, they were taken to the torture chamber and shown the instruments that were going to be used on them. Next, the manner in which the instruments would be used was explained to the suspect in great detail. Only then, if they continued to resist, would they undergo torture.[17]

Nicholas Eymerich, the Grand Inquisitor of Aragon, developed a "torture guide," called the *Directorium Inquistorium*, full of useful suggestions on how to obtain confessions. Before resorting to torture, he would undertake to persuade the suspect to confess, using an approach that, as you will see, could have been taken out of almost any interrogation manual or training class in the United States. Eymerich wrote that

> the inquisitor should behave in a friendly manner and act as though he already knows the whole story. He should glance at his papers and say "it's quite clear you are not telling the truth," or pick up a document and look surprised saying "How can you talk to me like this when what I've got written down contradicts everything you told me?" He should then continue: "Just confess—you can see that I know the whole story already."[18]

The inquisitorial courts were well aware of the danger of a suspect falsely confessing because of the mere threat of torture. This was the last thing that they wanted, as convicting and executing an innocent man would wreak havoc on the judge's chance at eternal salvation. Safeguards were put into place to try to prevent this. When questioning the suspect, the judges were not allowed to use any form of suggestive questioning. Such questioning could provide the suspect with details about the crime that only the true perpetrator would have known, thus calling into doubt the reliability of the confession.[19] We will see in later chapters how even today the "contamination" of a confession through the use of leading questions is a huge problem.

Another safeguard was the requirement of some courts that the information given by the suspect during their confession be verified to further ensure its reliability. However, this was not a universal practice.

As a procedural matter, any information obtained by torture or threat of torture was considered to be involuntary, and thereby inadmissible in court. In order for the confession to be used as evidence, the suspect had to repeat it in court, thus making it "voluntary." If the suspect refused, they would simply be taken back to the torture chamber until they came to their senses. In chapter 11, you will see parallels between this environment and with the plea bargaining process in the United States.

Over the centuries, much of Europe maintained the major components of the inquisitorial system; however, the use of judicial torture did not survive.

Now we are going to England, where they developed a quite different system that eventually led to the way we investigate and interrogate in the United States today.

ACCUSATORIAL SYSTEM

In England, they decided to go another route, mainly because of a system that they had in place as part of trials by ordeal. Rather than wait for the victim or the victim's family to accuse a suspect in cases of theft, robbery, and murder, and to prevent them from taking justice in their own hands, England established the "jury of presentment." If the jury decided that there was enough evidence to suspect that the accused committed the crime, then they underwent trial by ordeal. Once the trial by ordeal was abolished, it was an easy move for judges to accept the findings of the jury as the final deposition of the case.[20] Called the accusatorial system, it differed from the inquisitorial system in a couple of ways. One is that the judge acted as a referee. It was the prosecutor who questioned the witnesses and suspects in the presence of a jury in order to establish the suspect's guilt. The suspect could mount a defense, and if the jury had doubts, they could acquit. Which leads us to the second difference. The accusatorial system was not designed to determine the truth per se, but to determine if sufficient evidence existed to prove that a suspect committed a crime. This gradually developed into the present-day system that was exported to the United States.

Though torture did take place in the English judicial system, it was nowhere near as ramped up as in Europe. It was mainly used procedurally in the event that the accused refused to plead either guilty or innocent when first brought before the judge. This caused a quandary, because if they refused to plead one or the other, then the case could not proceed. A guilty plea, of course, allowed the judge to then pass sentence. A not-guilty plea led to a trial by jury. No plea, no resolution, and every case had to be resolved.[21]

The torture undergone by the accused in these scenarios was of such a nature that it could eventually lead to his death. One such means of torture was known as "pressing." The accused would be bound to the floor on his back with weights placed on his chest. More and more weight would gradually be added, increasing the difficulty of the accused to draw breath. Once the accused agreed to enter a plea, then they were released. Otherwise they died.

Since torture methods such as pressing were not being used to obtain a confession but simply to get the suspect to enter a guilty or not-guilty plea, what would be the reason for someone to refuse to enter a plea and thus subject themselves to torture? If the accused was a man of substance, a guilty plea or conviction would have in some cases resulted in his property being forfeited to the government. If he died while being pressed, or via some other means of torture designed to induce them to plea, they died without being convicted, and their property remained with their heirs.[22]

Judicial torture for the purpose of obtaining information for use at trial did occur, but it was relatively rare. For this to occur, a torture warrant was issued naming the crime and the method of torture to be used. The large majority of times it was used on political (including religious) offenders, mainly to uncover the identity of their associates and the details of ongoing plots.

It is believed that one of the reasons that judicial torture didn't catch on in England as it did in Europe was because in England, legal professionals were not bound to the "two witnesses or a confession" rule to obtain convictions. Other, circumstantial, evidence could be considered. Absolute proof of guilt was not required to obtain a conviction, thus rendering confessions less important. Judicial torture as a tool of justice gradually disappeared; the last record of its use in the investigation of a criminal case occurred in 1597.[23]

QUESTIONABLE CONFESSIONS

An interesting development occurred in the decades following the abolishment of judicial torture in England. Confessions, usually considered to be the "queen of proofs" when it came to confirming a suspect's guilt, began to lose its luster in the eyes of the court and juries. Judges would still accept confessions made directly to them through guilty pleas, but the reliability and voluntariness of confessions made to others outside of their presence were viewed more critically. In their book *Confessions of Guilt: From Torture to Miranda and Beyond*, George Thomas and Richard Leo list several cases in which confessions led a jury to render a "not guilty" verdict because there was evidence that they had been coerced or had been promised leniency of some sort. In one case that occurred in 1686, a man accused his maid of stealing a guinea (coin) from him. The man dragged the maid before the justice of the peace to whom she confessed the theft, saying that she stole the money to pay off a debt. When the maid appeared in court for trial, she recanted the confession and was acquitted. To the justice of the peace, the confession was considered invalid because it was "looked upon as the effects of Fear."[24]

As time passed, judges began suppressing confessions that they believed might have been coerced, not even allowing them to come before the jury. Judges during that time appeared to have had a more enlightened view of human nature, taking the position that it might be possible that one would confess to a crime that they did not commit even if they were not tortured or mentally ill. By 1778, Sir William Blackstone, the most widely read legal scholar in England, condemned confessions as being "the weakest and most suspicious of all testimony."[25] Thomas Leach, another prominent legal mind, wrote in 1784:

> The human mind, under the pressure of calamity is easily seduced, and is liable, in the alarm of danger, to acknowledge indiscriminately a falsehood or a truth, as different agitations may prevail. A confession, therefore, whether made upon an official examination or in discourse with private persons, which is obtained from a defendant, either by the flattery of hope, or by the impressions of fear, however slightly the emotions may be impacted, is not admissible evidence; for the law will not suffer a prisoner to be made the deluded instrument of his own convictions.[26]

Justices of the peace were told that in order for confessions to be admitted, they had to be shown to be voluntary. To try to meet the threshold of proven voluntariness, the justices began to warn suspects brought before them that they did not have to answer any questions. Thus was the humble beginnings of what much later became the English "cautions" and in the United States the Miranda warnings. However, these early warnings initially did not prove to be sufficient. In many cases, the warnings were not enough, and in fact they were thought by some to be coercive in and of themselves. As time passed, the pendulum began to swing the other way. The warnings were refined, and judges began to relax their restrictions on what they considered to be coercive.[27] It was about this time that the first police force came into being in England, and the responsibility for investigating crimes and interrogating suspects shifted to the police.

INTERROGATIONS AND CONFESSIONS IN EARLY AMERICA

With that background, it is time to shift our attention to the history of interrogations and confessions in America. The English principles followed the first colonists over, and the two systems of law evolved in close tandem for years. Like England, what was to become the United States did not adopt judicial torture, and like England, the courts had concerns about confession evidence. A Vermont court quoted an English scholar in one ruling, saying, "A confession must never be received in evidence, where the defendant has been influenced by any threats or promise."[28] However, in addition to concerns about the voluntariness of the confession, there was an increased concern regarding reliability. Several of the states required that the confession evidence be corroborated before it could be accepted by the courts, some even requiring corroboration even when the confession was totally voluntary. Confessions that could not be corroborated were called "naked confessions."

THE POLICE TAKE OVER

In the early days of the United States, justices of the peace or magistrates were the ones primarily responsible for the questioning of suspects. This began to change in the early 1800s with the rise of cities and the creation of organized police departments, the first in Boston in 1838, followed by New York City in 1845. By the 1880s all major cities had municipal police forces in place.[29] Unfortunately, for many reasons, many of these police departments became "notoriously corrupt and fragrantly brutal."[30] One reason for this was that it was considered the best response to an increase in crime. Civil unrest was on the rise. Between 1904 and 1907, the murder rate across the country tripled, and then increased again by 50 percent by 1919.[31] The implementation of Prohibition brought with it organized crime and additional police corruption.

The increase in crime had, back then, the same effect on the elected officials and the public as it does when crime increases today. Wars on crime generally lead to a harder stance on the rights of the individual and an increased tolerance by the general public for the use of "drastic" measures. Bit by bit, the various protections against involuntary and false confessions were removed, the primary one being the loss of long-held skepticism toward the reliability of coerced or uncorroborated confessions.

As time went on, and the courts became more permissive about coercion in the interrogation room, they also gave investigators another tool for their interrogation toolbox—the use of deception. In the 1920s and 1930s, the courts began to rule that the use of trickery, such as the investigators telling the suspect that his cohort had accused him of the crime even though he had not, was permissible. Basically the courts said that such trickery was fine as long as it was not "calculated to procure an untrue statement."[32]

The questioning of suspects by magistrates, what was mostly a public affair, had now become a private affair conducted outside of the public's view by investigators in police interrogation rooms. Investigators conducting interrogations were expected to solve crimes, and they had been given a great deal of leeway by the courts, the public, and the politicians as to the tactics they could use. In addition, another issue emerged that caused concern among those who were uneasy with this trend. In the late 1800s, prominent legal scholar Simon Green spoke out about the problem of investigators being so zealous in their pursuit to solve crimes, especially in egregious cases, that they would "rely on slight grounds of suspicion, which are exaggerated into sufficient proof."[33] What Green described is what is now called tunnel vision, a condition in which investigators become so fixated on a specific suspect, often based on minimal evidence, to the point that they ignore all evidence pointing to that suspect's innocence or the guilt of other suspects. It is one of, if not the, leading factor behind false confessions and wrongful convictions.

So it was under these conditions that law enforcement, with a not-so-discreet nod from the rest of the criminal justice system, turned to the widespread use of "the third degree."

THE THIRD DEGREE

Simply put, the third degree was the use of extreme coercive interrogation tactics used by an investigator to obtain a confession from a suspect, or a statement from an uncooperative witness. The only limits were the imagination of the investigator.

It is not known when the practice began or when it became widespread. Not even the origin of the name has been accurately determined. Some have attributed it to a take on the name of the rituals of the Freemasons. The Third Degree was a level of the highest order within the group. To reach it, members had to undergo extreme and grueling initiation rites, the secrets of which must never be revealed.[34] But then Thomas Byrnes, a famous New York police inspector from the late 1880s, well known for his brutal interrogation tactics, took credit for the name. Some say that it was a play on his last name as a third-degree burn (Byrnes) as the most severe burn one can receive.[35] A tamer explanation is that it was only the third step in the arrest process, the first two being arrest and transportation to the police station, and the third being the interrogation.

Documented third-degree tactics range from psychological coercion to physical threats, and go all the way to beatings and extreme torture. The suspect may be kept in isolation for long periods of time, forced to undergo hours of interrogation by multiple interrogators working in relays, or subjected to the famous "Mutt and Jeff" routine, otherwise known as "good cop/bad cop." In that scenario, one investigator is the aggressor, yelling, threatening, and/or physically beating the suspect. The other, the "good guy," intervenes, but can only keep the bad cop at bay if the suspect confesses.

"Sweat boxes" were a common tactic used in third-degree interrogations. These were rooms that were intentionally made either freezing cold or extremely hot where the suspect was kept for hours, or even days. The name itself is carried over into modern police lingo. The interrogation room is often called *the box* and the interrogation process is sometimes referred to as "sweating" the suspect.

Other tactics included beating the suspect with fists, rubber hoses, or phone books, the application of electrical shocks, waterboarding, and mock executions. Reporter Emanuel Lavine who, in the 1930s, was allowed to view interrogations conducted by the New York Police Department, documented his experiences in his book *The Third Degree*.[36] The book includes a case in which a resistant suspect was taken to a cooperative dentist. In a scene right out of the 1976 movie *Marathon Man*[37] featuring a Nazi dentist who used his skills to torture Jews in a concentration camp, the dentist used a drill on the suspect's teeth without the benefit of any Novocain until the suspect confessed. The dentist then filled the hole, the investigators knowing that the natural acids in the suspect's mouth would quickly act on the new fillings, making them indistinguishable from old ones and thus preventing the suspect from making credible complaints against them.[38]

Police interrogations during that time did not necessarily begin with third-degree tactics. Taking a page out of the torture handbook of Grand Inquisitor Nicholas Eymerich (discussed above), investigators would first try to verbally persuade the suspect to confess. They would then move on to verbal and visual threats, such as showing the suspect the "instruments of torture" (i.e., rubber hoses) before moving to even more brutal means.

In the majority of cases, investigators would take great pains to make their tactics undetectable. Some departments had "rules" about only striking the suspect on places where any bruising and swelling would not be readily evident. Or, the suspect may be beaten about the head with a phone book, which usually does not leave any visible clues. If bruising, swelling, or broken bones did occur, they were often explained by the suspect "resisting arrest" or "falling down the stairwell." Whether or not the third degree was used would come down to a "swearing contest" between the investigator and the suspect, with the suspect swearing under oath that they had been beaten and the investigator swearing otherwise.

Even though investigators would sometimes go to great lengths to conceal their activities, they could not have used the third degree with any regularity without the tacit (or at times explicit) consent of their supervisors, prosecutors, judges, and the public. The investigators' supervisors didn't care. They had probably used the same tactics themselves in their own careers, and if the result was a closed case, then all the better. Prosecutors and judges in the lower courts were often beholden to the local political machines. Prosecutors needed convictions, and judges, who in many places are elected officials, could ill afford to question confessions from the "obviously guilty." Defense attorneys would often not even raise the issue, knowing that it would get them nowhere. However, since the use of third-degree tactics was illegal, for this to work, investigators would have to lie under oath, and those lies would have to be accepted by the rest of the system. [39]

In spite of the official denials of most law enforcement personnel that third-degree tactics were used regularly, some flaunted it. They freely admitted the practice to reporters and even allowed some, such as Emanuel Lavine (mentioned above), to watch and observe. Inspector Byrnes was admittedly proud of his work and made no bones about his use of force. [40] Many investigators' biographies and autobiographies described their use of third-degree tactics. The memoirs of Cornelius Willemse, titled *Behind the Green Lights* [41] (referring to the green lanterns that hung by the doors of the police station), provide a good example of such braggadocio. Willemse was a New York City police detective in the early 1900s, retiring as the acting captain of the homicide branch in 1925. Regarding his interrogation tactics, Willemse wrote,

> Against a hardened criminal I never hesitated. I've forced confessions—with fist, black-jack, and hose—from men who would have continued to rob and to kill if I had not made them talk. The hardened criminal knows only one language and laughs at the detective who tries any other. . . . Remember that is war after all! I'm convinced my tactics saved many lives. [42]

Willemse's book was made into a movie of the same title in 1935 [43] and with a remake that was released in 1946. [44]

In some places third-degree tactics were practiced essentially out in the open. On March 30, 1934, a white farmer named Raymond Stuart was found murdered in Mississippi. At the time of his death, Stuart had three

African American tenant farmers in his employ. They immediately became suspects and confessed to the crime, but only after being brutally whipped by the investigators. One was even hung by his neck from a tree.

During the court trial, one of the investigators who was present admitted under oath that they had used the third degree to obtain the confessions, saying that the three suspects had been whipped, but "not too much for a Negro; not as much as I would have done if it were left to me."[45] The confessions, obtained through torture, were the only evidence of the suspect's guilt that was admitted at trial. The investigators, prosecutor, judge, and jury had no issues with how the evidence was obtained, and all three suspects were convicted and sentenced to hang. The sentence was appealed to the Mississippi Supreme Court, which upheld the verdict. Fortunately, the US Supreme Court heard the case, and overturned the verdict based on the methods used to obtain the confession.[46]

There were attempts at reform. Illinois attempted to pass several anti third-degree bills. One, proposed in 1917, was adamantly opposed by the Chicago police chief "on the grounds that it deprived the police power to secure proof against criminals."[47] The governor vetoed the bill. A second bill died in committee. One state senator complained that "there is too much sentiment for those accused of crime. . . . It is time we are paying attention to the law-abiding citizens."[48]

The relatively few times that a confession was determined by a lower court judge to be inadmissible because it had been obtained using third-degree tactics elicited a predictable response. When this happened in a case in Chicago in the early 1920s, "a Chicago police official announced that 95% of the department's work would be rendered useless if the [court's] decision was allowed to stand. 'We are permitted to do less every day,' the chief complained. 'Pretty soon there won't be a police department.'"[49] Unfortunately, law enforcement was unaware of the widespread and long-term impact that such attitudes and tactics were having, and the results still linger with us today.

UNACKNOWLEDGED REPERCUSSIONS OF THE THIRD DEGREE

The fallout from the use and tolerance of third-degree tactics was immense. First was the moral and ethical corruption of all those who participated or turned a blind eye. Next was the erosion of trust in the system by citizens and the general public. And third was the corruption of the investigative process itself.

The use of third-degree tactics to obtain confessions made for easy arrests and convictions. More and more cases were closed using confessions; some estimates of closure rates ranged as high as 95 percent for some police departments. Investigators used interrogations to cut corners, and the quality of investigative work dropped. A police officer in India once said that "it is far easier to sit comfortably in the shade rubbing pepper into a poor devil's eyes than to go out in the sun hunting up evidence."[50]

As we have seen, advocates of the use of the third degree contended that they were only used on the guilty, men who don't deserve to be treated the same as everyone else. Besides the obvious ethical and moral issue here, this comment begs the question, "How do you know they are guilty?" Remember Simon Green, who in the late 1800s criticized the police for falling victim to "tunnel vision" and determining a suspect's guilt based on little to no real evidence, or evidence that came to light only after third-degree tactics were applied? He was ahead of his time; this problem still exists today.

Advocates of the third degree also contended that investigators only accepted confessions as true when they contained the details of the crime that only the true perpetrators would know. This issue will be discussed in great length in other chapters, but the truth of the matter is that in many cases, the investigator can actually provide the suspect with the details during the interrogation in a phenomenon known as contamination. In order to escape the third degree, an innocent suspect could simply agree to the details being provided and the investigator would then incorporate them into the confession. This problem of "contamination" even manifested itself with truly guilty suspects. If the investigator was mistaken about the details of crime, they would force the suspect to adopt those false details just because the investigator believed at the time that they were true. This is called "overconfessing."[51]

In the end, it was the investigator who usually wrote out the confession, incorporating in a lie or "mistake" somewhere that the suspect would cross out and initial to prove that he had actually read and understood the confession, thus help validating it. In the early 1930s, one judge described it as happening this way:

The police decide on the details as well as the essentials and give a man whatever treatment they think necessary in order to make him come through.[52]

At the bottom of the statement, investigators will typically include a phrase like "This statement is made freely and voluntarily and is not made by me as the result of any form of threat or inducement." This can be compared with the "valid confession" requirements of the inquisitorial system in place in Europe, as we discussed earlier in this chapter. Remember, a confession obtained by torture was not valid until it was made "voluntarily" in open court. If the person recanted, then it was back to the torture chamber. Here, in more modern times, investigators sought to have the suspect adopt the voluntariness requirement into their confession by means of a statement at the end. The suspect knew that failure to accept this clause would probably result in a return to the third degree.

Finally, as already mentioned, investigators were all too willing to use third-degree tactics on witnesses who they believed were lying to them. This no doubt resulted in untold false witness statements that supported the investigator's theory of the case and thus likely made the tactics used against the suspect harsher, since the investigator had become more convinced of his theory from the outcome of the witness interview.

As you progress through this book, you will discover that, unfortunately, these are not issues that were only part of the "bad old days," but are present with us today.

THE EXPOSURE OF THE THIRD DEGREE

In 1929, the extent of the use of third-degree tactics by law enforcement was about to be exposed. It was that year that President Hoover ordered the formation of the National Commission of Law Enforcement and Observance. The purpose of the Commission was to focus on the widespread violations of prohibitions governing the treatment of detained suspects and to document law enforcement's response. Chaired by former Attorney General George Wickersham, the group became known as the Wickersham Commission. The Commission's report, released in 1931, was a scathing indictment of law enforcement, especially in the area of interrogations.

In its reports, the Wickersham Commission concluded that the third degree, which they described as "the inflicting of pain, physical or mental, to extract confessions or statements" was in widespread use by law enforcement investigators all across the country.[53] One detective who testified in front of the commission described the "old methods" as "brutal, and there wasn't any limit."[54] The Commission went even further, calling some of the techniques that they uncovered "torture."[55] The commission concluded that false confessions were not rare phenomena, and that "many things make it clear that a non-inconsiderable portion [of suspects who underwent the third degree] are innocent."[56]

The report sent shock waves through law enforcement. Police chiefs across the country denied the findings, yet went on to say that the use of such tactics was crucial to the ability to do their job. Books such as Edwin Montefoire Borchard's *Convicting the Innocent*[57] spoke of sixty-five cases of wrongful convictions, many of which resulted from false confessions. The courts began examining confessions more closely, and were more prone to questioning the methods by which they were obtained. This helped prior efforts at police reform to take on new energy. The "good guys" in law enforcement, the ones who promoted professionalism, integrity, and the "scientific methods" of investigation, were having a bigger say.

THE MOVE TOWARD PROFESSIONALISM

In 1935, four years after the Wickersham Commission issued its report, the Federal Bureau of Investigation (FBI) was created. It was also during this time that many of the forensic sciences were becoming available to law enforcement. Textbooks were published, including *Modern Criminal Investigation*[58] in 1935, that covered in detail topics, including processing and documentation of the crime scene, fingerprints, hair and fiber analysis, and "general rules" for the investigation of specific crimes, such as homicide and burglary. The authors were Harry Soderman, DSc, who was the head of the Institute of Police Science at the University of Stockholm, Sweden, and Deputy Chief Inspector John J. O'Connell of the New York Police Department and dean of the Police Academy.

Soderman and O'Connell also included chapters on "Aspects of Detective Work" and "Psychology in Detective Services," which contained sections discussing the interrogation of suspects and witnesses. Soderman and O'Connell harshly criticized the use of coercive tactics, writing:

> To force a witness to give information or a suspect to admit his guilt by threatening him, frightening him, injuring him, or by giving him false information regarding the state of the investigation, is discreditable, unnecessary, and unwise.[59]

Soderman and O'Connell wrote of the necessity for the investigator to always maintain an open mind, remembering that though the evidence may point toward guilt, it may have been misinterpreted and the suspect might actually be innocent. They wrote that the investigator's questions "should not be so formulated as to lead the questioned person to answer in a certain direction or suggest the answer to him."[60] Both recommendations address major problems that are present in interrogations to this day.

THE FIRST INTERROGATION TEXTBOOK IN MODERN TIMES

The very first full textbook on police interrogation was published in the United States in 1940. The author, Lt. William Kidd of the Berkeley, California, police department, wrote of the crossroads that law enforcement was facing at the time. Kidd said that they could either take the path of becoming a professional group or "raise our work to the same prestige as is enjoyed by medicine, law and other professions," or "become definitely an unskilled, day-labor group, capable of being replaced by any unskilled but physically able men."[61] Kidd's sentiments were echoed by Chief August Vollmer, ex-chief of the Berkeley Police Department, president of the International Association of Police Chiefs, and considered by many to be the father of the modern police department. In the foreword to Kidd's book, Vollmer emphasized the importance of professionalism in interrogations. He wrote that a "faulty approach by the interrogator" can turn a potentially cooperative witness hostile as well as contributing to "dangerous criminals" being turned loose on the public, two problems that will be discussed more in a modern context in later chapters.[62]

In his book, Kidd spoke out strongly against the use of both the physical and mental "tortures" that made up the third degree, tortures that he acknowledged were still in use nine years after the Wickersham Commission issued its report. As an example of "mental torture," Kidd wrote how an investigator once refused to let the suspect's sick wife know where he was unless he confessed. Kidd said that such tactics would not only cause innocent people to confess to crimes that they did not commit, it also caused great harm to the reputation of law enforcement as a whole.[63] Kidd wrote that "fairness and kindness" in the interrogation room often pays unexpected dividends in the future as "the vast majority of today's prisoners will be walking our streets tomorrow."[64]

Many of Kidd's ideas regarding interrogation were adopted, in one form or another, to one degree or another, by future interrogation text-books and schools. For example, Kidd recommended that the suspect be allowed to tell his version of events in as much detail as possible. The suspect would then be confronted with "justifying devices" that help the suspect save face. Such devices might include a suggestion that a theft was committed as a prank and not with the intent to really steal. Finally, the investigator would use "emotional appeal and tricks" to obtain the confession. Emotional appeals might include kindness and sympathy. A trick might include holding a line-up where a fake witness "identifies" the suspect, exaggerating the seriousness of the crime, or bluffing about what the scientific evidence will reveal about the suspect's involvement in the case.[65] These same or similar techniques are taught regularly at interroga-tion training centers throughout the United States.

Like future interrogation manuals, Kidd offers what are obvious contradictions. For example, when offering a "justifying device," he rec-ommends that the investigator suggest extenuating circumstances that would lead the suspect to believe that by agreeing with the suggestion that is being offered he might help himself (or at least get a lighter sentence). In modern interrogation training manuals this is known as *minimization* and *maximization*—a technique whereby the interrogator minimizes the suspect's involvement in the crime and maximizes the alternative theories. However, in the next breath, Kidd says that such a suggestion must not be made in a way in which a promise of leniency was even inferred[66]—a difficult trick to accomplish since the promise of le-niency is part and parcel of the entire technique.

Kidd also promoted techniques that investigators could use to talk suspects out of obtaining the assistance of an attorney during questioning. In these pre Miranda rights days, investigators did not have to tell sus-pects before they were interrogated that they had the right to have an attorney present, though that right was in place should they have decided to exercise it. Kidd suggested that if the suspect "immediately starts clamoring for his attorney" that the investigator might argue:

> Why should this very confidential matter get into the hands of a third person? Maybe this lawyer is your friend, but maybe he will use the information against you at some later time. You have nothing to fear if you are innocent. [67]

Kidd also talked about ways that investigators could detect deception. One way was by the careful observation of the suspect's physical reactions to questions and their body language. However, Kidd warned that such observations were far from being totally reliable. He also talked about the use of the so-called lie detector, a device that had come into vogue around that time and had actually been created by his own department. Kidd doubted the polygraph's reliability and pointed out that even if it indicated that the suspect was lying, without real evidence to bolster the case in court, the results were useless. Kidd pointed out that overreliance on the machine only weakened the detective's investigative skills. [68]

Despite the seeming contradictions within his recommendations—at once progressive and old school—Kidd, with one final recommendation, was decades ahead of his time. Kidd wrote about the advantages of making "sound recordings" or even "sound movies" of interrogations from beginning to end, primarily to protect the investigator from accusations of using the third degree. [69] This idea was largely ignored until decades later, when through DNA testing the confirmed number of wrongful convictions resulting from false confessions shot through the roof.

RISE OF THE POLYGRAPH

Though the first lie detector machine (still used by law enforcement to this day!) was invented twenty years before Kidd wrote his interrogation manual, it is discussed here because it is largely responsible for the development of the most widely used interrogation method used in the United States today. The machine, dubbed the *polygraph*, was invented in 1921 by John Augustus Larson, a medical student and police officer employed by the same police department as Kidd. The principle behind the device was that by measuring the body's reaction (i.e., blood pressure, pulse rate, breathing, etc.) to specific questions, the examiner could determine whether or not the subject being tested was being deceptive. However, since science has never been able to accurately determine what, if any, specific physical reactions occur in response to lying or other factors, the machine's usefulness has long been the subject of harsh criticism from the scientific community. In his book *The Lie Detectors: The History of an American Obsession*, Ken Alder writes that over the course of its history, the lie detector "has been perhaps the most investigated forensic technique."[70] According to Alder, a 1941 study by the National Research Council, a 1984 analysis by the Congressional Office of Technology, and a 2003 survey by the National Academy of Science all "concluded that the techniques of lie detection, as used in investigative work by polygraphs, do not pass scientific muster. Yet lie detection lives on."[71]

Investigators and prosecutors have long sought easy answers and shortcuts to the investigative process, and so were more than happy to buy into what the polygraph promoters promised. They would continue to do so in the future, when simpler, yet even more questionable, lie-detection machines such as the computerized voice stress analysis, or CVSA machines, were developed. The CVSA supposedly worked on the same principle as the polygraph, except that the machine "measured" the stress generated by the vocal cords as they reacted to the suspect's deceptive answers. Like with the polygraph, independent research has largely disproven the claims of its creators and supporters. None of these machines have ever achieved the level of scientific accuracy or support within the scientific community that would allow their findings to be admissible in court.

Over time, law enforcement agencies began using the polygraph as part of their interrogation tool kit, relying mostly on the mystique of the machine as a foolproof lie detection device. Investigators were taught to maneuver suspects into taking the test by telling them that only guilty people feared it. They would then work to convince the suspect of the machine's infallibility. The suspect would often be confronted with the machine's response (whether they were provided with accurate information or not was left up to the investigator giving the test), and then were repeatedly questioned until the confession was forthcoming.[72]

THE CREATION OF THE "REID TECHNIQUE"

The development of non third-degree tactics for use by investigators during interrogations took a huge step forward because of the work of Fred Inbau. Inbau was a native of New Orleans who obtained his law degree from Tulane University. While studying for an advanced degree at Northwestern University Law School in Chicago, he became interested in criminal investigations and forensics. Inbau joined the School's Scientific Crime Detection Laboratory in 1931. The laboratory became part of the Chicago Police Department in 1938, at which time Inbau became its director. [73]

Inbau's primary interest was in the area of interrogation and the use of the polygraph. While at the laboratory, he met and began working with John E. Reid. Reid was an attorney who joined the Chicago Police Department in 1936, later accepting a position at the laboratory as a polygraph examiner.

Through their use of the polygraph, Inbau and Reid developed an approach to interrogation that included some of Kidd's techniques. In 1942, Inbau published these techniques in his book *Lie Detection and Criminal Interrogation*. As the title suggests, the book was done in two parts: the first on the use of the polygraph and the second on interrogations. In the 1948 edition, Inbau wrote that the interrogation tactics he proposed could be used with or without a polygraph machine to obtain confessions of guilt from a suspect. [74]

In his book, Inbau outlined nineteen interrogation tactics to which he assigned letters of the alphabet. Later, in collaboration with Reid, these were reduced to what would later become finalized as the famous Reid nine-step program. This program will be discussed in detail in both this and subsequent chapters.

From the start, critics of Inbau (and later Inbau and Reid) called out the tactics as unethical and unfair. Both Reid and Inbau concede that the tactics are unfair, but justified their use due to their belief that "an interrogator must deal with a criminal offender in a somewhat lower moral plane than that in which ethical, law-abiding citizens are expected to conduct their everyday affairs." Furthermore, the two have always asserted that the use of the tactics that they propose will never cause an innocent person to confess. [75]

Reid left the Chicago Crime Laboratory in 1947 to form his own company, John E. Reid & Associates. Reid's company, often referred to as the Reid Institute, offered polygraph testing and interrogation services to both private companies and law enforcement agencies. They also began to offer training in interrogation techniques for law enforcement agencies, eventually becoming the largest provider of interrogation training in the country. During this time, Reid and Inbau continued working together. In 1962, they coauthored what was to become what many considered to be the "bible" of interview and interrogation, *Criminal Interview and Interrogation.* The book condensed Inbau's nineteen tactics into the Reid nine-step program.

THE REID NINE-STEP PROGRAM

The Reid Technique and the nine steps are discussed in great detail in the following chapters, but to understand the rest of our history, you need to have a basic overview of the process. The Reid Technique is broken down in two parts: the Behavioral Analysis Interview (BAI) and the interrogation. During the BAI, the investigator is supposed to attempt to build a rapport with the suspect, during which time the suspect is asked to provide their version of the event in question. While this is going on, the investigator is supposed to be testing the suspect for truthfulness and making a determination as to the probability of their guilt. To do this, the investigator carefully watches the person's body language and listens to how they verbally respond to questions. The investigator also has in their toolbox several predetermined "behavior-provoking questions." How the suspect responds to these questions will further assist in confirming the suspect's guilt in the investigator's mind.

Once the investigator has determined that the suspect before them is guilty, they will switch to the interrogation phase. To accomplish this, the interrogator is supposed to excuse themselves from the interrogation room for several minutes. The purpose of this is to increase the anxiety of the suspect. The interrogator will then reenter the room, maybe carrying a large file that may or may not contain anything of relevance to the case. The file is used as a prop to emphasize to the suspect the level of work the investigator has done on the case.

While he remains standing, the investigator will tell the suspect that the investigation has proven that he is the one that committed the crime. The investigator will go on to say that there is no doubt as to the suspect's guilt, the suspect can say nothing to change the investigator's mind, and that all the investigator wants to hear is why the suspect committed the crime.

Now the investigator will launch into what are referred to as "themes." A theme is supposed to be a psychological or moral justification as to why the suspect committed the crime. As an example, consider a case of theft: The interrogator might suggest that the victim left the money out in plain view, and anyone would have been tempted. If one theme does not work, then the investigator suggests another, then another, until the suspect latches on.

Any time the suspect attempts to deny the accusation or protest his innocence, he is cut off. The investigator would tell him to just listen, and would go on to suggest yet another theme. This goes on, with the investigator doing all of the talking, until they are ready to propose the "alternative question."

The alternative question is a form of a false dilemma, where the suspect is only given two choices, both bad, but one worse than the other. In our theft example from earlier, the suspect would be asked, "Did you steal the money because you are a low-life dope fiend who cares about no one but yourself, or did you take the money because it was out in the open, you were tempted like anyone would have been, you had bills to pay, and you would have paid it back anyway?" The goal of this question is to force the suspect to choose one, thus admitting guilt. Once the suspect makes the choice/admission, the investigator is supposed to obtain details about the crime and then formally document the confession.

According to the Reid Institute, the BAI allowed investigators to detect deception and determine guilt with over 80 percent accuracy, and the nine steps produced confessions approximately 80 percent of the time when used. In addition, the Reid Institute assured law enforcement agencies that the proper use of the nine-step program would never result in a false confession. One could conclude that law enforcement now had a safe and reliable tool to use in the interrogation room and the third degree was dead. Easy, right? As you might expect, these conclusions were too good to be true.

BEHIND CLOSED DOORS

False confessions continued to surface. For some examples, in 1952, after two weeks of on-and-off interrogation, at the end of which he was told that his mother would be arrested for complicity, Stanford Fenwell falsely confessed to the murder of his nine-year-old cousin. John Reid, presumably using his own technique, obtained a false confession himself during the investigation into the 1955 murder of Nancy Parker (detailed in chapter 6 of this book). In another city, during police interrogation following a highly questionable eyewitness identification procedure in which a victim falsely identified him, George Whitmore falsely confessed to the attempted rape of that victim. Under continued interrogation, Whitmore confessed to the 1963 brutal rape/murder of two young women in their Manhattan apartment.

In his biography, New York police detective Frank Serpico described an interrogation he witnessed when he was a patrol officer in the early 1960s. While on patrol, Serpico had come across several men raping a woman in a schoolyard. He gave chase but was only able to catch one of the perpetrators. After turning his prisoner over to the detectives for interrogation, Serpico's biographer described what happened next.

> There were three detectives in the squad room, one of whom was nicknamed "Blackjack" because of his enthusiastic use of that leather bound instrument. "OK, you fuck, who were your playmates?" the detective called Blackjack began. When there was no answer, he took his blackjack out and held it in his fist so that about two inches of its business end protruded and rammed it into the rapist's stomach. He crumpled over with a soft sigh. The blackjack came whistling in again and again to his stomach, his kidneys, and the back of his neck. He passed out. A pitcher of water revived him. He was put in a chair, and one of the other detectives came up behind him with a telephone book and slammed it against his ear. As the youth slowly shook his head in pain, the telephone book pounded his other ear. Back and forth it went. Occasionally the telephone book missed an ear, and his nose began spurting blood. Still he would not talk, and finally Serpico was told, "Get him the fuck out of here."[76]

In addition, during this time the Supreme Court was hearing more and more cases involving all kinds of questionable police conduct in the interrogation room. In 1966, the issue concerning what was really occurring in the interrogation room came to a head when the Supreme Court was asked to examine the case of *Miranda v. Arizona.*

THE *MIRANDA* DECISION

In 1963, Ernesto Miranda was arrested by the Phoenix Police Department and charged with the kidnapping and rape of an eighteen-year-old woman. After a two-hour interrogation, Miranda signed a confession to the crime. At the top of his signed confession was a typed paragraph stating "that the confession was made voluntarily, without threats or promises, and 'with the full knowledge of my legal rights, understanding that any statement I make may be used against me.'"[77]

At trial, the investigators testified that in spite of the above statement, they did not advise Miranda that he had the right to have an attorney with him during the interrogation. Miranda's attorney fought to have the confession thrown out, saying that because Mirada was not aware of his right to an attorney, the confession was not made voluntarily. The trial court ruled against Miranda, who was convicted of rape and kidnapping and sentenced to twenty to thirty years in prison on each charge.

The case was appealed and eventually made its way to the Supreme Court. What most people don't know is that in making their famous ruling, they were also considering three other cases at the same time. New York City police arrested Michael Vignera in 1960 on a robbery charge. Later, he was questioned by an investigator and then an assistant district attorney, and he confessed the crime to both. Neither time was he advised of his rights to have an attorney present. The second case being considered was that of Carl Westover. Westover was arrested by the Kansas City police in 1963 and charged with two robberies. Kansas City investigators and later the FBI questioned him for an extended period of time regarding other robberies. The court found no evidence that he had been advised of his right to an attorney. And in 1963, Roy Stewart was arrested in Los Angeles and charged with multiple robberies and a murder. He was interrogated nine times, after which he finally confessed. Again, the court found that he had not been advised of his right to have an attorney.[78]

To help them in their decision, the Supreme Court justices wanted to know exactly what was going on in the interrogation room that compelled these four men to confess, especially in light of recent cases that had come before them in which it was obvious that third-degree tactics were still being used. Since there were no verbatim recordings of the interrogations from start to finish, the Supreme Court turned to the interrogation manuals that were being used at that time to teach investigators the art of interrogation. The two primary manuals that they consulted were Inbau and Reid's *Criminal Interrogations and Confessions* (1962) and Charles O'Hara's *Fundamentals of Criminal Investigation* (1952).[79]

The justices made extensive references to the contents of the manuals and the tactics they taught. They concluded that "these tactics are designed to put the subject in a psychological state where his story is but an elaboration of what the police purport to know already—that he is guilty." It was obvious to them "that such an interrogation environment is created for no purpose other than to subjugate the individual to the will of his examiner."[80]

Though the primary focus of the justices was on whether or not the confessions were made voluntarily, the potential for their factual unreliability was also addressed. The justices noted that if the suspect had the assistance of a lawyer during the interrogation, the attorney could "mitigate the dangers of untrustworthiness by preventing coercion, and insuring that an accurate statement is recorded by the police and passed along to the prosecutor."[81]

In the end, the justices ruled that Miranda's and the other three subject's confessions were involuntary, and their convictions were overturned. The justices had decided that "without proper safeguards, the process of in-custody interrogation of persons suspected or accused of crime contains inherently compelling pressures which work to undermine the individual's will to resist and to compel him to speak where he would not otherwise do so freely. In order to combat these pressures and to permit a full opportunity to exercise the privilege against self-incrimination, the accused must be adequately and effectively apprised of his rights, and the exercise of these rights must be fully honored."[82]

Thus, the famous Miranda warnings so familiar to us through movies and television were born.

REACTION TO *MIRANDA*

The reaction of law enforcement personnel and prosecutors to now having to advise suspects in custody of their rights to have an attorney was predictable. Once again, they said, the hands of law enforcement are being tied. No one will ever confess now. But as each time before, investigators adapted in response to the new regulations (just not the way we would hope). As interrogation manuals changed to address the Miranda "problem," investigators creatively developed ways to get around it. As an example, since the new laws stipulated that investigators only had to give a suspect their Miranda warning if they were in custody, "noncustodial interrogations" became popular. The interrogation took place in the same room, and the same tactics were used, but the investigators were careful to work in the words "you are free to leave" somewhere in the conversation. Otherwise there was little change.

The Reid Institute and the nine-step Reid Technique grew in popularity. The company became the largest in the country to provide interview and interrogation training for law enforcement. With a few exceptions, other interrogation schools either taught the Reid Technique or a version that followed the same basic principles. It became part of the on-the-job training for many, with new investigators being taught Reid-style tactics by their co-workers who had taken the course. And as part of this interrogation training, investigators were being told that the tactics they were being taught would never produce a false confession. Those only occurred if the suspect was being tortured or was crazy.

However, false confessions continued to occur. Attempts to study the phenomena proved difficult. Scientists for the most part were not allowed to observe interrogations, and, for ethical reasons, it was extremely difficult to replicate in the laboratory the stressful and coercive conditions of the interrogation room.[83] This changed when many law enforcement agencies began audio or video recording part if not all of the interrogation or confession, and more importantly, because of DNA.

FIRST USE OF DNA BY LAW ENFORCEMENT

The very first time that DNA analysis was used by law enforcement was in the United Kingdom. On November 21, 1983, fifteen-year-old Lynda

Mann left her home in Narborough, Leicestershire, to go to see a friend. The next morning she was found raped and murdered on a path known as the Black Pad. Three years later, fifteen-year-old Dawn Ashworth was found near another path called Ten Pound Lane. She had also been raped and murdered. Investigators focused in on seventeen-year-old Richard Buckland, who, during interrogation, confessed to having murdered Mann, but not Ashworth.[84]

Semen was found on both of the girls' bodies. Investigators turned to Alec Jeffreys of the University of Leicester who, along with others, had just developed DNA profiling. Convinced that the new science would prove that Buckland committed both murders, the semen samples recovered from the two victims, along with a blood sample from Buckland, were submitted to the lab. Investigators were shocked to discover they were only half right. The DNA tests proved that the two girls were raped and killed by the same person, but that person was not Buckland. The DNA profile from the semen was later matched to Colin Pitchfork, who pled guilty to the murders.[85]

DNA AND FALSE CONFESSIONS IN THE UNITED STATES

The British investigators' experience would soon be replicated many times in the United States. One example was the case of Carolyn Hamm. Hamm was a lawyer who lived by herself in Arlington, Virginia. She was found raped and murdered in her home on January 25, 1984. When she was found, she was hanging by the neck from a water pipe in the basement.

A few days later, investigators learned that witnesses believed that they had seen David Vasquez in the area of Hamm's home around the time she was believed to have been murdered. Vasquez, who was later described in court as being of low intelligence, had lived in the neighborhood for several years before the crime.

Investigators picked up Vasquez at his place of employment and took him to the police station. He was not advised of his Miranda rights at first because he was not under arrest and the interrogation, until the end, was considered by them to be "noncustodial." After several hours of interrogation, Vasquez confessed to the murder, a confession he later recanted.

Vasquez was charged with capital murder and faced the death penalty. Once his attorneys were unsuccessful in getting the confession thrown out, they worked out a deal with the prosecutor. The prosecutor would drop the death penalty if Vasquez entered what is called an Alford plea[86] to second-degree murder. The plea would allow Vasquez to continue to maintain his innocence. He only had to admit that the prosecutor had enough evidence to convict him. Second-degree murder carried a sentence of twenty years, but with the time he had already served in jail awaiting trial and counting future "good time" in prison, Vasquez would have to serve only five years.

In 1987, while Vasquez was still in prison, a crime very similar to the Hamm murder occurred in the same Arlington neighborhood. An investigator then discovered that in the months preceding the second murder, three other similar murders had occurred elsewhere in Virginia. The investigator went back through the files and identified Terry Spencer, a local burglar who had been previously caught breaking into houses in the Arlington neighborhood. Spencer was supposed to have been in a halfway house, but the investigator discovered that he had checked out of the halfway house each time one of the 1987 murders in question had occurred.

Spencer's DNA matched the DNA recovered from all of the 1987 murder scenes. The DNA from the Hamm scene was insufficient to undergo testing, but there was other circumstantial evidence to indicate that Spencer was her killer as well.

Because the DNA in the Hamm case could not be tested, it could not be used to exonerate Vasquez. Instead, based on the evidence, the governor granted him a pardon.

However, that is not the end of the Vasquez situation. Unlike during most, the investigators recorded large parts of Vasquez's interrogation. The recordings revealed not only the extent to which the investigators used extremely coercive interrogation tactics on Vasquez but also that they actually provided him with all of the details about the crime that he later parroted back to them in his confession. With DNA and the videotape, researchers could begin to figure out not only why Vasquez confessed but also how he "knew" all of those details that "only the real killer would have known."

THE FLOODGATES OPENED

Now DNA testing was not only being used to solve crimes but also to exonerate innocent people behind bars. More and more research became focused on police interrogation tactics. The work of attorneys Barry Scheck and Peter Neufeld on the use of DNA to identify and litigate wrongful convictions led to the creation of the Innocence Project and like organizations. As the number of known wrongful convictions resulting from false confessions increased, the more that the tried-and-true interrogation tactics that had remained unchanged since the 1940s came under fire. And law enforcement and the Reid Institute fired back. Using the arguments that are discussed in greater detail in the next chapter, the Reid Institute was dismissive of the research and supported the contention that false confessions were nothing but a rare anomaly. They published articles critical of the research into false confessions, and, with the support of local and federal law enforcement, fought proposed reform such as the videotaping of interrogations from beginning to end. However, the growing number of confirmed false confessions, and the increasing number of agencies that were videotaping how those false confessions came about, could not be disregarded.

INTERROGATION TODAY

The state of police interrogations and the problems related to false confessions today is a topic that consumes the majority of the following chapters. Reform is slow, and law enforcement agencies typically do not respond to a problem until forced to. But as you will see, changes have been made. More and more agencies have begun videotaping interrogations in their entirety, thus not only helping to preserve the integrity of the process and the confession but also providing researchers with a ton of material to study. And even the Reid Institute has shown some major cracks in its tough veneer.

In their 1986 edition of *Criminal Interrogations and Confessions*, the Reid Institute barely mentions the words *false confessions*.[87] It is covered much more extensively in later editions. Included are cautions regarding the use of some techniques, such as lying about evidence, along with new topics such as the steps that should be taken to corroborate the confession once it has been obtained. The Reid Institute has even dropped its resistance to the videotaping of interrogations. However, they still contend, that if used properly, the Reid Technique will not produce a false confession.

But is that really the case? And are false confessions still an issue we should be worried about?

2

DO WE EVEN HAVE A PROBLEM?

In spite of the continuing advances in the forensic sciences, the large majority of crimes will continue to be solved through the interviews of witnesses and victims, and the interrogation of suspects. Over time, as we have seen, there have been attempts to identify and remove from the investigative toolbox those techniques, such as the "third degree" tactics described in chapter 2 that can obviously cause someone to falsely confess to a crime. We now have in place the Miranda warning, advising the suspect up front that they do not have to talk with the police, and that if they do, whatever they say might adversely affect them. The Reid Institute, which is the largest and oldest interrogation school in the United States, teaches a nine-step interrogation process that they say, if used correctly, will lead to confessions by the guilty, but will not induce an innocent person to falsely confess. Many law enforcement agencies videotape the interrogation process from beginning to end just to be sure that there are no shenanigans. But even with all of these advances and safeguards, false confessions still occur.

The tools and techniques that the investigator uses in the interrogation room are no different from any other process, procedure, or technique used in any other profession. All involve their own, unique problems and risks. From the medical field to the automobile industry, professionals attempt to identify those risks and work to minimize their impact. But seldom can all adverse effects can be eliminated. So the question becomes, What is an acceptable risk? What margin of error are we willing to tolerate? With all of the apparent enlightenment regarding interrogation practices and the court-enforced safeguards in place, should we be concerned about a "few" false confessions? Is there any reason for you to even be reading this book?

THERE IS NO FALSE CONFESSION "PROBLEM"

Paul Cassell would say no. A former prosecutor and federal judge, and currently a professor with the University of Utah Law School,[1] Cassell is a leading critic of much of the ongoing interrogation and false confession research. Cassell correctly point out that the number of false confession cases is one of the great unknowns. Cassell believes that the estimates of many false confession experts are greatly exaggerated. He says that their studies are flawed, basing their estimates on anecdotal information and the study of a limited number of cases. Cassell argues that many of the cases that the researchers used in their studies could convincingly be challenged as to whether or not the person was truly innocent and whether the confession they gave was actually false.[2]

In his estimate of the rate that false confessions occur, Cassell and others look to the number of arrests reported to the FBI each year as part of their Unformed Crime Reporting (UCR) program. UCR is a voluntary program in which law enforcement agencies across the country report the type and number of crimes that occur within their jurisdictions and the percentage of those crimes that have been closed by arrest. Cassell says that his studies show that "the available data indicate that about 80% of all arrested suspects will be interrogated"[3] by the police, and at least 33.3 percent will confess.[4] Based on the average number of arrests, this results in nine hundred thousand confessions.[5] He then takes the estimated number of persons convicted and the data collected by other false confession researchers and concludes that approximately ten people are convicted each year based on a false confession, or an error rate of 0.001 percent. Cassell compares this rate to the number of people killed by lightning each year, which is about fifty.[6]

Cassell believes that the researchers do not take into account how many of these false confessions that resulted in convictions were voluntary, the result of persons confessing to crimes in order to protect someone else, or for a multitude of other self-serving reasons. The assumption is that since these voluntary confessions were not the result of police interrogation, they should not be used to support any argument to restrict or modify the tactics used by the police to obtain confessions.[7]

In his argument, Cassell focuses only on the number of possible false confessions that result in a wrongful conviction. Cassell discounts the number of arrests that result from a false confession that for whatever reason do not make it to trial, or if they do, result in an acquittal. Cassell presumes that if a person was coerced by the police to falsely confess, then they would report this to their attorneys, who would then take the appropriate action. This appropriate action, combined with the checks and balances process of the judicial system, would prevent the false confession from resulting in a conviction, and thus would count as a success and the system worked.

Cassell is among many who say that the pendulum has swung too far the other way. Cassell contends that the Supreme Court's *Miranda* decision and other attempts at restricting the ability of police to interrogate suspects based on the insignificant number of wrongful convictions resulting from false confessions has not only prevented the apprehension of the guilty but also has actually helped increase the conviction of the innocent by preventing the police from interrogating those truly responsible for the crime.[8]

Cassell contends that on those "rare" occasions where an innocent person is either facing the possibility of a wrongful conviction or has been wrongfully convicted, the ability of the police to property interrogate the true suspect is an important means of exoneration. One example that Cassell uses in support of this is a study by Sam Gross on the miscarriages of justice resulting from faulty eyewitness identification. Cassell says that Gross found that over half of the eyewitness identification mistakes were only uncovered when the "actual criminal confessed."[9] Another example that he uses is a study by Arye Rattner of wrongful convictions in general, not just cases resulting from eyewitness identification error. In that study, Cassell says that Rattner found that confessions were the leading cause of the innocent persons being exonerated. One could conclude that restricting the police's ability to interrogate would only lesson that number.[10]

Additionally, because Miranda can allow a smart criminal to stop the police from trying to obtain a confession before it starts, what happens, Cassell says, is a crime goes unsolved because of what Cassell calls a "lost confession."[11] According to Cassell, Miranda has done nothing to protect the innocent. What it has done has allowed an untold number of criminals to go unpunished, and has severely restricted the ability of law enforcement to interrogate the real perpetrator and free the innocently accused or convicted.

Others have supported Cassell in his argument that the attempts by the Supreme Court and others to address this "nonissue" of false confessions have, and continue, to severely hurt law enforcement's ability to get the guilty off the streets. In 1986, a report was submitted to then–attorney general Edwin Meese by the US Department of Justice's Office of Legal Policy detailing the consequences of the Supreme Court *Miranda* decision. The report discovered that in Philadelphia, Pennsylvania, during a period prior to Miranda, "an estimated 90% of arrested persons made statements to the police," while only 41 percent did so once suspects were required to be advised of their right to remain silent. Pittsburgh, Pennsylvania, police reported a 50 percent drop in confessions in murder and in robbery cases. [12]

BUT AT SECOND GLANCE

At first glance, the arguments appear persuasive. Even today, we have no firm idea how many false confessions occur yearly. But in spite of these assertions that the police obtain approximately nine hundred thousand confessions or incriminating statements a year, we don't know if that number is true either. There is no central database that tracks the number of suspects who are interrogated, and of those, the number who provide incriminating statements or confessions. Nor do we track the numbers who were convicted or pled guilty based on those confessions.

Adding to the problem is the question, How do you determine that a confession is actually false?

CONFIRMING TRUE-FALSE CONFESSIONS

Actually, there are several ways that researchers can determine that a confession is truly false. An obvious one is when a person confesses to a crime that never occurred.

Confessions to Crimes That Didn't Happen

This has happened frequently in misdiagnosed "Shaken Baby Syndrome cases." In the 1970s, doctors believed that they had identified a series of internal conditions that, if found together, could only have come from someone violently shaking an infant. Armed with what they believed was scientific evidence, investigators would confront parents and caretakers and often obtain confessions in which the subject confessed to having shaken the child. Many times, these confessions came after the subject was confronted with the threat of having their other children taken from them, or because they were told that the doctor needed confirmation of the shaking to help save the child. Later research has disputed whether or not Shaken Baby Syndrome actually exists, and many convictions based on confessions were overturned when the child was found to have died from natural causes. [13]

Another example is documented in Edwin Montefiore Borchard's 1932 classic *Convicting the Innocent: Sixty-Five Actual Errors of Criminal Justice*. [14] In 1812 in Manchester, Vermont, a local resident, Russell Colvin, disappeared without a trace. Shortly afterward, rumors soon came to light that before his disappearance, Russell had been involved in a violent quarrel resulting from a long-term dispute with Jesse and Stephen Boorn. Years went by, and bit by bit, more evidence came to light that indicated that Russell might have been murdered.

In 1819, Jesse admitted to the townspeople that he was with Stephen when, during an argument, he saw Stephen beat Russell to death with a club. Stephen was arrested, and during his interrogations he was confronted with his brother's statement, as well as the statement of a jailhouse informant who said that Stephen had admitted the murder to him. Confronted with people telling him that his conviction was inevitable, Stephen confessed to having murdered Russell. Like so many false confessions, Stephen's account conflicted greatly with that of his brother and the informant. He was convicted and sentenced to death. Shortly before his scheduled execution, Russell was found alive and well in Dover, New Jersey. The charges against Stephen were dropped, but when he attempted to obtain compensation for his imprisonment, he was denied. The courts said that Stephen was convicted because he confessed, and so only had himself to blame. [15]

Physically Impossible to Have Committed the Crime

Another situation in which a confession can be confirmed to be false is when a person confesses to a crime but it was physically impossible for them to have committed it. We saw an example of this type of confession in the last chapter, when the physically incapacitated Robert Hubert confessed to starting the Great Fire of London in 1666. A more recent example is the 1988 confession of Bernard Ward to the murder of Edward Brewer.[16]

On November 16, 1988, a car belonging to Edward Brewer was found on fire in a parking lot next to an abandoned house in Anne Arundel County, Maryland. A gas can was found in the car, and Brewer was nowhere to be seen.

A few weeks later, a police officer went inside of the abandoned house, looking for a missing child. Instead of the child, the officer found Brewer's body. He had been stabbed over twenty times and his neck had been broken.

Investigators identified Bernard Ward as a possible suspect because of his prior arrest history for assault and homosexual solicitation. Ward's photograph was placed in a photospread with several other photographs and shown to various witness. Two witnesses said that they saw Ward and Brewer in a bar the night that Brewer's car was found. Other witnesses said that they saw Ward near Brewer's burning car.

The investigators tracked Ward down to Tallahassee, Florida, and arrested him for Brewer's murder. During his interrogation, Ward confessed to the crime. He told the investigators that he and a stranger met Brewer in the bar that night. Ward and the stranger rode with Brewer to the parking lot, where the stranger stabbed Brewer to death. Later, at his trial, Ward recanted his confession, testifying that all he did was parrot back the details he was provided by the investigators.

The problem with Ward's confession was that he was not in Maryland at the time of the murder. Not only did Ward have numerous witnesses, including his employer and local courthouse employees who placed him in Tallahassee at the time, the witnesses were further supported by phone records and court papers. Ward had signed the court papers, and FBI handwriting examiners confirmed that the signatures were his.

Ward appealed his conviction and won a new trial based on the new alibi evidence. He was acquitted.

Another Is Identified as the True Perpetrator

If after a person confesses, the police positively link another suspect to the crime and confirm that the person who originally confessed had no connection to the new suspect, that confession can be considered false. Such is what happened to twenty-five-year-old Jermel Lewis after he falsely confessed to having participated in the worst mass murder in the history of Philadelphia.

On Thursday, December 28, 2000, Philadelphia police received a 911 call for a shooting that turned out to be at 816 North Lex Street. The location was well known in the neighborhood as a place to purchase and use drugs. When the police arrived they found six people, ages ranging from fifteen to fifty-four, shot dead in a downstairs room. Three people survived, including a resident of the house named Yvette Long. The murders received national attention and quickly became known as the Lex Street Murders. [17]

Working off the theory that the murders were the result of local drug disputes, investigators began focusing on the neighborhood drug gangs. One of those gangs included Jermel Lewis, who when first interviewed by investigators admitted that he had been by the house earlier that evening. Other information surfaced regarding threats that persons associated with Lewis had allegedly made to some of the occupants of the house. Investigators also repeatedly interviewed Long, whose memory of the crime, as well as her descriptions of the shooters, evolved with time. [18]

On January 11, 2000, investigators located Lewis and asked if he would mind coming to the police station to answer a few questions. At the same time, they also had Long come to the station to view some photospreads of suspects. Long identified one of Lewis's associates as one of the shooters. [19]

By this time, the investigators had been questioning Lewis for six hours. They then confronted him, saying they had "new information." According to the investigators, Lewis admitted to having participated in the murders, naming the subject identified by Long and two others as his accomplices. Approximately seven hours later, Lewis signed a statement prepared by the investigators detailing his involvement and that of his associates in the murders. The three associates that he named were arrested soon afterward. [20]

As preparations for trial began in the case against Lewis and his code-fendants, the investigation hit a speed bump. Investigators were notified by the Philadelphia Police Firearms Investigation Unit that a shell casing recovered from a separate shooting was confirmed to have been fired from one of the guns used in the Lex Street murders. Shihean Black had been arrested for that shooting. Investigators reinterviewed Black, confronting him with the firearms report. Black confessed that he had participated in the Lex Street murders, along with a person he identified as Charles and two others. Black provided numerous details about the events of that night before suddenly changing his mind, telling the investigators that he was lying. The investigators dismissed Black's confession, believing that he was crazy. [21]

The investigation hit another speed bump when Lewis recanted his earlier confession. His version of how the confession came about differed from that of the investigators. Lewis said that the investigators "roughed him up, lied about the evidence. Lewis alleged that the investigators had written the confession and threated him with the death penalty if he did not sign it." [22] Lewis said neither he nor the others he named had anything to do with the murders.

The prosecutor still planned on using Lewis's confession at trial. They also had the testimony of eyewitness Yvette Long, who, due to her constantly "improving" memory, was able to identify or otherwise connect the other suspects to the murder. The prosecutor was confident of a conviction, but some investigators were not so sure that they had the right men.

Some of the investigators who worked the case began to have doubts about Lewis's confession. They looked closer at Black, and began to see more and more connections between him and the Lex Street murders. A major break occurred when federal agents arrested a gun dealer named Dawud Faruqi, who they learned had given Black the gun that was traced to the Lex Street murders. Dawud Faruqi admitted to having committed the Lex Street murders, along with Black and two other subjects, one of whom also confessed after he was arrested. Additional shell cases, determined to have been fired from one of the same guns used at Lex Street, were recovered and linked to the new suspects. [23] Long later admitted that she had been smoking crack the night of the murders, and attributed her misidentifications to the "effects of 'getting high.'" [24]

In the end, the charges against Lewis and his codefendants were dismissed. Black and one of his codefendants pled guilty. Faruqi and the other codefendant went to trial and were found guilty.

Scientific Evidence Excludes the Confessor

Finally, a confession can be considered false when scientific evidence positively excludes the confessor as the perpetrator of the crime. The case against Danial Williams for the murder of Michelle Bosko is a great example. The DNA from the semen recovered from the crime scene matched the DNA of Omar Ballard. Ballard confessed to the crime, saying that he committed it alone and that Williams had nothing to do with it. But for the investigators and prosecutors, that didn't matter, which just highlights the power that a confession has.

FOR SOME—NOT GOOD ENOUGH

Even when a case matches one of the above criteria, there can still be debate. Many times, law enforcement and prosecutors will go to great lengths to defend the original confession, asserting that in spite of all the evidence to the contrary, it still must be true. Such reasoning gymnastics have led to some pretty amazing theories, especially when the confession is proven to be false when the DNA from semen recovered from the victim does not match the confessor. The prosecutor and/or police will switch their original theory of a single perpetrator to multiple perpetrators, even when the DNA is matched to someone that can be found to have no connection to the confessor. Some of the more outrageous theories I have heard include: the DNA came from a mysterious person who found the body afterward and had sex with the corpse, it somehow drifted down river and landed on a body that was discovered in water, or the crime scene was located in a "lovers lane" and the DNA got on the victim's body when they rubbed up against what must have been a semen-coated tree.

The problem is that a large number of highly questionable confessions do not easily fit into any of these categories. Or, because of the lack of a video or audio recording, or other documentation (such as police files or court transcripts), it is impossible to positively determine the validity of the confession to the satisfaction of the researchers, thus adding to the problem of getting anywhere near determining the true number of false confessions that occur.

WHAT IS AN ACCEPTABLE NUMBER OF FALSE CONFESSIONS?

Even so, there is no doubt that false confessions do occur. As discussed in the last chapter, false confessions have occurred throughout history, and with advances in the forensic sciences (especially DNA) and the increased videotaping of interrogations from start to finish, the number of confirmed false confession cases is steadily growing.

The problem inherent in identifying the rate of false confessions has not stopped researchers from trying to identify the scope of the problem using various approaches. Some look at how often confession evidence played a part in confirmed wrongful convictions. The National Registry of Wrongful Convictions, run by the Northwestern University School of Law, works to identify wrongful conviction cases nationally and studies their causes. As of December 15, 2015, they had identified 1,717 wrongful convictions, of which 218, or 13 percent, involved a false confession.[25]

Other studies include self-reporting surveys of inmates (12 percent report having made a false confession at some time in their lives) and laboratory experiments with college studies (1 percent to 7 percent). One very interesting survey was done of over six hundred North American police officers, a group that is usually very skeptical of the false confession phenomena. In that survey the officers reported that, based on their personal experience, false confessions resulting from interrogations occur 4.78 percent of the time.[26]

While even the researchers caution that this research must be taken with a grain of salt, the numbers do support the data obtained from the study of confirmed wrongful convictions that indicate that "a small but significant minority of innocent people confess under interrogation."[27]

But what is a "small" number, and when does it quality as "significant"? Though now almost universally recognized as an extremely low estimate, for argument's sake let's assume that Cassell's estimate of people being convicted bases on false confessions only occurring .001 percent of the time. Is that a sufficient enough number of cases for us to worry about? Should we look to other areas of our lives to determine what an acceptable risk is?

In 2014, General Motors issued a recall of 2.6 million vehicles because of a faulty ignition switch. This recall was prompted by "only" thirteen deaths,[28] creating a baseline error rate of .000005 percent.

Cassell's estimate of false confession cases base rate only includes those that resulted in a conviction. Like the GM recall, he does not mention the number of injured. Cassell fails to estimate or account for the number of false confessions that were uncovered by the police or prosecutors before trial, that were ruled inadmissible by a judge, or where the jury found the confessor "not guilty." Many in the criminal justice system point to these cases as "successes" of the system. "No harm, no foul."

COLLATERAL DAMAGE

Actually, the "collateral damage" from such "successes" is widespread. In these cases, innocent people often suffer from unjust incarceration, resulting in disruption of family life, loss of a job, loss of housing, damaged reputation, or other hardships. They may have to pay thousands for legal representation, often going deeply in debt. Unlike what Cassell suggests, the fact that the innocent person confessed will not be discovered because of the diligent and thorough work by the prosecutor or police, their name will never be cleared of suspicion, and the real perpetrator will go unpunished.

This damage is largely caused by the fact that, in the majority of these cases, just like in false confession cases that result in a conviction, law enforcement is unable to bring themselves to acknowledge that the confession is false. The power that a confession has over us, combined with tunnel vision and the criteria by which law enforcement judges itself, contributes to this blindness. These same factors are the reason behind the difficulty in overturning a wrongful conviction in which there is a false confession, in spite of overwhelming evidence of innocence.

"Why would someone confess to a crime they did not commit unless it was true" is one of the central questions that this book attempts to address. It is that belief among the public and most police officers and prosecutors that makes confession evidence so powerful, and yet so dangerous. In 1986, Supreme Court Justice William Brennan wrote:

> No other class of evidence is so profoundly prejudicial . . . the introduction of a confession makes the other aspects of a trial in court superfluous, and the real trial, for all practical purposes, occurs when the confession is obtained.[29]

Confession evidence has been repeatedly shown to trump all evidence of innocence to the contrary, including DNA evidence, both in and out of the courtroom. But when asking the question, "Why confess if you are innocent?" people don't think of what would make someone think it was a good idea to confess to a crime you did commit, thus subjecting yourself to jail time, or in some cases, even death.

One would think that cops would be more skeptical of confession evidence, and they tend to present themselves as such. David Simon, a reporter who spent a year embedded in the Baltimore Homicide Unit, noted the detectives' cynicism when it comes to believing anyone. He wrote that one of the "ten informal rules of homicide" is that "everyone lies. Murderers lie because they have to; witnesses and other participants lie because they think they have to; everyone else lies for the sheer joy of it, and to uphold a general principle that under no circumstances do you provide accurate information to a cop."

In reality, law enforcement is perhaps less skeptical than the general public. Part of this is because of the training they receive. As you will see in upcoming chapters, almost all formal interrogation training taught in the United States includes training in techniques that supposedly allow the officer to detect deception and determine if someone is guilty, techniques that have largely been discredited. The other reason is because law enforcement are the ones who obtain the confession. The investigator develops a theory of the case, believes that the suspect is the guilty party, and goes into the interrogation room with the goal of confirming his belief with a confession. This may work well if the investigator is correct in his reasoning, but it can cause problems if he is not. Verification bias is the very human reaction in which we tend to seek evidence to confirm what we already believe, and to reject or ignore any evidence that contradicts that belief. This is why so many investigators are able to accept the most outrageously inaccurate false confessions as fact when if the same information had come from a person claiming to be a witness or informant, they would reject it out of hand as not making any sense. The power of those words "I did it" can blind us to a lot of things.

Investigators and prosecutors also believe that they are quite able to detect a false confession if one occurs. Investigators are taught to identify "hold-back" information during their investigation. This is information that is not known to the general public and that only the true perpetrator would know. If a person was not there, that hold-back information would not be in the final confession.

As will be discussed in later chapters, this is not always the case. False confessions usually contain a great deal of the hold-back information. This is because, during the interrogation, the investigator provides it to them in one way or another. This most commonly occurs when the investigator, through tunnel vision, is convinced of the innocent person's guilt and becomes frustrated with their lack of "cooperation." Verification bias allows the investigator to "explain away" the lack of details or any incorrect information that is given as part of the false confession.

CONFESSIONS MAKE FOR LAZY COPS

There are other reasons why law enforcement and the prosecutors don't want to "look a gift horse in the mouth." Confessions make life easier. For the investigator and his agency, it means the case is closed. Law enforcement agencies and investigators are judged by their "clearance rate," which largely means the rate by which cases are closed by arrest. The FBI's UCR tracks and reports to the public clearances, not convictions. Once the confession is obtained, the investigation ceases and it's time to move on to the next case. The work necessary to follow-up and corroborate the confession, something that is routine with witness and victim statements, and, if done properly, could help identify a confession as false, is just not done.

Prosecutors also rely on the power of the confession for an easy win. They know that defense attorneys know that fighting a confession case is an uphill battle, especially when the entire interrogation is not video or audio recorded, as is still the case in many jurisdictions. In those instances, what happened in the interrogation room that may have led to a false confession boils down to the word of the investigator against the suspect. The defense attorney has to overcome the jury's belief that since they know that they would never confess to something they didn't do, why would the suspect? The innocent suspect is faced with a choice similar to the one that made them falsely confess in the first place. The innocent suspect is told that they can either face probable conviction or attempt to cut their losses by pleading guilty. As many as 95 percent of criminal cases are resolved this way,[30] with no additional independent critique of the confession or other evidence. The decision to plead guilty is not an admission of guilt as much as it is a loss/gain business calculation.

If the innocent suspect decides to go to trial and the judge determines that the confession is not admissible, the confession is not looked upon by the prosecutor or law enforcement as a potentially false one. To get to this stage, both had to believe that the false confession was true, otherwise the case would not have gone this far. Instead, such as in the case of an acquittal by a jury, they would have considered it to be a bad judgment call by the judge or the jury, no further work would be done, and the truly guilty would go unpunished.

False confession cases that are dismissed after the confession occurs and before the innocent suspect goes to trial fair no better. The reasons for such dismissals are hard to identify, as the details are not generally made public. The confession may not be identified as false but rather problematic; the result of the tactics that were used to obtain it, or other problems with the case. Where Cassell cites sources that say that, in the era before DNA testing became as widespread as it is now, the false confessions were discovered when the true perpetrator confessed, his sources do not say that those confessions came about through additional investigation, police interrogation, or as an admission to a third party such as a witness or informant. Case studies have shown that such post false-confession admissions usually have little impact on the investigator's or prosecutor's belief in the reliability of the original false confession. Such is the case of Danial Williams, whose story we are following throughout this book. In Williams's case, you will see how even when the real perpetrator, the only person whose DNA was found on the crime scene and who confessed voluntarily to a third party and to the police after only minimal interrogation that he had committed the crime alone (and told the police that Williams and his codefendants were "idiots" for confessing), the prosecutors just changed their theory of the case to include him. The real perpetrator was then threatened with the death penalty unless he incorporated Williams and the others into his story.

An exception to this usual course of events can be found in the Lex Street murder investigation discussed above. After obtaining multiple confessions from one group of suspects, the investigators learned of a confession from someone else. In spite of the prosecutor's assurance that they "had the right guys" and that he would prosecute them "come hell or high water," the investigators launched their own independent investigation. The result, which cleared the original suspects who had falsely confessed, has been acknowledged not to be the norm, and it is held up as a case study on the proper corroboration of confession evidence.

Confession evidence can reach out and contaminate other evidence as well. Known as *postconfession contamination*, sharing the fact that a suspect confessed can impact the testimony of witnesses, victims, and as you will see in later chapters, even forensic scientists. Sharing details of the confession makes the situation worse. Influenced by the all-powerful confessions, eyewitnesses have been known to increase the certainty of their identification of the subject, and victims are known to include details that they did not originally report but were part of the suspect's confession. After all, since he confessed, the detail must be true. The victim just didn't remember it at first. Through postconfession contamination, false evidence is unintentionally created, or real evidence manipulated, thus providing what is believed to be corroboration for a false confession and helping to ensure a wrongful conviction.

DOES MIRANDA REALLY INHIBIT THE POLICE?

What about the role of the *Miranda* decision in not only tying the hands of the police and prosecutors to convict the guilty but also in their ability help the wrongfully accused or convicted? Many researchers and other experts agree with Cassell in some areas, but not for the reasons he has proposed. The research to date has proven him wrong in others.

Earlier studies showed that, once the police were forced to start advising suspects of their right to remain silent, there was a sharp decrease in the number of suspects making statements and confessions to the police. Over time, these numbers have not remained low. Law enforcement is quick to adapt and improvise. More recent studies show that approximately 80 percent of suspects waive their Miranda rights.[31] I have described Miranda as only a "speed bump" in the interrogation process. If an investigator is able to talk someone into confessing to a crime that could put them in jail for life, and then convince them that it is a good idea to put that confession on paper or repeat it on tape, they have little trouble talking them past Miranda. Techniques for getting a suspect to waive their Miranda rights are passed from investigator to investigator, and are often presented in classes and seminars.

The claim that the *Miranda* decision has helped to increase wrongful convictions is now actually supported by many interrogation and false confession researchers, but for reasons other than those proposed by Cassell. Judges are often less likely to be critical of even the most coercive of interrogations if the suspect was read and waived their Miranda rights.

Additionally, as in the case of Danial Williams and our hypothetical case from the first chapter, innocent persons, in their naïvety, are usually less likely to invoke their right to remain silent, thus opening the door to being subjected to harsh interrogations.

CONFESSIONS CLEARING THE WRONGFULLY ACCUSED AND CONVICTED

One contention by the critics of Miranda and any further restrictions on police interrogation techniques is that these restrictions prevent them from interrogating and obtaining confessions from the real perpetrator in cases in which an innocent person has been wrongfully accused or convicted.

This argument would depend on the contention that law enforcement was actively investigating and interrogating alternative suspects in cases in which an innocent person was wrongfully accused or convicted. In Edwin Montefiore Borchard's 1932 study of sixty-five cases of wrongful convictions that had occurred around the turn of the century, in twenty-six of those cases the innocent person was exonerated because the real perpetrator confessed. However, only in five of those cases was the confession obtained through a police interrogation or other law enforcement act. In nineteen of the cases, the confession was a voluntary one, made directly to the police or to a third party (in two of the cases, there was insufficient information to make a determination of how the confession came about).[32] So in the large majority of these cases, which occurred during a time when law enforcement had fewer restrictions on their interrogations than they do now, the rate of exonerations would not have been impacted by any additional restrictions placed on law enforcement's ability to interrogate suspects.

As we have, and will continue to see, law enforcement is not known for going out of its way to reinvestigate closed cases or convictions. In the case of Danial Williams, when Omar Ballard, the real perpetrator, was finally identified through DNA, he did confess during his interrogation to having raped and murdered Michelle Bosko on his own. His confession did not lead to the release of Williams. Instead, the investigators and the prosecutors used those interrogation techniques that were, according to Cassell and others, supposed to have exonerated Williams to convince Ballard to adopt their theory that he committed the crime with Williams and the others.

INTERROGATIONS: NOT JUST FOR SUSPECTS

In later chapters you will see more about the very things that can lead to a false confession can also lead to unreliable statements from crime victims, witnesses, and informants. If the investigator believes that any one of these people is not saying what the investigator believes to be true, then the investigator will go into "interrogation mode." The Reid Institute teaches this practice, and recommends that when "all other methods have failed," the investigator should accuse the subject of committing the crime (or of being implicated in it in some way) and proceed with an interrogation as though that person was, in fact, considered to have involvement in the crime.[33] Other tactics that have been used include telling the subject that if they don't cooperate they will be reported to Child Welfare Services and have their kids taken away, they will be harassed at work and at home, and even being told that the investigator will falsely spread the word that they were "snitching."

For informants, the incentives to "cooperate" can be much higher. Some informants are providing information in an attempt to get a criminal charge dismissed or their prison sentence reduced. As you will see in chapter 9, their motivation to provide the investigator or prosecutor with the exact information that they want to hear, even if that information is wrong, is pretty high.

SIGN OF A BIGGER PROBLEM

Bottom line is, even though we do not know how frequently false confessions occur, we know that they do. Additionally we now know that the problem extends far beyond what goes on in the interrogation room and can severely and adversely impact the outcome of a criminal investigation, as well as individual lives. The evidence is there, and it is growing. For decades, law enforcement has been treating the evidence like that annoying noise that your car starts to make. You turn up the radio to drown it out, not knowing that the cause of the noise is a symptom of a serious underlying problem. Either way, refusing to acknowledge the problem and actively resisting reform leads to both more wrongful convictions as well as the truly guilty going unpunished.

3

TYPES OF CONFESSIONS AND STATEMENTS

Whatever scientists study, whether it is animals, natural history, or other phenomenon, they look for similar patterns or characteristics. They use these like characteristics to create classifications. The study of police interrogation and false confessions is no different. The researchers have been able to identify three classifications of false confession—the voluntary, the compliant, and the internalized.[1] In this chapter we will break them down to make sense out of them. By being able to distinguish among the different types, you will be in a better position to understand the mechanics and dynamics by which they occur, which are discussed in the following chapters.

Though at first glance the three classifications may seem to be separate and distinct entities, like everything in which human nature is involved, there is sometimes a blurring of the lines and crossover. Additionally, although the classifications were created to help facilitate the study of false confessions, they can also be applied to confessions in general, as well as to reliable and unreliable statements from witnesses, victims, and informants. It is for that reason that as I go through each one, I will first discuss them as classifications of confessions and statements followed by how they apply to false confessions and unreliable statement evidence.

As I go through the list, I will occasionally touch on another topic that will be discussed in more detail at the end of this chapter, that often not all confessions and statements are totally false or totally true. This will help you understand later on how, through the use of standard US interrogation tactics, an investigator can unintentionally take a good confession or statement and totally screw it up.

VOLUNTARY CONFESSIONS AND STATEMENTS

A witness comes forward to the police to report that they witnessed a hit-and-run accident. A suspect walks into a police station and confesses that he just killed his neighbor. These, of course, are considered to be voluntary confessions and statements. The witness acts out of a sense of civic duty, the suspect out of remorse and a guilty conscience. However, investigators are not supposed to take even voluntary statements or confessions of this nature at face value. In later chapters, we will see how prudent investigators must always check all statements and confessions against the evidence and other statements. The old saying "trust but confirm" always applies. While statements like this more often than not turn out to be trustworthy, that is not always the case. Where voluntary confessions of this nature do occur, it always pays to be extra cautious.

As will be discussed more lately, people confess falsely to crimes, and witnesses and others lie for a reason. Typically that reason is to escape some real or perceived consequence or to obtain some real or perceived benefit. When the reasons are identified, the false confession or statement often turns out not to be so voluntary after all. However, researchers continue to lump them in the voluntary classification because the coercion that led to the confession was typically not caused by the actions of the police. Some of the reasons that someone might give a voluntary false confession or statement involve mental illness. Others include the following.

A Desire for Fame or Notoriety

Here, the subject has a pathological need for fame (or to be infamous), even if it means going to prison. Over two hundred people tried to falsely confess in the famous Lindbergh kidnapping case. An example of a false witness statement occurred in Washington, DC, in 2002. Over a three-week period, the area was terrified by a series of murders known as the Beltway Sniper. Victims were being shot down as they went about their daily affairs by a sniper who investigators and the public believed was operating out of a white van.[2]

On October 11, 2002, Linda Franklin was shot and killed while in a parking lot of a Home Depot store in Falls Church, Virginia. A subject came forward, told the police that he witnessed the shooting, and gave them a description of the white van as well as the suspect. Investigators later determined that the witness was inside the store at the time of the shooting and could not have been a witness. When the two men who were responsible for the murders were caught, it was discovered that they were shooting their victims from a blue Chevrolet Caprice, and had no connections to a white van.[3]

A Desire to Aid and Protect Someone

A witness might lie and provide a friend with a false alibi or otherwise falsify their account of an event to support a friend or family member's version. A witness or victim may also lie about why they were at a certain place at a certain time, not wanting their wife to know they were in an area of town famous for its street prostitution. People also confess to crimes to protect others.

Sometimes the relationship between the confessor and the person they are protecting is personal, other times professional. I have encountered situations in which a subject who was already serving a long prison sentence confessed to a crime committed by an associate or fellow gang member. The confessor has nothing to lose, and at the very least, their confession might produce enough "reasonable doubt" in the mind of the jury that they let the real perpetrator go.

In another case, a mother had killed the boyfriend of her daughter during a fight. The daughter falsely confessed, saying that she and she alone committed the crime. The mother and the daughter both knew that since the daughter was only fifteen years old at the time, she would spend only a few years in jail, while the mother faced at least twenty.

A Desire to Receive a Benefit

It is understandable that a witness might lie to receive reward money. Or an informant might give false information to get their sentence reduced. But besides the benefit of protecting someone or gaining increased status within a gang, what benefit can come from confessing to a crime that you did not commit?

It depends on what you perceive to be a benefit. I worked a case involving a woman who was found stabbed to death in a stairwell. Some time later, a patient who had been involuntarily committed to a state-run mental institution confessed to the crime. DNA extracted from a blood trail leading away from the crime scene excluded the patient. He later admitted that the only reason he confessed was because he wanted to get out of the mental institution and thought that the local jail offered better accommodations.

COMPLIANT CONFESSIONS AND STATEMENTS

Compliant confessions and statements are the ones that we hear about the most. The investigator believes that a witness or suspect is not telling him what he believes to be the truth. The investigator uses coercive interrogation tactics to convince the witness or the suspect to tell him what he wants to hear. The suspect or witness is stuck between the proverbial "rock and a hard place," with the only escape possible is through telling the investigator what they want to hear. You have already heard some about these tactics, and they will be covered in even greater detail in later chapters.

The problem is, even the most coercive, most inappropriate interrogation tactics can produce factually true confessions and statements. If an investigator puts a gun to the head of a suspect and tells him to confess, what comes out of the suspect's mouth could be the truth. It could also just be what the suspect knows the investigator wants him to say. You will see in later chapters the steps that must be taken to determine if the confession or statement is one or the other. For the suspect or witness, the biggest difference between a coerced compliant and the next type of confession/statement is that at the time the suspect/witness knows they are lying.

INTERNALIZED CONFESSIONS AND STATEMENTS

This type of confession or statement is perhaps the hardest for people to understand. Through the interrogation process, the person comes to believe that they committed a crime or had knowledge of/or witnessed something even though they have no actual memory of having done so. What happens is that the suspect or witness begins to distrust their memory, and begins to look to the investigator for suggestions or answers. By the time they give their final confession, the suspect or witness actually believes that what they said is true. This condition might last, or it may dissipate once the suspect or witness leaves the interrogation room and is no longer subjected to its coercive influence. The internalized classification is usually associated with false confessions and statements.

Memory manipulation is not that hard, and is discussed more in chapter 9. It can be done simply through the way we ask questions. Leading questions such as "Was the suspect's hat blue?" suggest or provide the answer. There have been experiments that prove that fictional events, even criminal ones, can be inserted into a person's memory of their childhood. Many of the subjects who participated in such experiments even interjected additional details and emotions when asked to describe the event to the researcher.[4]

In the interrogation room, the suspect who respects and trusts law enforcement and authority in general seems to be more susceptible to making a coerced internalized confession. Think about what you know so far about how interrogations are conducted. The investigator, an authority figure many have grown up being told to trust, tells the suspect that there is no doubt that they committed the crime, and all of the evidence points to their guilt. The investigator is absolutely confident, and will not let the suspect get a word in edgewise. The investigator confronts the suspect with evidence of their guilt, some if not all of it false. There are eyewitnesses, scientific evidence . . . there is no way that all of this evidence could be wrong. The suspect believes, and is often told by the investigator, that it is against the law for the investigator to lie, so all of this must be true. Doubt begins to enter the suspect's mind. The investigator asks if the suspect has a drinking problem. Maybe they were on drugs. Maybe the crime was so horrific that the suspect has tried to push it from their mind. There is no way that anyone would forget something like that.

Faced with this, and leading questions and other sources of contamination that provide the suspect with the details that "only the true perpetrator would know," the suspect, with the help of the investigator, "reconstructs" his "memory."

THE CONFESSION OF JOE DICK

This is exactly what happened to Joe Dick, the roommate of Danial Williams who had been charged with the rape and murder of Michelle Bosko in Norfolk, Virginia. When the DNA from the semen found on the crime scene did not match Williams's DNA, the investigators didn't consider that there might be a problem with Williams's confession. They just concluded that someone else had to be present.

Dick had grown up in Baltimore, Maryland, before joining the navy. Some of the people who knew him were "shocked" when he got accepted. Dick had cognitive and intellectual limitations, and required what his immediate supervisor called "intense supervision." As a child, he was in an accident that resulted in frontal lobe damage to his brain. Some said he was "extraordinarily gullible and naïve."[5]

It was six months after Bosko's murder that the investigators decided to interrogate Dick as a suspect. In the interrogation room, Dick was asked to account for his whereabouts around the time of the murder. Dick said that he thought he had been on duty, a detail that if the investigators had checked his supervisor would have confirmed. The investigators challenged Dick's memory from six months prior as to where he was, and he began to waiver. The interrogators became hostile, repeatedly accusing Dick of having been part of Bosko's murder. The investigators told Dick that they knew he was not on duty that night (which they didn't) and that he failed a lie detector test (which he had passed).

Faced with the "evidence" presented by people he was brought up to trust, Dick began to doubt his memory. One of the investigators suggested that Dick might have blacked out. Dick began to accept this as a possibility, and with the help of the investigators he began to construct his false confession.

Dick truly believed that he had committed the crime. That belief was not shaken when later it was proven that it was not his DNA either that was found on the crime scene. The investigators were undaunted. They just went back and had Dick modify his memory even more, adding more and more suspects into the mix. Much later, he told his probation and parole officer that he had "forgotten about the entire incident" until he was reminded of it by the investigators. [6]

Now that we know the different classifications of false confessions and statements, the following chapters will discuss the steps that the investigator must take to get there.

4

TAKING THE FIRST STEPS

Random and unforeseen events—natural, manmade, and a combination of both—can suddenly and unexpectedly uproot the lives of anyone at any time. The term *struck by lightning* can refer to a real occurrence or serve as an analogy for a disastrous event that seemingly comes out of nowhere. Even though, because of our decisions and lifestyles, we may increase our chances that such things happen to us, such as the golfer who continues to play in an approaching thunderstorm or the pedestrian who continually jaywalks, thus increasing their chances of being hit by the proverbial bus, even the average person is not totally immune. As the saying goes, s*#t happens, and looking back, one can see that it happened because of apparently random acts and events that came together in the perfect storm.

On July 8, 1997, such a perfect storm was brewing for US Navy sailor Danial Williams. Up to that point, nothing in Danial's life would have led anyone to believe that on that date he would suddenly be accused of murder.

Danial was born to Rhea and Normal Williams of Owosso, Michigan, located near nowhere in the center of Michigan.[1] A town of approximately fifteen thousand, one of its most famous residents was author James Oliver Curwood. Curwood built an elaborate and eccentric castle that he used only for entertainment and as a writing studio, neglecting to include any sleeping or eating quarters. Every year, the town holds a four-day celebration in his honor. The majority of his works can be obtained for free as an Amazon e-book.

Danial grew up in a two-parent household and had a typical American childhood. Described as shy, introverted, and easygoing, he was never known to be rebellious or a troublemaker of any kind. He had been taught by his parents to trust and respect authority figures, especially the police. Danial liked to hunt and fish with his family, played coronet in his high school marching band, and was on the high school freshman football team. Faced with a difficult local job market, Danial decided to follow the example of many of his relatives and go into the military, enlisting in the navy as part of an "early start" program before he graduated high school in 1991.

Danial first served on an aircraft carrier and then a marine carrier, rising to the rank of Machinists Mate Petty Officer Third Class. He was transferred to Norfolk, Virginia, in 1992. Fond of country music, he enjoyed spending time with friends at a local bar called The Banque, and the group became known as The Banque Crew. As so often happens, Danial began having problems with his drinking and soon went into a rehabilitation program to get help. He was soon sober and on a path to recovery.

In 1994, Danial met Nicole Masterson, and they fell in love. Danial took Nicole home to meet his parents, and they quickly became engaged. The relationship wasn't perfect, though. The two broke up for a brief period of time but reunited before Danial was deployed to the Mediterranean.

Danial and Nicole received what they thought was good news. Nicole was pregnant. But their world soon came crashing down when they discovered that what they thought was a pregnancy turned out to be ovarian cancer.

Now faced with a life-threating illness and mounting medical bills, Danial and Nicole decided to rush their engagement, getting married on June 27, 1997. Nicole went into the hospital for surgery four days later on July 1, 1997.

A few days later, Danial's parents came to Norfolk from Michigan to help with Nicole's recovery. Because Danial and Nicole had taken in a roommate, another sailor named Joe Dick, to help with the rent, Rhea and Norman stayed at a campsite about forty-five minutes from the house.

Nicole came home from the hospital on July 6, 1997, and Danial and his parents spent the day with her at their apartment. The next day, Nicole felt well enough that she and Danial went out to see Danial's parents at their campsite. They stayed most of the day, stopping for dinner at a local Cracker Barrel restaurant. Exhausted, they both went to sleep as soon as they got home.

The next day, Tuesday, July 8, Danial and Nicole ran various errands. When they returned, they found Rhea and Norman waiting for them in the parking lot of their apartment complex with a microwave oven and other wedding presents. All four were sitting around the apartment when a neighbor, Billy Bosko, frantically banged on the door. When they answered, Billy said that his wife, Michelle, was dead, and that he needed to use the phone.

Billy was also a sailor with the US Navy. He and nineteen-year-old Michelle lived across the hall from the Williamses. Billy had been on a cruise on the USS *Simpson* and had just returned home that evening. He had expected Michelle to meet him at the dock, but when she did not, he assumed that she was stuck at work. When he arrived home, Billy discovered his wife's partially clothed body in the bedroom.

When he couldn't find the house phone, Billy ran over to the Williamses' apartment. Danial called 911, and then followed Billy back into the apartment, where he saw Michelle's body in the bedroom. Together, Billy and Danial covered her with a blanket. Danial went home and waited for the police.

The police arrived a few minutes later and began their investigation. One detective talked briefly to Danial and his family, discovering that Danial was the one who had placed the 911 call.

Later that evening, as the police were still collecting evidence, Danial and his family were preparing to leave to go to dinner. Before they were able to leave, Danial was approached by Det. Maureen Evans, who had just finished up her work on the scene. Det. Evans explained to Danial that since he was the one who made the 911 call and had also entered the apartment and seen the body, she would like to take a sworn statement from him at police headquarters. Danial wanted to help in any way that he could. He agreed to go to police headquarters to give a statement, telling his family that he would meet up with them later. When he left his family at 6:30 pm, Danial had no idea that the first step to his making a false confession had been taken. In the mind of the detectives, Danial had become their primary suspect in the murder of Michelle Bosko.

MAKING THE FIRST ERROR

Criminal investigations are fluid things, theories ever changing as new facts become available. Or at least that is what should happen. But investigators are human and are subject to all of the frailties and flaws that come with that. These can be exacerbated by outside pressures and influences, such as lack of experience, the horrific nature of a crime, or artificial time constraints placed on an investigator to close a case. All of these contribute to the many mistakes that can lead to an investigation going astray, including that first step that it takes to getting a false confession: identifying an innocent person as a suspect.

How often does this happen? We don't definitively know how often false confessions occur, but we do have a better idea as to how often law enforcement may initially get it wrong when it comes to identifying their suspect. It comes from a survey of DNA Laboratories conducted by the National Institute of Justice (NIJ) and published in their 1996 report *Convicted by Juries, Exonerated by Science.* The survey was done years before the DNA database CODIS (Combined DNA Index System) came online. CODIS allows law enforcement to automatically submit any potential suspect DNA profile that was recovered from a crime scene into the database. CODIS does automatic and ongoing comparisons of that unknown DNA profile to other crime scene profiles, as well as to the DNA profiles of known offenders. CODIS looks for DNA profile matches between different crime scenes, as well as matches to specific offenders.[2]

Before the advent of CODIS, the submission of material that had the potential for containing the suspect's DNA to a laboratory for the development of a DNA profile was not done automatically. With no database, any profile that was developed was useless, unless you had identified a potential suspect and submitted their DNA sample as well. Then the laboratory could do a one-to-one comparison, DNA profile from the crime scene to the DNA profile from the suspect.

In their survey of laboratories that were analyzing DNA samples for law enforcement (and this included the FBI DNA laboratory), NIJ learned that out of 21,621 cases that had been submitted for DNA comparisons, 23 percent excluded the person who law enforcement had identified as a suspect in the case. In 16 percent of the total number of cases, the laboratory was unable to develop a sufficient enough profile from the crime scene DNA to make a comparison, so the results were inconclusive.[3]

Though there are many variables that that must be included when considering this exclusion rate, some have argued that this survey reveals that law enforcement appears to initially "get it wrong" at a higher percentage than you would think. But in attempting to use these numbers to get an idea as to how often an innocent person might be subjected to interrogation, it is also worth considering what it takes to obtain a suspect's DNA sample versus what it takes to get someone into the interrogation room.

Unless a suspect voluntarily provided a sample of their DNA to law enforcement, some sort of court order or search warrant was required. Court orders and search warrants require that the investigator be able to articulate to a judge or magistrate the evidence that exists that establishes the fact that some level of probable cause exists to believe that it is that suspect's DNA that was recovered from the crime scene.

JUMPING TO CONCLUSIONS TOO SOON

A common definition for *probable cause* is "a reasonable amount of suspicion, supported by circumstances sufficiently strong enough to justify a prudent and cautious person's belief that certain facts are probably true."[4] Probable cause is more than a hunch, more than a rumor. Being the neighborhood "weirdo" does not count.

Unfortunately, innocent people often become the primary focus of an investigator's suspicions because of hunches, neighborhood suspicions, anonymous tips, unreliable informant information, or just because. In many cases, the innocent person became a suspect because, in the mind of the investigator, they just were not "acting normal." People have become suspects in murder cases because they acted "too upset" or "not upset enough," either in the eyes of the investigator or family members and associates of the victim. In hindsight, things that normally would not justify a second thought suddenly become highly suspicious.

In Danial's case, he became a suspect because of Tamika Taylor, a friend of Michelle's. While at the crime scene, Det. Evans told Taylor that it was her belief that Michelle had known her killer and asked Taylor for her "gut feeling" as to who would have killed her.[5]

Taylor told Det. Evans that she thought that they should check out Danial. Taylor said that she believed that Danial was obsessed with Michelle "in a creepy sexual way." She told Det. Evans of times that Danial had stopped by Michelle's apartment, and once, when Michelle had a party, Danial had stopped by, danced in a "sexual manner" and "leered" at Michelle.[6]

Taylor also told Det. Evans about another person besides Danial that she thought the police should check out, Omar Ballard. But Ballard wasn't there, Danial was. So the investigation would begin with him. Ballard's name would not surface in the investigation again for quite some time.

At this point, there is nothing wrong with Det. Evan's reasoning. There were no signs of forced entry, and based on how Michelle was found, the crime was clearly of a sexual nature. It was logical to investigate anyone who Michelle might have let into her apartment, and Taylor's comments about Danial would have peeked anyone's interest. More investigation was clearly warranted.

One of the most critical points in any investigation is when it shifts from being "evidence based" to "suspect based." Evidence-based investigations are what we typically think of when we think of "detective work." Clues are sought, information uncovered, theories are developed, and then put to the test. A good detective, like a good scientist, does not go out to prove a theory but to test it. As new evidence becomes available, old evidence and theories are reevaluated, then modified or discarded as required.

A shift to a "suspect-based" investigation occurs when, based on the evidence and information gathered during the investigation, a suspect has been identified. The emphasis now becomes the gathering of evidence and information to bring the case to court. Though the investigation has become more focused, the good detective continues to critically examine the evidence and is open to the possibility that they might still be wrong.

If this sounds like Basic Investigations 101, that's because it is. It is a topic covered in many basic textbooks on investigation and interrogation. The book *Criminal Interrogation and Confessions* published by John E. Reid and Associates, Inc. (commonly known as the Reid Institute; more about them later) is considered by many to be the "bible" of interviewing and interrogation in the United States. In their book, the Reid Institute cautions about the overreliance on potentially faulty eyewitness accounts and the possible misinterpretation of circumstantial evidence. They say that if there is to be a bias in an investigation, the bias should lean toward a suspect's innocence.[7]

Many other textbooks that teach the type of interrogation tactics used in the United States mirror Reid. In his textbook *Criminal Interrogation: A Modern Format for Interrogating Criminal Suspects Based on the Intellectual Approach*, Warren Holmes warns of the danger of being "married to a theory," warning that "in the pursuit of truth, ego is an insidious, undermining influence."[8] Holmes also cautions investigators about the problems with eyewitness identification, possible misinterpretation of forensic evidence by scientists, and the problems inherent with the use of informants, all causes of wrongful convictions.[9]

Law enforcement in the United Kingdom goes as far as to formally incorporate this "investigator's mindset" into their investigative process and documentation. A timeline for the investigation is created. Each critical decision point in an investigation is documented, including the justification for that decision. As new evidence becomes available, the prior decisions are reviewed to see if the new evidence would require that the earlier decision be reversed or modified.[10] This process has been used to help investigate alleged wrongful convictions and other investigative failures here in the United States by helping to identify evidence of confirmation bias. Once the timeline has been developed, the order in which evidence was discovered is established, and critical decision points are plotted, the order in which the evidence was discovered is switched around. If by reviewing the case with the evidence coming to light in a different order the conclusions drawn at the critical decision points are significantly altered, then there is a high probability that confirmation bias is present.

WRONG WAY TO THEORIZE

Unfortunately, this idealistic picture of the proper way of conducting evidence and suspect-based investigations is more difficult to accomplish than it sounds. It is natural for an investigator to begin to construct a narrative as to how the crime happened from the moment they arrive at the scene. A story is formed based on their interpretation of the scene, assessment of witnesses, personal experience, and mindset. But because the investigator failed to follow the advice of the famed fictitious detective from the late 1800s, Sherlock Holmes, and began to theorize before having all the facts, initial theories are often partially, if not completely, wrong.

Investigators often pride themselves on their intuition, the "sixth sense" that they feel that they have developed over the years, believing that it allows them to accurately read people and situations. This sixth sense is real, but it is not some paranormal ability, some special "cop knowledge." We all have it. It is a cognitive shortcut, allowing us to respond quickly to situations in which we have minimal information, using past learned experiences to reach immediate conclusions.[11]

Intuition has its place in investigations, but also its drawbacks. One is that "it is easily influenced by emotion and is often error prone."[12] Another is that the "experience" that we may be using to make intuitive decisions may not be real. In the mid-1990s, several seasoned homicide detectives attended a crime scene reconstruction class in Orlando, Florida. The detectives were being taught the basics of blood spatter analysis, bullet trajectory, and other skills that would assist them in using the physical evidence left at a crime scene to recreate the events leading up to and occurring after the crime. The class was being held at a local motel, and several of the rooms had been set up to simulate different types of crime scenes.

One of the rooms was supposed to replicate a double murder in which the killer used a shotgun on the victims at close range. As the detectives were combing the room for clues, they came up with multiple and often diverse theories as to what happened. With each new theory, the instructor became more and more amused.

Finally, the instructor called the examinations to a halt and began to walk the detectives through the process. The instructor placed two detectives, one petite in build and one structured like a linebacker, where the victims were thought to be when they were shot. The instructor placed the "shooter" with the shotgun only a few feet from the victims, and asked how far back the shotgun blast would propel each victim when it struck them. The class agreed that the big detective, because of his bulk, would only stagger back a few feet, while the smaller detective would be "blown back into the wall." The instructor laughed even more.

The instructor then showed the class several filmstrips of people being shot. Some of the filmstrips were taken by police during tactical operations and showed people being shot by snipers or by shotguns in SWAT operations. Others were news footage that captured close-range shootings, including suicides. In all of the clips, the person who was shot was not forced back by being struck by the bullet, but dropped straight down. The instructor explained that firearm projectiles do not carry the force required to blow a human off their feet. For years, the detectives had been interpreting their crime scenes based on the physics they learned from movies and Road Runner cartoons.

We also have a tendency to take minimal experience of a type of crime and apply it across the board. Because may law enforcement agencies are small and cover jurisdictions that don't have a lot of crime, their investigators might only investigate a few crimes such as a murder in their careers. This problem exists even in large departments, where child sex murders and other such crimes are, in reality, rare occurrences. The vast majority of investigators have little experience in both analyzing the crime scene and the type of person who would commit such a crime. Again, they often rely on "experience" they obtain through the popular media or through seminars that only touch on the topics. This is why there are organizations like the National Center for Missing and Exploited Children and the FBI's Behavioral Analysis Unit. These organizations study thousands of such crimes and make their findings and expertise available to investigators, services that are often not used.

IN COMES TUNNEL VISION

Once an incorrect theory or assumption is rooted in the mind of the investigator, it can be very difficult to shake. Tunnel vision, that narrowing of focus that prevents us from seeing possible alternative theories, kicks in. The investigator does not seek to test the theory, but, because of confirmation bias, to confirm it. "Confirmation bias is a type of selective thinking in which an individual is more likely to search for evidence that confirms his/her hypothesis while ignoring or refusing to search for contradicting evidence."[13] Tunnel vision, and the accompanying confirmation bias, has been identified as a leading cause of wrongful convictions.[14]

In addition to this are the often artificial pressures that are on an investigator to close a case. One is the "closure rate." The safety of a city, town, or county is judged by the crime rate. The ruler by which the efficiency of a law enforcement agency is measured is not only how much they can reduce the crime rate but also how many cases they solve, or the closure rate. In most, if not all, law enforcement agencies, the worth of an investigator is based on their closure rate. Their personal reputation, self-esteem, ability to stay within or be transferred to a choice assignment, and sometimes even the ability to earn additional overtime can be adversely impacted by a low closure rate. Because law enforcement management usually takes into account only the statistical number and not the other factors that differentiate one case from another when it comes to their solvability, investigators may look for the simplest and quickest way to get that closure.[15]

Combining with closure rates is often the artificial time constraints that law enforcement officials, the media, and the public place on investigators who are working on high-profile cases, especially murders. Television shows such as A&E's *The First 48* hype the belief that if a homicide case is not solved within forty-eight hours, it will most likely never be solved. In 2014, the *Miami Times* reported on how the deadline imposed by the show contributed to wrongful arrests in some of the cases they featured.[16] Quickly identifying a suspect and obtaining a confession helps to avoid time-consuming investigatory work.[17]

Cognitive biases, inexperience, and external pressures all contribute to taking that first step to getting a false confession to identify the wrong person as a suspect. Another contributor is the result of the training law enforcement receives, both formally and on the job, when it comes to deciding who to interrogate. It is that training that leads investigators to believe that they are capable of being human lie detectors.

YOU ARE SAYING ONE THING BUT YOUR BODY SAYS ANOTHER

The popular perception is that a trained investigator can determine if someone is being deceptive, or even determine that they are guilty, by closely watching and evaluating the suspect's movements, body position, and verbal responses. Just about every interrogation school and textbook used in the United States spends an enormous amount of time teaching these techniques under various scientific-sounding names, such as "Behavior Symptom Analysis"[18] and "Forensic Assessment Interview Technique (FAINT)."[19]

Behavior Symptom Analysis (BSA) is one of the most popular and widely taught deception detection techniques. Initially developed by polygraph examiner John E. Reid and Fred E. Inbau in the 1940s, instruction on the use of the BSA is offered as a component of interrogation training by John E. Reid & Associates, Inc., often referred to as the Reid Institute. They are the oldest and largest interrogation training facility in the United States, and have provided training here and abroad. The Reid technique of interviewing and interrogation textbook was one of the interrogation training textbooks cited in the *Miranda* decision of the Supreme Court as an example of how typical interrogations are conducted by law enforcement. Researchers in the field of police interviewing and interrogation usually reference the Reid Technique in their work. The large majority of other interrogation schools models their deception detection training along the same lines as that taught by the Reid Institute.

Though it is supposed to be used throughout the investigator's interaction with the suspect, the BSA comes into its own during the Behavioral Analysis Interview (BAI). This is a preinterrogation interview during which the investigator uses the BSA to determine if a suspect is being deceptive as well as the likelihood of their guilt. It is like a screening interview, in which the investigator makes the determination as to whether or not to move on to the more accusatory interrogation stage.

The Reid Institute teaches that during the BSA, the investigator is supposed to evaluate the suspect's behavior in three different areas of communication: verbal, "paralinguistic," and nonverbal.[20]

Regarding verbal behavior, the Reid Institute says that the investigator must carefully note the suspect's word choice and arrangements. They teach various propositions, such as "truthful subjects will offer spontaneous responses; deceptive suspects may offer rehearsed responses," and "truthful suspects respond to questions directly; deceptive suspects may answer evasively."[21] Paralinguistic behaviors are things such as how quickly or not the suspect responds to a question and the tone and rate of their response. An example they use is if the subject says, "Listen, I did not steal any money" and each word is separated for emphasis, that is supposed to be a response from an innocent person.[22]

Nonverbal behavior is all of that body language stuff made popular by books such as *How to Read a Person Like a Book*[23] published back in

1971. Deception and truthfulness can be detected by the way a person sits, folds their arms, touches their face, and numerous other acts. Some interrogation schools go further, and teach that by observing the direction a suspect's eyes move (i.e., up and to the right, down and to the left) indicate what "side of the brain" they are using to formulate their answer.

In addition to watching for verbal, nonverbal, and paralinguistic indicators, the investigator is taught to use "behavior-provoking" questions. It is alleged that innocent subjects will respond differently to these questions than the guilty. One such question is "What do you think should happen to the person who committed this crime?" An innocent person would say that they should have the "book thrown at them," while a guilty person would suggest that maybe they deserved a second chance (an answer that my all-forgiving mother would probably give no matter what the circumstances).

DOES IT REALLY WORK?

Most interrogation schools claim that through the use of their system, an investigator can correctly identify the guilty and determine when they are being deceptive 85 percent of the time or higher. In one recent study that used a Reid-trained interrogator, the rate was 100 percent.[24] This is in stark contrast to over fifty years of lie detection research in which using the same tactics taught by the interrogation schools the rate was 54 percent, slightly better than the flip of a coin.[25] At least one study showed that participants who relied on the behavioral signs taught by the Reid Institute actually fared worse.[26]

Accusations fly between the two groups. The pro-BSA side claims that the opposition's experiments do not reflect real-world conditions, a claim also issued against the pro-BSA side. While there are only a small handful of experiments that support the pro-BSA aide, there are numerous more that support the opposition. In addition, the opposition's experiments have been replicated many, many times over five decades, producing the same results.

Interestingly, the pro-BSA experiment that produced the 100 percent accuracy results used a similar model, as did many of the opposition's experiments, with some important changes. In this experiment, the participants played a trivia game with a partner who, unknown to them, was in on the experiment. The participants were paid cash for each right answer that they gave. At one point, the researcher who was conducting the game left the room, at which point, the participant who was the "plant" suggested to the unsuspecting participant that they cheat. The participants that agreed were the "guilty" subjects, because by cheating they were stealing money.

Afterward, a Reid Institute–trained interrogator interviewed the participants. He observed their behavior as he asked them a series of questions, one of which was what questions did they get right and how they knew the answer. Afterward, as trained, the interrogator left the room. Returning a short time later, the interrogator accused the participant of cheating and went into "interrogation mode" (as will be discussed more in the next chapter) for several minutes. Afterward, the interrogator announced his decision as to the guilt or innocence of the participant. Not only was the interrogator 100 percent right but also he was able to obtain confessions from all of the guilty parties.

Taking this 100 percent confession rate (and the associated claim of 0 percent false confession rate) at face value is problematic, and I will discuss the confession issue in the next chapter. But for now, I want to focus on this apparently remarkable success rate of the BSA, except that the interrogator's conclusion was not based solely on his BSA. As mentioned above, the purpose of doing a preinterrogation interview at which the BSA is used is to prevent the first step of getting a false confession, to identify the honest and innocent and not subject them to a coercive interrogation. Instead, everyone, regardless of whatever opinion may have been formed, was interrogated, using tactics that are not supposed to be part of the BSA and thus skewing that side of the experiment. This scenario mimics exactly what the Reid Institute says should not happen.

THE "SMALL PRINT"—USE WITH CAUTION

Putting the "accuracy" debate beside, some interrogation schools do caution that there are some factors and conditions that can lead the investigator to misinterpret the signs and symptoms of guilt or deception. The Reid Institute says in their textbook that the following situations and conditions may adversely affect the normal interpretation of the standard guidelines for behavioral assessments:

- Use of medications by the subject
- Mental illness
- Antisocial personality
- Low intelligence
- Low social responsibility and/or maturity
- Young children
- The emotional condition of the suspect
- Cultural differences
- A subject who is trained in or aware of the signs and symptoms used in Behavioral Analysis[27]

The researchers who conducted the 100 percent success rate experiment did not report if any of their participants had any of these issues. In my world, this probably composed over 90 percent of my suspect and witness pool. Many interrogations are conducted with the investigator having minimal or no background information on the subject, either through lack of time or preparation, thereby making it difficult for the investigator to know if their subject fell into some of these categories.

There is also debate on what constitutes a young subject. In their textbook, the Reid Institute calls for caution when using the BAI on a suspect "less than nine years old," but also says that the person's "degree of maturity" must be considered.[28] Most places place the cutoff age for becoming an adult at the age of eighteen but allow for suspects as young as fourteen or sixteen years old to be charged as an adult with a criminal offense. The International Association of Chiefs of Police uses the research conducted by several experts and acknowledges in its model policy for interviewing and interrogating juveniles that the term usually includes someone up to the age of eighteen years old, but that "youths as a whole" are typically more impulsive, less mature, less able to weigh risks and consequences, and more vulnerable to pressures such as are found in the interrogation room.[29] However, as any parent knows, maturity and good decision-making skills just don't kick in when someone reaches the magical age of eighteen.

Typically, investigators receive little to no training on identifying mental health issues or other cognitive problems, such as Attention Deficient Disorder or autism. When the signs and symptoms of these problems manifest themselves in the interrogation room, they are often misinterpreted as indicators of deception and/or guilt.

Add to this the problems that tunnel vision and confirmation bias add to the picture. Investigators are naturally suspicious. After all, that suspect is in that interrogation room for a reason, no matter how tenuous. And the cop's mantra of "everyone lies, even when they don't have to" is usually the starting point of the exchange between the investigator and the suspect.

A good example of this can be found in David Simon's book *Homicide: A Year on the Killing Streets*. Simon was a *Baltimore Sun* reporter who was imbedded in the Baltimore Homicide Unit for approximately one year, and the book documents his experiences and observations. Simon documented the behavior patterns that the investigators would use to detect deception. They include:

- Uncooperative
- Talks too much
- Gets their story perfectly straight
- Blinks too much
- Avoids eye contact

Other indications of deception include:

- Too cooperative
- Talks too little
- Fucks his story up
- Doesn't blink
- Stares[30]

Because of confirmation bias, we see what we seek.

The actual training classes offered by the Reid Institute and others does little to discourage this problem.

The dangers of confirmation bias and the factors that might result in the misinterpretation of the signs of deception go virtually unmentioned. Students are not required to practice any of the BAI techniques themselves, are told what to look for, and then are shown videos in which the subject exhibits that specific behavior.

RELIANCE ON "SCIENCE"

Along with using the BAI to help who is guilty and should undergo interrogation, investigators often turn to the "science" of the polygraph, or other "lie detection" devices discussed in the last chapter. During criminal investigations, investigators typically use polygraphs in one of three ways. The first is to confirm the accuracy of the information that a suspect or witness has provided. An example would be subjecting an informant to the polygraph before acting on the information that they provided.

The second way the polygraph is used, which overlaps with the first, is as leverage either before or during the interrogation itself. The suspect has denied any involvement in the crime or has provided an account that the investigator does not believe is the truth. The first step for the investigator is to ask the suspect if they will take a polygraph exam. If the suspect hesitates or refuses, the investigator includes the refusal into the "guilty column" of behavior by the suspect. If they do agree to take the exam, the suspect is first reinterviewed by the polygraph examiner. The main purpose of this reinterview is for the examiner to convince the suspect of the infallibility of the machine. For some, this serves the same purpose as the inquisitor showing the suspect the instruments of torture and how they will be applied. Often, admissions are made even before the test is run. It doesn't matter if the polygraph works at all as long as the suspect believes that it does.

The third way is what I call "investigation by polygraph." The investigator drags in all of the "usual suspects" and subjects them all to a polygraph examination. The investigator separates the innocent from the guilty and conducts accusatory and coercive interrogations based on the results. Even if the polygraph examination did have an 80 percent, or let's say 90 percent accuracy rate, that still leaves a lot of innocent folks who are being exposed to the possibility of falsely confessing.

Though as discussed in chapter 1 the accuracy and reliability of such devices is highly questionable, many in law enforcement have a great deal of faith in these machines—unless, that is, they don't produce the results expected by the investigator. As you will see in the next chapter, investigators will, as one of their interrogation tactics, tell suspects that they have failed the polygraph, even when they pass or the results were "inconclusive."

Since polygraph and other "lie detector" machines don't actually detect lies but measure the body's physiological responses, the interpretations of those responses are subjective. Being human, polygraph examiners are subject to the adverse effects of tunnel vision and verification bias just like everyone else. A good example is a case I was working when we were using both the polygraph and the computerized voice stress analysis (CVSA) machines. The suspect was believed to have participated in a murder based on what turned out to be misinterpreted forensic evidence. The suspect continued to deny any involvement in the murder, and agreed to undergo a CVSA test. An investigator who had no involvement in the original investigation administered the test. According to that investigator, the test showed that the suspect was not being deceptive when they denied any involvement in the murder. Another investigator who had participated in the interrogation of the suspect was a CVSA instructor. That investigator interpreted the findings differently, pointing out the indicators on the tape that showed deception. Confronted with these findings, the suspect confessed but later recanted.

Because they were now saying that his confession was false, the suspect was offered a chance to take a full polygraph exam. After consulting with his attorney, the suspect agreed. The polygraph examiner, who was aware of the earlier confession when he gave the test, said that the suspect once again failed. Evidence uncovered later in the investigation proved unequivocally that the suspect was not in any way involved in the murder. Both the polygraph and the CVSA were wrong.

I have worked with many polygraph examiners in the course of my career, including many considered to be at the top of the field. The best polygraph examiners, who not by accident were also excellent interviewers, would always tell me that when it comes to using polygraph examination results in an investigation, an investigator should always listen to what the evidence is saying over the polygraph. The same applies to the BAI as well.

WILLIAMS BECOMES A SUSPECT

In the very early stages of the investigation into the murder of Michelle Bosko, Det. Evans had begun to fall victim to confirmation bias. Even before the crime scene investigators had finished processing the apartment, even before the autopsy on Michelle's body was completed, Danial had become the suspect.

Acting on Tamika's "gut feeling" that Det. Evans should look closer at Danial (as well as Omar Ballard), Det. Evans approached Danial and asked him if he would mind coming down to the police station to talk with the detectives. In their book *The Wrong Guys*, Tom Wells and Richard Leo describe Det. Evans's mindset.

> Williams appeared overly cooperative to her. "I was actually kind of shocked that he gave in that easy," Williams recounts. "He didn't ask me any questions whatsoever," like, Why do I have to come down right now? the kind of thing that Evans had come to expect from criminals. She thought that Williams might have been trying to appear cooperative so as to avoid looking suspicious. "But to me that looked suspicious," she says. [31]

At this point, Danial didn't realize it, but he "couldn't win for losing." His willingness to be a good citizen and try to help the police was held against him. Even the bumper sticker on his truck, a typical macho/juvenile one that said "Sex is like pizza, when it's good, it's very good. When it's bad, it's still good" just reinforced Det. Evans's forgone conclusion of Danial's guilt. [32] The next step that was required for Danial to give a false confession was about to happen.

5

GOOD POLICE WORK OR COERCION?

Once at the police station, Det. Evans asked Danial to wait. For over an hour he sat, drinking soda and smoking cigarettes. Danial didn't mind. He, as he figured most people in his situation would do, was willing to do what he could to help the police solve Michelle's murder. Unknown to him, the detectives were using this time to strengthen their belief in Danial's guilt, continuing to interview Tamika Taylor, picking her brain for what she knew for sure and thought she knew about Danial. At approximately 8:00 pm, they were ready. Danial was led into the interrogation room. Danial didn't know it, but he was about to engage in the most important conversation of his life. He was moving to the second step necessary in obtaining a police-induced false confession: the coercive interrogation.

But so what? It is generally accepted by everyone that an interrogation is inherently coercive. How else can you expect the police to convince a guilty suspect to admit to a crime, knowing such an admission could result in loss of liberty and sometimes even their life? The Supreme Court has said that "[a]ny interview of one suspected of a crime by a police officer will have coercive aspects about it, simply by virtue of the fact that the police officer is part of a law enforcement system which may ultimately cause the suspect to be charged with a crime."[1] As we discussed in chapter 4, the largest interrogation school in the United States, the Reid Institute, blatantly admits that successful interrogations "frequently require the use of psychological tactics and techniques that could be classified as 'unethical,' if evaluated in terms of ordinary, everyday social behavior."[2] Such unethical tactics include, within limits, the investigator lying about evidence of using deception. The use of physical force or threats of such force, are, of course, condemned across the board.

Besides, there are lots of safeguards in place to prevent an interrogator from going too far, or an innocent person confessing to a crime they did not commit, right? The fact that a suspect must be advised of and then voluntarily waive his right to remain silent and the right to have an attorney with him before any interrogation can take place is a major one. Another major safeguard is what the investigator perceives to be a successful end result or goal of the interrogation. Any investigator will tell you that the purpose behind an interrogation is not to obtain a confession, but to elicit "the truth." A false confession is therefore counterproductive, something that no one wants to have happen.

The actual interrogation tactics that are generally taught to police allegedly provide yet another safeguard. The major interrogation school in the United States is adamant in saying that the process and tactics they teach will not cause someone to falsely confess. However, as they warn in what appears to be a confusing contradiction, these tactics should only be used on a person that the investigator believes to be guilty.

But are these safeguards enough? Do they keep an innocent person from falsely confessing to a crime and ensure that the information obtained from the guilty person is "the truth?" What happens in that interrogation room that would get someone to confess to a crime that they did do, much less one that they didn't? What do we know, or think we know, about what goes on in the interrogation room? In this chapter we will examine what is supposed to happen versus what often happens, and how both scenarios can lead to false confessions.

PUBLIC PERCEPTION VIA THE MEDIA

The fifth season of the Baltimore-based crime drama *The Wire*[3] opens with a close-up of the impeccably dressed Det. Bunk Moreland, aka "The Bunk," in a claustrophobic interrogation room. He is explaining to De-Shawn, the young and obviously scared African American suspect, that keeping silent is "not all that it's cracked up to be," not when you are "seen, running from the deed." And when your own "running partner is in the next room, putting you in . . . telling it like a little bitch." Exuding confidence, Bunk tells DeShawn that his running buddy, Monell, was so helpful that they took him to "Mickey D's." Bunk correctly rattles off Monell's McDonald's food preferences: "Quarter Pounders, big fries, McDonald Land cookies, Dr. Pepper," saying "that's how your boy rolls, right?" This "inside knowledge" increases Bunk's credibility and causes a flicker of doubt to cross DeShawn's face. Could his partner in crime really be giving it up?

The camera switches to the squad room, where Monell, hands full of McDonald's bags, is speaking with another detective. Asking where he is going, Monell is told "the break room" so that he can enjoy his food. Monell tells the detective, "All right, but I still ain't saying shit to ya'll." The move is clearly scripted to allow DeShawn to see Monell with the food, acting friendly and cooperating with the detectives in the hope that he will become nervous and try to beat Monell to the punch, providing a confession or, at the very least, incriminating details about the crime.

Bunk arranges for DeShawn to take a "false detector" test, consisting of his hand being taped to a copy machine with preloaded sheets of paper that say "true" or "false." "The Professor," who is actually Bunk's sergeant, administers the "test." The Professor assures DeShawn that the machine can measure his pulse, and that "the machine tells the tale."

Bunk starts with "easy questions," such as asking DeShawn to confirm his real name. The copy button is pushed and the preprinted "true" sheet comes out. Bunk asks a few more simple ones, and then lobs the big one, "And did you and Monell shoot your boy Pookie down on Carrie Street just like Monell said you did?" Rattled, DeShawn answered, "Na, no!" A pause, and the "false" sheet comes out of the machine. The detectives tell DeShawn that he is a liar, backed by the Professor telling him that "the machine is never wrong." DeShawn breaks, saying that Monell "can't never keep his mouth shut. I should have put a cap in Pookie's ass my own self, left Monell at home." Case closed. Score one for the good guys.

For the majority of us, our knowledge of the interrogation room extends no further than television, movies, novels, and "true crime" stories. We perceive interrogation as involving high drama, a battle of wits between good and evil, with all the rules favoring the side of evil so that when good prevails it is a significant victory. We enjoy watching the game, and since the playing field is portrayed as tilted, we applaud the creativity and ingenuity of the Bunks of the world. Even when, through passion, our favorite detectives cross the line, we give them a pass.

And cross the line they do. In shows and movies such *Law and Order* and *LA Confidential*, investigators succumb to their emotions, resorting to threats if not physical violence. But even in these cases, we all know that the suspect is guilty, and we silently support the investigator's efforts to get justice. In one scene in *The Wire*, multiple investigators beat a confession out of a suspect and justify the resulting injuries in their paperwork as having come from "resisting arrest." But of course he was guilty, so what did it matter? Another murderer was off the street.

Still, Hollywood is not reality, or is it? Law enforcement investigators are often hired to act as consultants in movie and television productions to help add a sense of reality to the finished product. And many in the law enforcement field acclaim *The Wire* as one of the most realistic cop shows ever produced. Still, it would be unfair to pass judgment solely based on television and movie depictions, especially when they get so much else wrong all for the sake of a good story line.

To learn what investigators are supposed to do to convince someone to confess, let's begin by examining what is supposed to happen during a textbook-perfect interrogation. But even here we have a problem. In the United States, there are no formal, nationally accepted interrogation training programs, no model standard, and no nationally recognized best practices. Interrogation tactics that might be accepted in the courts in one jurisdiction could be rejected in another. Some investigators receive extensive training in interrogation, others just on the job. And investigators, like everyone else, are influenced by what they see in the movies and television, especially "real crime" TV shows.

Since there are no national training standards, quality varies quite a bit from school to school. First, anyone can set themselves up as an instructor in interview and interrogation tactics. Second, there is no standard as to the number of hours that an investigator must spend learning and practicing. Training programs can run anywhere from a few hours to a week. It used to be the practice of my old agency to send its investigators to a couple of different interrogation schools and let the individual investigator pick and choose the techniques that they like the best (or use no specific techniques at all).

In spite of this, there is actually some consistency in the way interrogations are supposed to be conducted. Certain basic principles are found in almost all formal training, and even in the interrogation tactics of investigators who have received no such training. These principles, and the interrogation tactics that arise from them, are often structured into numbered or alphabetized "steps" or "parts." The most well known is the Reid Technique of Interviewing and Interrogation, more commonly known as the Reid Nine Steps of Interrogation.

Initially developed by polygraph examiners John E. Reid and Fred E. Inbau in the 1940s, the training is still offered through John E. Reid & Associates, Inc., often referred to as the Reid Institute. They are the oldest and largest interrogation training facility in the United States and provide training in their nine-step program both here and abroad. *The Reid Technique of Interviewing and Interrogation* textbook was one of the interrogation training textbooks cited in the *Miranda* decision of the Supreme Court as an example of how typical interrogations are conducted by law enforcement. Researchers in the field of police interviewing and interrogation usually reference the Reid Technique in their work. And as mentioned above, the techniques developed by the Reid Institute can be found in one form or another in most non-Reid interrogation training.

A frequent criticism of false confession experts by interrogation schools like the Reid Institute is that they believe that the experts misrepresent the interrogation tactics that the schools teach. So using Reid[4] as a general guide, let's see what a textbook interrogation is supposed to look like in the United States.

INTERROGATION BY THE BOOK

Preliminary Matters

Before going into the interrogation room, the investigator has done his or her homework. He has reviewed the file and has a thorough understanding of the crime and the evidence. It is during this review that the investigator identified what is often called "hold back" information. These are details that, as law enforcement personnel love to say in murder cases, "only the killer would know." These hold-back details will later help the investigator determine the reliability of the confession.

The investigator has also completed as much background research on the suspect as is possible. Information regarding the suspect's education, employment, relationships, past criminal history, and any substance abuse problems will all be helpful during the investigator's interaction with the suspect.

The Location

Just like in the movies and on TV, interrogation rooms are small (usually around ten feet by ten feet), windowless structures. In some there is a one-way mirror, allowing others a way to observe without being observed. If there is recording equipment, it is usually video, and is located so that it is unobtrusive.

Furniture consists of a table and chairs, one for the suspect and others for the interrogators. Often the suspect's chair is bolted to the floor, and a ring bolt is mounted nearby to secure cuffs to the wall or floor if necessary. It is recommended that the table be off to the side so that there are no physical barriers between the suspect and the interrogator(s). No clocks should be on the walls so as not to give the suspect a sense of passing time.

The stated purpose of the layout of the room is to afford the suspect privacy, much the same as a Catholic confessional. Privacy is instrumental in helping to get someone to confess, but so is the sense of helplessness and isolation from the outside that the layout of the room naturally generates. No investigator wants to interrogate a suspect in surroundings that are comfortable to them. They want to make sure that interrogations are done on the investigator's turf.

Phase 1: The Interview

Before any interrogation, there should be an interview. As the two words are often used interchangeably, some confusion about this is natural. In general, an interview is a fact-gathering conversation whereas the interrogation becomes accusatory. This difference will become important as we go on.

For the investigator, the interview serves several purposes. It allows the investigator and the suspect to get to know each other, build a rapport. The investigator's observations of the suspect's physical and mental state, combined with the earlier background investigation, are supposed to help the investigator determine any issues that might impede the interview. The interview phase also provides an opportunity for the suspect to provide their version of events or an alibi. The interview allows the investigator the chance to ask for details that will permit further investigation of the alibi or the suspect's side of the story. It is usually during this time that, depending on local laws, policy, and/or whether the suspect is in custody at the time, the suspect will be given their Miranda warnings: told of their right to remain silent and their right to an attorney. If they waive those rights, the interview will continue. If not, that's the end of it.

During a proper interview, the suspect should do most of the talking. The investigator should use open-ended questions or requests, such as "Tell me what you did that day," in order to elicit the most information from the suspect.

The interview also gives the investigator an opportunity to "size up the suspect" and develop a baseline of their behavior, which will be used to compare how they act in the interrogation. Using the training described in the last chapter, the investigator will look for behavioral signs of deception. They will ask those specific questions that are supposed to help determine the suspect's probability of guilt, such as "What do you think should happen to the person who committed this crime?" They may infer that evidence might be forthcoming that could point to the person's guilt, through questions like "We are now processing the gun that was used in the crime for fingerprints. Is there any reason that we would find your prints on that gun?" The suspect's answers, along with their behavior, will help the investigator decide whether or not to move to Phase 2, the interrogation.

Phase 2: The Interrogation

The investigator moves to the interrogation phase only if they are certain (or reasonably certain) that the suspect is guilty and they did not admit their guilt during the interview phase. This certainty of guilt may be the result of the investigator's interpretation of the suspect's behavior during the interview, the information (or lack thereof) provided by the suspect, evidence obtained during the investigation independent of the interview, or a combination of the three. The goal now becomes getting the suspect to admit to the truth.

If the suspect was already under arrest, the move to interrogation is a natural next step; unless, of course, the interview uncovered information that led the investigator to believe in the suspect's innocence.

Before beginning the interrogation, the investigator would leave the suspect alone in the interrogation room for several minutes. This allows them to contemplate the crime, the investigation, and the possible consequences of their actions, thus increasing their level of anxiety. When the investigator returns to the interrogation room, they bring with them a case file or folder filled with documents (even blank papers) or other similar props to help emphasize the preparedness of the investigator. It is now time for the interrogation to begin.

Phase 2, Act 1: We Know What You Did

The interrogation begins with a simple proclamation—"Our investigation has revealed that you did it." This opening salvo can take many forms as long as it conveys certainty in the mind of the investigator. By saying "our investigation," the investigator lets the suspect know that it is not his opinion alone. He may assert that all the evidence leaves no doubt of the suspect's guilt. There is nothing more to say. Game over, you're toast. However . . .

Phase 2, Act 2: Here Is Why You Did It

The investigator knows that in most cases, it will not be easy to get the guilty party to admit to the truth and provide incriminating information against themselves. The investigator needs to help them along, help them perceive that there is a benefit to confessing. But here the investigator must walk a fine line. The benefit that they offer must be of a psychological or moral nature. It cannot involve any suggestion that confessing will minimize any criminal responsibility that the suspect may face or decrease the likelihood of punishment. The investigator cannot tell the suspect that the judge will go easier on them if they admit responsibility, even if in the past experience of the investigator it might be true.

The investigator proposes the benefit in the form of a rationalization, or "theme." In keeping with the idea that the benefit could be obtained by accepting the theme involves only a moral or psychological justification, and such rationalizations might include: (1) others in the same situation might have done the same thing, (2) emphasizing that we all make mistakes, (3) blaming the victim, and (4) the suspect's judgment was clouded because of alcohol or drugs. A theme may be presented as part of a third-person narrative, where the investigator tells a story about a person in a similar situation as the suspect and the relief that person felt when they finally told the truth.

Almost every textbook on interrogation tactics offers numerous suggestions for rationalizations for even the most reprehensible crimes, such as child sexual abuse. But the investigator knows that the theme they proffer to the suspect is not the truth, but only a device used to move the suspect's mindset to the point in which they will finally tell the truth.

Phase 2, Act 3: I Can't Hear You and Repeat as Needed

At the moment the investigator starts the interrogation, their focus is to move the suspect toward the goal of the truth. Denials of guilt or protestations of innocence are not going to help this process along. The investigator has to block those denials from the beginning. If the suspect starts to state their innocence, the investigator will hold their hand up in a blocking action, telling the suspect that they just "need to listen for a minute," and then offering the suspect another rationalization. If the suspect is able to sneak in an objection as to why they would not have committed the crime, such as "I would never have taken the money, I have plenty in the bank," the interrogator turns in around and incorporates it into their theme or rationalization.

> I know you have plenty of money in the bank. That is why I know that this was a spur-of-the-moment thing. They left it out and you were tempted. If you had been thinking, I know that you would have never taken it, am I right?

An interrogation is not intended to be a conversation. It is a one-sided monologue. The investigator does not want to hear the suspect's denials of guilt, protests of innocence, or objections as to why he could not or would not have done it. To do so would only strengthen the suspect's resolve not to tell the truth about their involvement in the crime. Themes and rationalizations are offered over and over, new ones taking the place when old ones are rejected. Hopefully one theme will resonates over the others.

Phase 2, Act 4: Evidence Does Lie

In order to learn "the truth," the courts have ruled that within limits, the investigator can lie. They lie about witnesses identifying the suspect as the person who committed the crime. They can lie and say that forensics unquestionably linked the suspect to the scene. They can lie and tell the suspect that they failed a polygraph examination when they didn't. They can even lie and tell the suspect that it is against the law for the police to lie to a suspect in an interrogation room. But the ability of the police to lie, believed by many in law enforcement to be an essential tool in obtaining confessions, does come with risks.

A bad lie can blow the interrogation. The investigator must make sure that the lie is believable. If the investigator lies and tells the suspect that his fingerprints were found in the house and the suspect knew he wore gloves the entire time, the investigator's credibility is blown.

To safeguard against this, some investigators infer rather than lie. They will ask the suspect something like "What would you say if I told you we found your fingerprints in the house?" If the suspect calls their bluff, then the investigator has the wiggle room to say that he did not say that they did, he was just curious as to how the suspect would respond to such evidence, if it existed.

Phase 2, Act 5: Going in for the Kill

During his entire monologue, the investigator will continuously evaluate the verbal and physical behavior of the suspect. These behavioral cues will alert the investigator as to when the suspect's interest is waning, what theme or rationalization seems to be working, and if his presentation of false evidence strikes home. His analysis, which is solely focused on identifying signs of guilt or deception rather than innocence, will therefore provide additional validation of his belief in his theory of the crime. When the time is right, the investigator will move in and present the suspect with an "either/or" choice, sometimes called by some as the "alternative question" but can be referred to as the "kill question."

To accomplish this, the investigator will reassert that despite any attempts at denials and explanations, the evidence clearly shows that the suspect committed the crime. And he could have committed it for only one of two reasons. Both reasons admit guilt, but one reason makes the suspect look really, really bad, versus the second, which is more in line with the themes and rationalizations that the investigator had been presenting throughout the interrogation. As an example, if a suspect is believed to have stolen money from his employer, the either/or option might be:

> You either stole the money because you are a lowlife who cares about no one but himself, who would steal from a man who trusted you and gave you a break, and probably spent the money on booze and hookers, or . . .

> You took the money, because it was lying out in the open, and you were tempted like anyone would be. You had pressing bills, and you were going to pay it back anyway. That is what happened, isn't it?

No other option is presented. As always, any attempt at denial or insistence upon innocence is blocked. It is either/or.

Often, as in many high-pressure sales pitches, a time constraint is introduced. Like a car salesman saying that the sale ends tomorrow and they will never be able to get a deal like this again, the investigator might tell the suspect that this is their only chance to tell their side of the story. The time constraint may be connected to the either/or question, for example:

> If you stole the money for booze and hookers, then I'm out of here. I'm finished, I want nothing to do with you, but . . .

Sometimes the investigator will follow up the kill question with a statement designed to further emphasize the fallout of them not admitting to the more "positive" alternative. The Reid Institute suggests that the investigator could say, "If you want your family and friends to believe that you are dishonest and can never be trusted, then my advice to you is to say nothing."[5]

The kill question is designed to take advantage of all the groundwork laid by the investigator during the interrogation up to this point, to push the suspect over that hump to taking that first step toward them telling the truth.

Phase 2, Act 6: Baby Steps

If all has gone well, the suspect will admit that they committed the crime, choosing the "lesser of the two evils" option offered by the investigator during the kill question act. But in the language of interrogation, this admission is not a confession. The suspect thus far has provided no details about how or why the crime was committed. They have only said that they did it and for the reason or reasons suggested by the investigator—a reason that, since the investigator proposed it, he has no real reason to believe is the truth. Paradoxically, the sole purpose of the interrogation so far has been getting the suspect to agree to an excuse for the crime that originated not from the suspect himself but from the interrogator. Now the investigator has to backtrack and get the suspect to admit that the reasoning he just admitted to is a lie, to give the real reason, and get the additional details of the crime that are necessary to secure a conviction in court.

Phase 2, Act 7: Just the Facts

Up to this point, the interrogation has been nothing more than a monologue controlled by the investigator. The suspect has not been allowed to get a word in edgewise. Now that the suspect has admitted guilt, even though the excuse for the crime was provided by the investigator himself, the interrogation has to switch focus back to talking about those details that "only the true perpetrator would know." These are the hold-back details that the investigator identified when he was preparing for the interrogation. They are the details that the investigator believes to be true and are supposed to have been kept secret from anyone outside the investigation. In addition to obtaining hold-back information from the suspect, the investigator will try to obtain new information from the suspect that was previously not known to the investigator, such as the location of the murder weapon or the stolen items. This previously unknown information is considered the gold standard of corroboration of a confession.

During this stage, the investigator will now challenge the suspect on his concession to the kill question, since the investigator himself instead of the suspect posed that question. Since the investigator posed the admission that the suspect has merely agreed to, the admission is, in and of itself, a lie. In doing so, the investigator may resort back to interrogation mode and the use of more themes and additional alternative questions.

In an example used in the Reid textbook, the investigator believed that the suspect, Jack, went over to his estranged wife's house and stabbed her to death. The "theme" that the investigator used to get the admission was that while being screamed at by his wife, Jack lost control, grabbed the knife from the table, and stabbed her. It is the investigator's belief, however, that the knife was not on the table, and Jack had to search until he found one in a drawer, thus increasing Jack's criminal culpability from a spontaneous crime of passion to first-degree murder. The Reid textbook suggests the following alternative question be used to make the admission that Jack had to look for the knife a "more acceptable" choice.

> Jack, you said earlier that the knife was on the table and not in the drawer. . . . we know the knife was not on the table. My concern is whether it was just in the drawer or if you brought it there with you, knowing all along that you were going to use it. Now, Jack, was the knife in the drawer or did you bring it with you? It was in the drawer, wasn't it?[6]

After working with the suspect to extract the details about the crime that the investigator knows to be true, it is time to move on to the end game.

Phase 2, Act 8: Closing the Deal

As the old saying goes, no job is over until the paperwork is done. Once the investigator has obtained what they consider to be an acceptable confession (or as close as they feel that they are going to get), they need to lock it in. Different law enforcement agencies do this in different ways. Some have their investigators prepare a written confession for the suspect to sign; other agencies might have the suspect write it out in their own words. Some agencies might bring in a court stenographer to take down the final confession verbatim, while others prefer to videotape it, creating what is often referred to as a recap video. Within some agencies, it is the investigator who obtains this finalized confession statement. Others bring in a prosecutor who is responsible for the final documentation.

When there is a written confession, the investigator has been trained to intentionally make a few minor mistakes within the confession. The suspect is asked to read the written confession before they sign it, and to correct any mistakes that they find. These corrections allow the prosecutor to later argue in court that the suspect had to have read and agreed to the contents of the confession; why else would they have corrected the mistakes? In cases in which the suspect misses the mistakes or reads poorly or not at all, the investigator has been trained to point out the mistakes so that they can then be corrected.

Besides containing the suspect's admission and details about the crime, almost all of these recap confessions include the Miranda warnings or some mention that the suspect had previously been advised of his rights and agreed to talk with the investigators. At the end, the investigator or prosecutor will almost always ask the suspect if they were treated fairly, if anyone threatened them or promised them anything, and if they gave the confession of their own free will. Invariably the answers to these questions will be acceptable to the prosecutor or investigator.

As icing on the cake, an investigator may suggest that the suspect write a letter of apology or remorse to the victim or their family. The prosecutor later uses this letter as additional proof of the suspect's guilt.

If the entire interrogation is electronically recorded, preferably by videotaping, the above forms of capturing the final confession are unnecessary. But law enforcement, like most long-established cultures, is slow to change. Many agencies still have the suspect sign a written statement even when they videotape as well.

QUICK SUMMARY

With some variations, what was described in this chapter is how law enforcement agencies in the United States are supposed to conduct interviews and interrogations. To summarize:

1. Conclude that the suspect is guilty.
2. Tell them that there is no doubt of their guilt.
3. Block any attempt by the suspect to deny the accusation.
4. Suggest psychological or moral justifications for what they did.
5. Lie about the strength of the evidence that points to the suspect's guilt.
6. Offer only two explanations for why he committed the crime. Both are admissions, but one is definitely less savory than the other.

7. Get them to agree with you that they did it.
8. Have them provide details about the crime.

This basic approach to interrogation has pretty much remained unchanged since the 1940s. Proponents have described it as "an art whereby through the use of persuasion and observation the truth is elicited from a suspect by sound reasoning and understanding without the use of threats or promises."[7] However, as we have seen and will continue to see, this method has serious problems and flaws that can lead to an innocent suspect confessing to a crime that they did not commit. To take it one step further, not only can this result in an innocent person serving time in prison, it amounts to a get-out-of-jail-free card for the actual guilty party.

That said, this method is also purposed to be extremely effective. In their classes, Reid instructors tell their students that those using their technique have a 70 to 75 percent confession rate.[8] Another survey conducted by the Reid Institute claimed that 99.4 percent of confessions obtained by Reid-trained investigators were found by the courts to be voluntary and admissible as evidence.[9] But a confession being ruled admissible does not mean that it is true. Behind every wrongful conviction resulting from a false confession, there is a judge that ruled that confession to be voluntary and admissible.

In response to critics and the increasing number of confirmed false confessions, the Reid Institute and others who teach similar courses continue to steadfastly assert that there is nothing about this process that would cause an innocent person to confess to a crime that they didn't commit. They contend that it is when investigators deviate from this technique and use improper or illegal tactics that false confessions occur. But is that true? Is this interrogation process as benign as they claim? We will next look at what the critics have to say. Later, in chapter 11, we will look at the way another law enforcement system uses interview and interrogations and see if they get it better (hint: they do). But before we begin, let's first look at a case in which a false confession was obtained by one of the founders of the Reid Technique.

FALSE CONFESSION OBTAINED BY A REID INSTITUTE FOUNDER

On Tuesday, December 13, 1955, Darryl Parker returned to his home in Lincoln, Nebraska, to find that his wife had been raped and murdered. The police cleared the initial suspect, Wesley Perry, an ex-convict who owned a car that was identical to the one seen in the neighborhood before the murder, after he passed two polygraph exams. Based on a "feeling," the prosecutor then focused on Parker as the primary suspect. [10]

Polygraph examiner and cocreator of the Reid Technique John E. Reid was brought in to assist in the investigation. Reid administered a polygraph exam to Parker, but he was unable to get a definitive result. During his subsequent interrogation by Reid, Parker confessed to raping and murdering his wife, a confession he later recanted.

In his book *Barbarous Souls*, [11] David L. Strauss describes the testimony of both Reid and Parker regarding the interrogation. Though the accounts differ, both say that Reid used the same tactics described above— tactics taught by the Reid Institute that purportedly would not induce an innocent man to confess and include blocking denials, offering only two excuses for the crime, neither of which were offered by the suspect, and stating total confidence in the suspect's guilt. In his testimony, Parker added that Reid informed him that he had failed the polygraph, a false evidence ploy taught as an approved tactic by the Reid Institute and others. On the strength of the confession, Parker was convicted of murder.

While Parker sat in prison, Perry, the original suspect in his wife's murder, went on to commit other, horrific crimes, was caught, and was sentenced to death. In 1978, while waiting in prison for his sentence to be carried out, Perry contacted his attorney. Perry said that he wanted a book written about his life of crime. After soliciting an agreement from his attorney that no details would be released until after his death, Perry confessed to numerous crimes, including thirteen murders. One of those murders was that of Nancy Parker. Perry's confession to the Parker murder contained numerous details that coincided with the evidence found on the scene.

When Perry died ten years later, his confessions were released to the public. Parker was granted a full pardon, and in 2012, he was fully exonerated by the state of Nebraska. [12]

If one of the founders of the Reid Technique, a technique that allegedly if used property will not lead an innocent person to confess, can obtain a false confession, what of the investigators who receive only superficial training in the technique? Let's move from what the textbooks say to what really goes on in the interrogation room.

THE REALITY OF THE INTERROGATION ROOM

It is only until fairly recently that the details of what really happens in the interrogation room have been made publicly available, not only through the proliferation of videotaping but also through true crime television shows such as the A&E production *The First 48*, the Biography Channel's *The Interrogators*, documentaries such as *The Central Park Five*,[13] and personal stories told by those who have falsely confessed and then been exonerated. But because interrogations were not, until very recently, electronically recorded in their entirety (and still not every agency complies), judges and juries were left with what is often referred to as "dueling testimony" between the investigator and the suspect. Their accounts would frequently be polar opposites of each other, the suspect claiming that he was beaten and threatened and the investigator saying that all he did was ask "What happened?"

The increasing movement toward videotaping interrogations from beginning to end has opened up the world of the interrogation room to both the public and researchers. You can watch actual interrogations of suspects on YouTube, and entire television programs are devoted to them. Psychologists, sociologists, behavioral scientists, and others now have a treasure trove of raw, unfiltered material to study and analyze. What they have discovered is that the interrogation tactics used by law enforcement personnel in the United States are extremely effective in convincing someone to confess, but are these confessions the truth?

Increased videotaping of interrogations, along with the growing number of exonerations in wrongful convictions involving confessions, has also resulted in some of the interrogation schools rethinking their attitude toward their tactics and how they relate to false confessions. To their credit, the Reid Institute has taken the lead here. In the third edition of their textbook, *Criminal Interrogation and Confessions*, published in 1983, there was nary a mention of the problem of false confessions or the need to confirm the reliability of the details contained within. [14] Later editions are almost double in size, dedicating much of the new space to the discussion of these topics. The Reid Institute website also contains numerous publications regarding the avoidance of improper interrogation tactics and confession evidence contamination. [15]

Tactics such as threats of physical harm or inevitable consequences or promises of leniency are, of course, considered by Reid teachers and other experts as improper, as well as denying the suspect any of their rights or the opportunity to satisfy their physical needs, such as thirst or having access to a bathroom. Juveniles and persons with mental disabilities are now recognized as having a higher likelihood of falsely confessing. Where, in the past, Reid Institute teachers advocated the need for prolonged and persistent interrogations, they now recognize that such interrogations contribute to false confessions. Where they were once a vocal opponent of videotaping interrogations, they are now a supporter.

Though beginning to find some common ground, Reid Institute and other interrogation schools still strongly disagree with the researchers and experts in many areas. Reid textbooks minimize the overall problem, saying that false confessions only account for between .001 percent to .04 percent of wrongful convictions per year. [16] They also teach in their classes that people using their Behavioral Analysis techniques can determine that a suspect is being deceptive with over 80 percent accuracy, [17] whereas every other study shows that the accuracy is about the same as a coin toss. [18] Reid Institute teaching points disagree with the characterization that the goal of an interrogation is only to get a confession, and they still contend that there is nothing in the Reid Technique that will lead an innocent person to confess—but remember, don't use it on anyone *but* the guilty.

TWO SIDES TO THE INTERROGATION STORY

We have just gone over how a textbook interrogation is supposed to work according to its creators. Now we are going to look at what goes on in the interrogation room through the eyes of the scientists and researchers, those who study actual interrogations and the interrogation process, and attempt to make sense of the false confession phenomena. We will see how the tactics taught by the Reid Institute and other schools are applied in real life, how investigators can use manipulation and trickery to circumvent the rules that are in place to protect suspects from coercive tricks, and the other things that can happen in the interrogation room that can convince the guilty to confess to a crime they did do and the innocent to one they didn't. First, we will examine what is the real goal of an interrogation.

The truth, the whole truth, it just has to match my truth.

In any trial involving a confession as evidence, one particular question from the defense attorney is inevitable. Attempting to illustrate the investigator's tunnel vision, the defense attorney, full of self-righteous indignation, will ask, "When you interrogated my client, all you were trying to do was get a confession, right?" And any investigator who has been on the stand more than once knows how to answer. Oozing sincerity, they say, "Counsel, I didn't interrogate the defendant, I interviewed him. And all I was trying to do was get to the truth." *Interrogation*, with its many unpleasant associations, is a word to be avoided in public. As to the truth, which truth is the investigator talking about? The truth as to what actually happened at the scene of the crime? Or the truth of which he became convinced of before even speaking to the suspect?

I have no doubt of the sincerity of the investigator. Outside of the rare rogue cop, that is the goal, to learn the truth. But is the way that law enforcement officers interrogate suspects the path to that truth, or does it hinder more than it helps?

Consider what we have discussed so far. The first step to getting a false confession is identifying an innocent person as a suspect. We have seen how that can happen. Investigations can be messy things. Information comes in piecemeal. The investigator may be under a time constraint. As the investigation progresses, the investigator may latch on to a suspect because of incomplete information, a rumor, a neighbor's suspicion, a bad informant's tip, or just their own gut feeling, as is what happened when Danial Williams became the prime suspect in Michelle Bosko's murder.

Or the investigator may be working off what they perceive is more solid ground. There may be eyewitness identification that later turns out to be wrong. Or other, seemingly indisputable evidence, that may not be "all that." A good example of this can be found in the investigation of the 2002 murder of Denise Mansfield.

Denise Mansfield ran her accounting business from her home, located in Prince George's County, Maryland. On June 29, 2002, she was found bound and strangled in her living room. Investigators determined that the murder probably occurred on June 22, the same day that her debit card was last used at a local ATM.[19]

The investigators pulled the computerized bank and video surveillance records for the ATM. Based on the time stamp on the videotape, they discovered that Mansfield's ATM card appeared to have been used to withdraw funds from the machine by an adult woman and two female juveniles. Still pictures of the three were broadcast by the local media, but without success.

The investigators got a break in March 2003 when the Fox television program *America's Most Wanted* featured the case. A viewer called in to say that he recognized the three as Virginia Shelton, her daughter, Shirley, and a friend, Jennifer Starkey. The viewer told the investigators that the three lived in Sierra Vista, Arizona, where the two girls attended high school.[20]

The Prince George's County investigator flew out to Arizona where, with the help of the Sierra Vista police department, brought the three women in for questioning. They learned that the three had been in the Prince George's County area at the time of the murder, and that the three readily admitted that it was they pictured in the ATM photographs.[21]

The Prince George's County investigators notified other investigators in their office what they had uncovered during the interrogations. Taking that information, an investigator back home typed up an affidavit for arrest warrants for the three women in which he swore that during questioning, the three had admitted to using Mansfield's ATM card. All three were arrested. Virginia Shelton and Jennifer Starkey were extricated back to Prince George's County where they were held in jail awaiting trial. Shirley Shelton was held in an Arizona juvenile detention center.[22]

It was Jennifer Starkey's father and Shelton's father that uncovered the mistake. He was able to obtain copies of the computerized bank transactions and the surveillance video. What he discovered was that the time stamps on the computerized bank transactions were not synchronized with the ATM's video camera—they were actually several minutes apart. The suspect who actually used Mansfield's ATM card was an unidentified male who had a cap pulled low in an attempt to cover his face. All charges against the three women were dropped soon afterward. [23]

In cases such as these, the investigator enters the interrogation room with what they consider to be a pretty good idea of what comprises "the truth." They know the evidence and what others are saying, and they have developed their theory of the crime. Additionally, investigators are taught that they should not go into interrogation mode unless they are reasonably certain of the subject's guilt.

Let's look again at the way a classic, approved textbook interrogation is structured. Simply, the investigator tells the suspect that they know that the suspect committed the crime, and all they want to know is why. The suspect is actively discouraged from saying anything that is not a confirmation of what the investigator believes to be true. The suspect is provided with inducements to tell the investigator what they want to hear— inducements that, as you will see in a bit, can be pretty powerful. And if the suspect then admits to the crime, the investigator takes steps to ensure that the admission contains the details that the investigator believes to be true. But what if the investigator is wrong, either about any of the facts or about the guilt of the suspect?

Unfortunately, a major flaw exists in the way that law enforcement personnel are taught to conduct interrogations in that the methods taught actively encourage tunnel vision and confirmation bias, the conditions that cause an investigator to focus in on one theory and ignore or play down any evidence that might contradict that theory. The investigator is no longer seeking information but confirmation of what he already believes to be true. If a confession is defined as an admission to a crime, then it is a confession that the investigator seeks.

The Reid Institute and others argue that sometimes it is only through an interrogation that a suspect's innocence becomes apparent. They say that "if a suspect can be eliminated based on his or her behavior or explanations offered during the interrogation, the interrogation must be considered successful because the truth is leaned."[24] However, interrogations are structured to prevent the suspect from offering explanations, and the suspect's behavior is being judged by an investigator who, if he has followed his training, has already used the suspect's earlier behavior to determine that he is lying.

This confrontational approach to interrogations is dangerous in and of itself, but even more so when combined with some of the other practices commonly used by law enforcement that will be discussed as we move through this chapter. This approach cannot only contribute to an interrogator obtaining a false confession but also it can screw up a guilty person's confession as well. As we will explore more in the next chapter, if an investigator is mistaken about how or why a crime occurred but insists that the guilty suspect include that mistake in their final confession, it can make a good confession appear unreliable.

But there is a safeguard for both the guilty and the innocent. The investigator cannot compel a suspect to talk to them against their will, or can they?

The Shield of Miranda

Even though law enforcement personnel were supposed to have stopped using the "third degree" and switched to tactics such as those taught by the Reid Institute, the courts continued to be concerned that police interrogations might be too coercive. This came to a head in 1966 when the Supreme Court heard the case of Ernesto Miranda.

We have already discussed in chapter 1 the 1963 case of *Miranda v. Arizona* that resulted in the creation of the famous Miranda rights, well known to anyone who has spent a day binge-watching *Law and Order* or any other cop show. For those who have not, they generally go like this:

> You have the right to remain silent. Anything you say can and will be used against you in a court of law. You have the right to speak to an attorney for advice before questioning and have an attorney present with you during questioning. If you cannot afford one, an attorney will be appointed for you.
>
> If you want to answer questions now without an attorney present, you also have the right to stop answering at any time and to consult with an attorney at any time during questioning.

As you will remember, this decision caused an uproar within the law enforcement community. Just as they did when told that they were forbidden from obtaining confessions through the use of the third degree, law enforcement officials declared that this ruling would eliminate their ability to obtain confessions and solve crimes. Civilization as we know it would come to an end.

At first it looked like it might. Some early surveys taken after the Supreme Court's ruling showed a dramatic decrease in confessions.[25] How much of this was the result of law enforcement's self-fulfilling prophecy is unknown. But investigators are very creative at developing workarounds for whatever gets in their way, and the *Miranda* ruling is no different. Today, over 80 percent of people waive their Miranda rights,[26] many because of the tactics of the investigator. Ways to get suspects to waive their Miranda rights are taught in the classroom, during on-the-job training, and shared during war-story time at the local cop bar. We will go over some of them now.

It's all in the delivery.

You have been sitting with the investigator for a while, making small talk as he rummages through a file. He has thanked you for coming in, offered you a cup of coffee, and even said you could smoke (as if anyone still did anymore). Taking out a form, he begins to fill in the blanks, asking you your address, place of employment, and so on. Suddenly he stops and says, "Oh, I almost forgot. Where is that thing?" Pulling out another form, the investigator says absently "Let's go on and get this out of the way. Just more paperwork but we got to do it with everybody you know. Makes you feel like you are on one of those cop shows. You have the right to remain silent . . . "

This is one of the most commonly talked about and used techniques. Bury Miranda in the conversation. Minimize it. Just make it a routine procedural thing that you have to do for everyone. And this technique is very effective, especially since we have all become so numb to the process through TV and the movies. The cops always read the suspect their rights, and the suspect waives them. If they didn't, that would really screw up the story line.

People who are innocent, or, like Danial Williams, are not yet aware that they are even considered a suspect, are much more likely to waive their rights than people who are guilty. When Danial was later asked why he waived his Miranda rights, he said, "I was there under the pretenses that they just wanted to get more information. . . . I had nothing to hide and had done nothing wrong and never thought of asking for a lawyer."

So you have just been read your rights. The investigator slides the form over to you, hands you a pen, and asks you to sign right there. You take the pen, and he begins rummaging through the file again, mumbling to himself. You begin to sigh, but for some reason you hesitate. "Do you think I should talk to a lawyer?" you ask. The investigator pauses, looks up. "I'm not allowed to tell you what to do," he begins. "Do you really think you need one? I just have a few questions. And besides, like the paper says, we can talk now and if you change your mind, we can stop at any time. You are in charge here." That sounds fair to you, so you sign.

As long as you don't specifically say, "I want a lawyer," the investigator is allowed to dance around the issue all he wants. He knows that no self-respecting attorney is going to allow his client to be interrogated by the police. And as for the "you can change your mind anytime" part, it sounds reassuring, but once the interrogation starts, people seldom ask for it to stop. They too often get caught up in the belief that they have to prove their innocence, and even if they are not yet under arrest, they don't want to leave until that happens.

In many jurisdictions, there is no obligation on the part of the investigator to make sure that the suspect fully understands the Miranda warnings. Simply responding "yes" to the question, "Do you understand your rights?" is enough. When glossed over as a mere formality, for many, understanding what you are signing away is like understanding the fine print on a credit card agreement. You figure it's something you just accept and get on with.

The problem is especially pronounced with juveniles, those with low IQs, or other cognitive or mental health issues. Suspects that fall within these categories are least likely to understand what they are agreeing to and are more likely to falsely confess. Some law enforcement agencies and associated organizations such as the International Association of Chiefs of Police have developed practices and model policies addressing the special needs of such suspects in regard to Miranda warnings and interrogations. Though currently not widely accepted, at least there is an attempt to get investigators to follow the spirit of the Miranda ruling and not just the letter of the law.

Another interesting phenomenon is how, even in the midst of the most psychologically brutal and accusatory of interrogations, the suspect will not say, "Stop, I've had enough. I want to talk to a lawyer now." By the time the interrogation has reached this stage, the suspect often believes they have to stay. To terminate the conversation at this point would only further convince the investigator of their guilt. To leave now would be to bring down upon them the inevitable consequences that the investigator has told them will follow, and deprive them of any benefit or help from the investigator that would come from their cooperation (and more on this in a bit).

I really want to answer your questions but I can't.

Another favorite tactic is the offer to trade information for a Miranda waiver. This is often done when a suspect has decided to remain silent, or even as a preemptive move by the investigator.

Being under arrest (or even under suspicion) is an anxious time for anyone. You want information, even if just to know if you are going to be able to call someone or what is going to happen next. And the investigator would really like to tell you, but he can't. You see, there is this Miranda issue . . . procedure, you know. He can't talk to you and answer any of your questions because he is really concerned about protecting your rights. But if you just sign this paper right here . . .

Rack up the pressure.

There are also ways to increase the desire of the suspect to tell their side of the story.

Some investigators will leave a copy of the arrest warrant affidavit with the suspect, telling them, "Read that, I'll be back in a minute." The affidavit usually contains just enough information for the judge who issued the warrant to determine that sufficient probable cause exists for an arrest. The document is a one-sided narrative, presenting only the evidence that points to the suspect's guilt. When the investigator returns to the interrogation room, the suspect is told that this is their chance to tell their side. Of course, there will be no mention that there will be plenty of other opportunities for the suspect to tell their side, such as in person or through their attorney in court, and that this opportunity is conditional upon waiving the right to have an attorney present when they do it.

One trick that has several variations is sometimes used if the investigator believes that the suspect may be close to asking for an attorney, especially if more than one person was involved in the crime. The investigator will cut the suspect off, telling him that he is going to talk to the accomplice for a bit. The suspect is left alone. When the investigator returns, he has with him a file, along with a videotape or CD. "Your buddy was really helpful. Told me everything I need to know," he says, and begins to remove the suspect from the interrogation room. This is a more subtle variation of the trick of telling someone that his buddy ratted him out and put the whole thing on him. Its sole purpose is to make the suspect want to talk.

POSTCONFESSION MIRANDA

Early on in my career, one tactic that was in common use was to postpone advising the suspect of their Miranda rights until after they confessed. The logic was this: Once you got the confession you wanted you would then read the suspect their rights and have make the same confession again. By this time most figure, "Heck, I've already confessed, what difference does it make?" Seldom would anyone refuse.

This was a win-win for the investigator. They got the confession. If the judge ruled that the first confession was inadmissible because the suspect had not been read their Miranda rights, the second one would be allowed in. If the suspect refused to repeat the confession the second time, or the judge, for whatever reason, refused to allow both the pre- and post-Miranda confessions in, then the investigator has still kept the suspect from testifying on their own behalf in trial. If the suspect did decide to testify and their story was any different from their confession (especially if the original confession was false), by the rules of evidence the prosecutor could now tell the jury that the suspect had confessed, and present them with the original confession.

MAKING MIRANDA WARNINGS UNNECESSARY

When exactly an investigator is required to advise someone of their Miranda rights before questioning varies based on local law and the policies of the individual agencies. In the military, investigators are required to read the Miranda warning before questioning anyone that they consider to be a suspect in a crime. In other places, investigators have more flexibility.

In many agencies and jurisdictions, the only time a suspect absolutely must be read their Miranda rights before questioning is when they are in police custody. And they don't actually have to be under arrest for this to apply. The courts have basically said that all the suspect has to have is a reasonable expectation that they are not free to leave at the time the investigator is questioning them. The suspect is not technically under arrest but might not understand or be made to understand that they are free to leave at any time.

For some reason, some investigators fear the process of providing suspects with Miranda warnings even though most people are going to agree to talk with them in spite of it. They use this loophole of noncustodial interrogation in an attempt to avoid the whole issue. The investigator will *invite* or *suggest* that a suspect come down to the police station "for a little chat" or to "help clear this up." Once there, the suspect will be placed in the same interrogation room as would someone in custody, but the investigator will repeatedly, often with great fanfare, tell them that they are free to leave at any time. One tactic that I have seen used many times is the "no matter what" approach. The suspect is told that no matter what they say, even if they admit to being part of the Lindbergh kidnapping and murder, they are going home today. Of course, the investigator doesn't dwell on what will happen to them tomorrow if they confess.

When the conversation becomes accusatory and increasingly coercive, the person at that point may try to leave. Investigators are taught that what many average citizens would consider to be a commonsense decision is actually a sign of the person's guilt. The idea that any lack of cooperation is a clear indicator of guilt is also a common belief of most people, and it in and of itself is often enough to keep the suspect in the room.

If the suspect does try to leave a noncustodial interrogation, the investigator has been trained in how to keep them in the room. When the suspect begins to move toward the door, the investigator is taught to remain seated and continue to talk to the suspect's now empty chair for thirty to sixty seconds. At this point, the investigator is taught to turn to the suspect and ask him to take a seat, so that they can get this straightened out.[27] The reasoning behind this is something we have all encountered, especially at a bar or social function. Someone who you have no interest in having a conversation with is talking to you. They ignore all of the unspoken signs that you want go (i.e., turning away from the person, trying to start a conversation with someone else) and keep talking. Unless you are very assertive to the point of being socially rude, it is very difficult to terminate the conversation. That is what the investigator is relying on.

The problem with these approaches, especially when the interrogation is videotaped, is that the subtle (and not so subtle) inferences of some of the language used by the investigator might not be lost on the judge. Though the investigators may riddle their interrogation with reminders that the suspect is free to leave, statements like, "I will take you home once we get to the truth," or "We need to get to the bottom of this now" (especially when combined with some of the more coercive tactics discussed throughout this book) might lead a judge to conclude that the suspect had good reason to believe that they were not free to leave and thus were essentially in custody, and that the requirement for reading Miranda warnings applied.

This exact situation occurred during one of the most coercive interrogations that I have been asked to review as an interview and interrogations consultant. The suspect had suffered frontal lobe damage during childbirth and had obvious severe cognitive issues. What helped to cement the judge's eventual decision to suppress the confession was that, on a couple of occasions, the suspect indicated that he wanted to leave but was told that he would be allowed to go home once he "told the truth." The suspect was totally dependent on the investigators for his transportation home, located several miles away. The interrogation continued, with the investigators becoming more and more accusatory and coercive. Because of these facts, the judge ruled that the confession could not be used at trial. The judge did say that if the investigators had taken the time to advise the suspect of his Miranda rights and the suspect had waived them, that he had no problems with the blatant threats that the investigators used to obtain the confession.

FUNCTIONAL EQUIVALENCE OF INTERROGATION

Once a suspect says that they want a lawyer, all questioning by the investigators is supposed to stop. But again, there are some loopholes. If the suspect chooses to say something on their own that is not in response to a direct question from the investigator, then that can be used against them in court. Or the suspect can change their mind about wanting a lawyer and the interrogation can resume. The catch there is that the suspect has to change their mind on their own. They can't be helped or nudged along in their decision making by the investigator.

The tactics that investigators have developed over the years to take advantage of these loopholes have been referred to as the *functional equivalent of interrogation*. This occurs when investigators use nonquestioning words or actions in the hope of getting the suspect to make an incriminating statement.[28] We saw some examples of this that are used to get a suspect to waive his Miranda rights, such as providing the suspect with a copy of their arrest warrant affidavit and saying nothing more. When the use of such tactics is uncovered, the judge often suppresses a confession or statement.

One of the most famous cases involving the functional equivalent of interrogation is commonly known as the "Christian Burial Speech" case. The suspect, suspected of murdering a young girl whose body had yet to be found, had been picked up by investigators. The investigators were instructed by the suspect's attorney that he was not to be interviewed without an attorney present. While the suspect was being transported to another location by the investigators, the investigators began talking between themselves about the upcoming Christmas season, and what a shame it was that the family of the dead girl could not give her a Christian burial. In response to that conversation, the suspect directed the investigators to where the girl's body was hidden. The evidence that was obtained by this tactic was later thrown out on appeal.[29]

In one case in Washington, DC, that was captured on videotape, the investigator went into the interrogation room, uttered the words, "Your buddy talked," and then sat in silence. Where it might be argued that the investigator was only notifying the suspect of a fact, the judge ruled that the investigator's actions were clearly intended to get the suspect to talk without having first waived his Miranda rights, and threw out the confession.

Another very effective tactic that can be used both in the interrogation room and on the street is to "let the judge decide." Say the police get a tip that drugs are being sold from a home. They execute a search warrant on the house, which at the time is occupied by several people, including the grandparents of most of the occupants. Because of where the drugs were found, the investigators cannot link them to any specific person. The investigators might begin to have a conversation between themselves, but loud enough for everyone to hear. One says, "Since no one wants to take responsibility for the drugs, just lock them all up [including grandma] and let the judge decide," hoping that this would provoke an admission from someone.

We have discussed the mindset created by the confirmation-seeking model of interrogation and the workarounds that some investigators use to get past the Miranda hurdle. The innocent suspect is now ready to begin the second step toward their false confession. Now let's finally get to the question that caused you to buy this book: Despite being told outright that they don't have to talk to an investigator or being able to leave at any time, if not in custody, why on earth would someone ever confess to a crime that they did not commit?

MISTAKEN PERCEPTIONS OF AVAILABLE OPTIONS

Though many might expect a complicated psychological analysis accompanying stories of those who have falsely confessed to crimes they did not commit, the answer is actually simple. People falsely confess for many of the same reasons that someone would confess to a crime that they did commit, and for the same reasons that we make many of the bad decisions in our lives. Simply put: They conduct a bad cost-benefit analysis.

The Reid Institute and other interrogation schools admit that suspects confess because they believe that they will obtain some sort of benefit from doing so.[30] Even with voluntary confessions, confessions that occur without any coercion by law enforcement, the suspect might be seeking relief from guilt and remorse, notoriety, or the protection of an associate or loved one. The perceived benefit from confessing outweighs or at least helps negate the cost of the outcome.

In the interrogation room, just like during a high-pressure sales pitch or business negotiation, the investigator is seeking the advantage and hoping to achieve their goal of obtaining a confession by manipulating the suspect's perception of the cost-benefit ratio. This is what the Reid Technique and other similar interrogation approaches do. They manipulate the suspect's knowledge of their situation, creating the perception that it is in the suspect's best interest (even if only temporarily) to tell the investigator what they want to hear. While different interrogations use different steps or processes in their methods, researchers have broken down all of those steps into two parts: maximization and minimization.[31]

Maximization

Maximization is the term used for the tactics that, for the suspect, increase the severity of their situation to its maximum level.[32] As we have seen with the Reid Technique, maximization begins at the very beginning of the process. The suspect is told that without a doubt, the investigation has proven that he committed the crime, and the investigator refuses to hear anything that the suspect might have to say that would prove otherwise. The suspect is provided with two possible reasons for why he committed the crime, one much worse than the other, and if he refuses to admit to the lesser motive then everyone, including the jury who will convict him and the judge who will sentence him, will only believe the worst.

Many investigators go against the recommendations of their training and use tactics that ratchet up the cost even higher. Real or implied threats of a sure conviction by the jury, a lengthy sentence from the judge, loss of a job, separation from family members, and even the likelihood of prison rape are all tactics used by interrogators to convince the suspect of the seriousness of their situation. Some investigators combine such tactics with expressing extreme anger, yelling at the suspect, calling them liars, and banging their fists on the table, even when the interrogation is being videotaped.

Threatening the suspect with the death penalty is not an uncommon occurrence. The investigators used that and other threats to get Danial Williams and others to confess to murdering Michelle Bosko. Illinois State Representative Jim Sacia, a retired FBI agent who argued in 2011 that Illinois should not abolish the death penalty because the threat of it helped law enforcement obtain confessions during interrogations, accepted this tactic.[33]

Use of False Evidence Ploys

As we have seen, lying about evidence that doesn't exist is a maximization tactic that, with few limitations, is allowed by the US judicial system. Also known as "false evidence ploys," they could include telling the suspect that he had been identified by eyewitnesses as the perpetrator, that he failed the polygraph test, or that his buddy snitched him out. The only purpose behind falsely telling the suspect that three eyewitnesses put him on the scene of the crime is to increase his belief in the inevitability of his conviction, which would then make it easier to convince him that confessing would provide him with some sort of benefit that might outweigh that cost.

The most effective false evidence ploys are those that involve scientific evidence rather than circumstantial. A suspect might discount a claim of eyewitness evidence, knowing that no witnesses were present or, in the case of an innocent suspect, believing that the eyewitnesses just made a mistake that will be easily explained. Scientific evidence such as DNA or fingerprints is much harder to disregard. It is usually presented as infallible, not open to dispute.

The Machine Says You Are Lying

The most commonly used scientific evidence is the polygraph, the accuracy of which is questionable, as discussed in chapters 1 and 4. The polygraph examiner, who usually works for the law enforcement agency conducting the investigation, first sells the polygraph machine to the suspect as scientifically proven and impossible to fool. This usually does not take much doing, as we have become so acclimated to the alleged accuracy of the device through daytime television shows such as *Jerry Springer*, who use it in cases of infidelity and paternity. The polygraph examiner might tell the suspect that the machine is unbeatable. In one case I was asked to review, the suspect expressed doubt about this claim, asking the examiner that if the machine was that accurate, how come the results were not admissible in court. The examiner explained, "That is because it would be a violation of your constitutional rights to a trial by jury. The judge would just accept the results and that would be that."

Aside from the questionable validity of the polygraph itself, there is no requirement that the investigator or the polygraph examiner tell the suspect the true test results. When Danial Williams was polygraphed during his interrogation regarding the rape and murder of Michelle Bosko, he passed. The investigators chose to ignore the results, using a false evidence ploy in telling him that he failed, and used that as an excuse to continue the interrogation.

Accidental False Evidence Ploy

Sometimes the scientific evidence has been misinterpreted, or is just wrong, especially when the testing is subject to individual examiner or analyst interpretation. There have been numerous false confessions documented in so-called shaken baby and other child abuse cases. I was once called to an emergency room to investigate the sudden death of an infant. The child was severely emaciated and had an enlarged rectum. The emergency room physician and nurses were adamant that the child had not only been starved but sexually assaulted as well.

The child's parents were young, poor, very uneducated, and had obvious cognitive issues. All they knew was that the child had been sick since birth and was undergoing treatment for some condition that they could not name. I could have taken the emergency room physician's diagnosis and interrogated the couple, accusing them of a horrific crime and confronting them with the scientific evidence. Instead, I first had the child's body examined by a pathologist who specialized in injuries and illness of children. The pathologist said that the child suffered from a medical condition that prevented him from property digesting his food, causing it to back up in his intestine. The massive bowel movements that resulted caused the enlarged rectum. The parents of the child were almost subjected to an interrogation for a crime that never occurred, and in all probability might have confessed if I had used the tactics we have been learning about in this chapter.

A now infamous series of both scientific and nonscientific evidence ploys were used to get seventeen-year-old Marty Tankleff to falsely confess to the murder of his mother and father. Tankleff had woken to find his mother beaten and stabbed to death in her bedroom and his father beaten and stabbed in his office, alive but unconscious. Tankleff immediately became a suspect because in the eyes of the investigator, he was not acting appropriately for someone who had just learned of the death of his parents.

Because the investigators did not find any blood on his clothing or body, they theorized that Tankleff had committed the murder in the nude and showered shortly before he called 911. Tankleff told the investigators that he had showered before he had gone to bed. The investigators said he was lying, because they used a so-called humidity meter in the bathroom that proved he had showered just before the police first arrived (no such meter exists). Later in the interrogation, one of the investigators faked a telephone call from the hospital where Tankleff's father had been taken for treatment. The investigator told Tankleff that the hospital had given his father a shot of adrenalin, causing him to wake up and name Tankleff as his attacker (this never happened).

Told by the investigators that they had no doubt that he murdered his parents, the false evidence from both the humidity meter and the adrenaline shot, along with trusting that his father would not lie, Marty began to believe that he actually might have committed the attacks, but during a blacked-out state. In his subsequent confession, Tankleff provided numerous details of how the attack took place, details that were believed by the investigators at the time of the interrogation to be true but that were later proven through crime scene analysis not to be correct.

Your Looks Give You Away False Evidence Ploy

Another sort of evidence ploy is the investigator's use of "demeanor evidence."[34] This is done by the investigator voicing his observations of the suspect's behavior based on the "behavior analysis" signs discussed in previous chapters. The suspect is told that the investigator "knows" they are guilty because the suspect won't look them in the eye, or because of their response to seeing a photograph of the victim's body.

One favorite "indicator of deception" that investigators like to point out is when a suspect invokes God in their responses. "I swear to God I'm telling the truth" is met by the investigator saying, "Any time someone swears to God, that is a sure fire sign they are lying." There are several such "absolutes" that are passed from investigator to investigator. Another is if a suspect falls asleep when left alone in the interrogation room, that is a sure sign of guilt. It doesn't matter that it is 3:00 am and the interrogation has been going on for hours, that guy is guilty as sin.

Like "scientific" evidence, this demeanor evidence is presented to the suspect as having come from an authority who has training and experience and is infallible in their interpretation. But while "this is the weakest type of evidence ploy, it is also the easiest to claim, and the safest."[35]

As discussed earlier in this chapter, false evidence ploys can backfire with guilty suspects who see through them, but they have been found to induce false confessions from innocent suspects for not-so-obvious reasons. Both research and actual case studies have found that a suggestive evidence ploy as described above can actually contribute to an innocent suspect falsely confessing to a crime. An innocent suspect, told that DNA was found on the scene and was currently undergoing testing, may confess to the crime at that point just to escape the pressure of the interrogation. The innocent person may feel that the short-term benefit of confessing and ending the interrogation will be worthwhile, knowing that the DNA tests will prove them innocent. Unfortunately, no DNA was found on the scene, and they are effectively screwed by their decision.

Duration of the Interrogation

The duration of the interrogation is another form of maximizing the seriousness of the situation. Back when I was first receiving interrogation training, we were told that the only time an interrogation should end is when the suspect asks for a lawyer, or the investigator runs out of things to say. Interrogations lasting ten, sixteen hours, and even longer are not unheard of, especially in more serious and higher-profile cases. Many of the most famous false confession cases occur after such interrogations, though I have seen some occur after less than an hour of questioning. You just have to hit the right buttons with the right person.

Though some may say differently, I include lengthy interrogations as part of the maximization process. Besides physically wearing him down, isolation and intense questioning for such long periods of time can emphasize the seriousness of the situation for the suspect. Lengthy interrogations are often accomplished by rotating investigators through the interrogation room. This can be beneficial for the lead investigator, as it gives him time to confer with any colleagues who are observing the interrogation—find out what tactics they think are working and points that the investigator might be missing. It also gives the investigator a break while not allowing the suspect one. This tactic creates additional problems, however, in that it can contribute to the confession contamination issue. Essentially, the more time two people spend talking, the more information is exchanged—in both directions. This will be discussed more in the next chapter.

The "Alternative Question"

"It can be only one of two things. You either committed the crime be-cause of A (a really reprehensible option) or B (a much kinder, gentler, understandable, and acceptable option). Which one is it?"

Though it is true, as the Reid Institute and other interrogation schools argue, that the suspect always has the option of choosing neither, the alternative or "forced choice" question (referred to earlier as the kill question) has one purpose, which is to eliminate in the mind of the suspect that they have any other option other than to pick one or the other. In addition, in a textbook interrogation, any attempt to choose the third option would be blocked by the investigator who would simply continue to repeat the forced choice options over and over.

When using the forced choice or kill question, it is easy for the interrogator to slip into the forbidden realm of real or implied threats of inevitable consequences. As an example,

Alternative #1: "Right now all the evidence points to this being a cold-blooded, heartless, premeditated murder. Is that what it was? Is that what you want people to think, that you are a monster? Well that is what the jury is going to hear. What do you think they will do when they hear how you killed that man, made him suffer?"

Alternative #2: "But if there is a different side to it, if he had threatened you, came at you, and you knew it was him or you, you need to tell me. If you do, that is what I will put in my report for the District Attorney. Personally I think that is what happened, but I need to hear it from you."

The greater the real or implied threat, the greater the incentive to choose the lesser of the two evils.

This is a one-time offer . . .

Like any slick salesman, the investigator is going to increase the pressure on the suspect to confess by stressing the necessity of acting now. This maximization tactic is usually combined with the minimization tactics (discussed next). Basically, the investigator would tell the suspect that the situation is very, very bad, and any chance they have to make it any better expires once the investigator leaves the room. Statements like "This is the one chance to tell your side of the story," or "Once I leave, there is nothing I can do for you," are essentially untrue, but they effectively minimize the perception of what options the suspect thinks they have open to them while maximizing the severity of the situation, causing desperation to increase. Poor choices made because of such pressure is why laws are in place that allow a person to reconsider a sales contract for a couple of days after signing and withdraw from it without penalty.

Minimization

Whereas maximization techniques are designed to increase the perceived severity of the situation, minimization is the way out, a ray of hope, the light at the end of the tunnel.[36] In the Reid Technique, minimization begins right after the maximization tactic of telling the suspect that there is no doubt that they are the one who committed the crime. The investigator is now supposed to suggest to the suspect a theme for why they committed the crime, a theme that makes the suspect's actions seem not to be that awful, but only if they accept the theme and confess.

According to Reid, the theme is only supposed to suggest that the suspect had a moral or psychological justification for their alleged actions, not a legal one that would possibly negate any potential punishment.[37] The theme does not have to have any basis in the truth. Its only purpose is to provide the suspect with a perceived benefit that they would receive by confessing. Such benefits might include a relief from the emotional distress associated with continuing to lie, placing the blame for the suspect's actions elsewhere, the suggestion that people will respect them for taking responsibility or that by confessing they will prevent themselves from doing something worse.

Some themes are common for almost any crime. For example, the suspect succumbed to peer pressure, stress, or was influenced by alcohol or drug use. Or the investigator could offer a theme as a form of an alternative question: this was the first time, and not one of several crimes suggesting a habitual offender. It was a just spur-of-the-moment thing, and not something you planned out. It was only money, not like anyone got hurt.

Where most interrogation schools only offer a few theme suggestions, the Reid Institute does one better. In their book, *Anatomy of Interrogation*

Themes by Louis C. Senese,[38] they offer close to two thousand different themes for just about every crime imaginable, from animal cruelty to workplace violence. Having a multitude of different themes available allows the investigator to keep suggesting a different one if he finds that the one he is using isn't hitting home with the suspect. The more themes the investigator has, the less of a chance they will run out of things to say.

Samples of the themes that the Reid Institute suggests for certain crimes include:

- *Credit Card Fraud.* Blame the carelessness of the victim; that is, leaving their credit card at a retail establishment, and so on.[39]
- *Child Abuse.* Suggest the intent of the action was to correct a behavior as opposed to abuse.[40]
- *Domestic Violence.* Blame the victim for not following orders, being too independent.[41]
- *Homicide.* Blame video games for promoting or normalizing violent behavior.[42]
- *Workplace Sabotage.* Blame the employer for not promoting the suspect or promoting less qualified individuals.[43]

The above-mentioned "spur of the moment" or "not planned out" theme is one that I see frequently used in alleged sexual assault cases. It is frequently pitched as an alternative question. The investigator, who has already told the suspect that there is no doubt of their guilt, then says that because the suspect is "not that bad a person," the rape must not have been planned in advance, but was something that just happened. This theme can also take the form of a question: Was it just this time or has it been going on for a while? The investigator would then go on to hint (or outright say) that if there was planning, or if the act was done more than once, then the suspect is an awful person. This effectively forces the suspect to choose to confess so that he can defend himself from being a repeat offender—it was only one time, it was not that bad. But the confession is made.

THEMES THAT ARE SUPPOSED TO BE AVOIDED—BUT FREQUENTLY ARE NOT

While the investigator is supposed to stay away from any theme that even implies any sort of leniency, these can slip their way in way too easily. One way, especially in sexual assault or child abuse cases, is through the offer of help. An example of such a theme is:

> Not everyone who does something like this goes to jail. There is help out there, but first you have to admit that you have a problem. I want to help you, but you have to take the first step.

Another theme that implies leniency is how the judge and jury will respond to the suspect taking responsibility or showing remorse for the crime. The investigator will hammer home that a suspect's confession and expression of remorse is bound to create a favorable impression in court in contrast to the suspect remaining silent about his role in the crime. As discussed earlier, this ploy is often used to induce the suspect to write a letter of apology to the victim or the victim's family. This letter will later be used to argue the reliability of the confession to the judge and jury. After all, why would someone not only confess to a crime they didn't do but also apologize?

Leniency can also become part of a theme when it states or implies the possibility that the assault or murder resulted from the suspect trying to defend themselves or that it was not an intentional act but an accident.

A theme that has been shown to be hugely problematic and its use discouraged by the leading interrogation schools is suggesting that the suspect committed the crime while intoxicated or on drugs. This is called the *blackout theme*. In this scenario, the overwhelming evidence definitively points to the suspect, but they just don't remember committing the crime. The reason could be drugs, alcohol, or maybe the crime was so horrific that they just blocked it from their mind. "Could that be a possibility?" suggests the interrogator.

The Desire to Get It Over With

Ending the interrogation is also a benefit that comes from confessing. In many confirmed false confession cases, the innocent suspect said they confessed just to get the interrogation to stop. Juveniles are especially prone to confessing for this reason. Many have reported that they confessed because they believed that once they did, they would be released to their parents.

A note when it comes to juveniles: some jurisdictions require that a parent or other responsible person must be present during the interrogation. Intended to be a safeguard, it can actually increase the effectiveness of the interrogation process. Instead of directing their tactics toward the suspect, investigators talk to the parent, either directly or indirectly through their child. The investigator emphasizes the seriousness of the situation, and if, with the parent's help, the investigator can get to the truth things will work out. Through this tactic the investigator is often able to enlist the parents' help, and they actually become cointerrogators.

BUT COULD THESE THINGS REALLY LEAD TO FALSE CONFESSIONS?

Naysayers of the phenomena of false confessions downplay the research that claims that these tactics have any real impact on causing an innocent person to confess to a crime that they did not commit. They say that the simple studies of confirmed false confession cases have produced only anecdotes that show no real correlation between the individual tactics used by the investigator and false confessions in general. They say that the laboratory experiments that attempted to show such correlation were unrealistic and did not reflect what actually goes on in the interrogation room.[44] And on this point, they are right . . . somewhat.

Let's take one of the earlier experiments that was conducted to determine if lying about evidence would increase the likelihood of someone confessing to something they did not do. Several college students were asked to participate in what they thought was a speed typing experiment. The students were told that they were to type as fast as they could on a keyboard, but under no circumstances were they to strike the Alt key. If they struck that key, then the system would crash.[45]

At a predetermined point while the student was typing, the system was intentionally crashed by the instructor, who would exclaim, "You must have hit the Alt key."

Of course the student had not, and they would say so. The instructor would insist that they must have. After several denials, another student who was in the room, who was actually working in collaboration with the instructor, would confirm that they saw the student hit the key.

Confronted with this false evidence in conjunction with the accusation, not surprisingly, the majority of the students confessed to striking the Alt key and causing the computer system to crash. Many who confessed actually came to believe that they did hit the Alt key, and some even developed a false memory of having hit the key.

The critic's response was "So what?" These students were not faced with criminal penalties, so the consequences of confessing were low. Besides, they could have just concluded that they did hit the key by accident. In their viewpoint these experiments proved nothing.[46]

One thing that the experiment did show was that isolating and testing specific interrogation tactics in the laboratory is extremely challenging. First, it would be unethical to recreate an actual police interrogation in a laboratory to see, under controlled conditions, if an innocent person would confess. That would require accusing an innocent person of a crime and subjecting them to conditions that would never receive approval from any university or research review panel. Second, as we have seen, no interrogation tactic is ever used in isolation. Each tactic is codependent on the other, and the investigator often uses multiple tactics in the same breath.

Other experiments were devised. In one, the students were told they were taking part in a problem-solving experiment. Some of the problems they would solve together as a team and some separately. It was made clear from the onset that a critical component of the experiment was that the students did not collaborate on the tasks in which they were supposed to work separately. If they did, that would be considered cheating, exposing them to the potential of disciplinary action.[47]

On each team of two students, one of the team members was in cahoots with the researcher. During some of the times when the students were supposed to be working individually, the researcher's participant would suggest to the other student that they work together. If the other student agreed, they would become the guilty component of the experiment. Other times, there was no effort to get the other student to break the rules, so they were the innocent component.

After they finished the task, both the guilty and innocent students were accused of cheating. All were interrogated using varied approaches and tactics. As expected, more guilty people confessed than innocent. But when minimization tactics were used during the interrogation, the researchers found that the rate of true confessions shot up, but so did the number of false confessions.

In another interesting variation of this experiment, the interrogators were training in a variety of interrogation tactics, including the use of both maximization and minimization. The interrogators were allowed to apply those tactics freely during their fifteen-minute interrogations of both the guilty and innocent students. This time, before they began, the interrogators were provided with information that indicated the likely guilt or innocence of their suspects. As before, more guilty suspects confessed than innocent, but the interrogators who were given information that their suspect might be guilty used harsher accusatorial interrogation techniques and obtained more false confessions than interrogators who were given information that their suspects might be innocent. Additionally, the level of detail that the first group obtained in the confessions from the truly guilty was less than the confessions obtained by the second group of those presumed innocent.

DOES LAW ENFORCEMENT TRAINING ACTUALLY CONTRIBUTE TO THE PROBLEM?

Beyond the fact that researchers contend that many of the interrogation tactics taught by the Reid Institute and other interrogation schools can lead to false confessions, is there anything else that might contribute to the problem? Here we will discuss the actual training undergone by investigators and examine whether or not it actually makes things worse.

Types of Training

During their careers, investigators receive extensive and vigorous training in some areas, and minimal training in others. When it comes to their firearms, a tool that the majority of investigators will never be called upon to use in their careers, the training is quite extensive. Usually it involves a week or two of basic training with retraining and practical testing in firearms proficiency done two to four times a year.

Though obtaining accurate, reliable, and admissible information from witnesses, victims, and suspects is critical to the success of an investigation, and something that an investigator usually does every day, most formal training is superficial, if any exists at all. Classes range from one or two hours at a seminar to up to a week if offered by formal interrogation schools. Instruction is provided through lectures and videos. Seldom are there any practical exercises done by the students, nor testing to see how well they absorbed the material. Basically the investigator sits, listens, and then checks the box saying that they are now a trained interrogator.

The majority of the instruction usually focuses on the behavioral analysis of the suspect, which, as we have seen, is supposed to teach the investigator how to become a human lie detector. The rest focuses on the actual steps and tactics that are supposed to be used to obtain the confession. Mentions of the problems of false confessions are minimal and downplayed as a rare phenomenon.

In a recent Reid Technique training class put on by the Reid Institute in Boston, the instructor mentioned that false confessions typically occur in cases in which the suspect was very young, immature, or had very low intelligence. Later in the class, the instructor went around the room and asked each of the students if they would confess to a crime that they did not commit. Each student responded that they would not. The instructor used this as proof that short of physical harm, or the offer of total leniency, it was impossible to get an innocent person to confess to a crime that they did not commit. The instructor was heard as saying that "[The suspect] will keep denying it and never admit it."[48]

Herein lies the crux of the problem. Some interrogation schools, with Reid in the forefront, have attempted to address many of the problems that can lead to false confessions. However, these updates to curriculum do not make it into the classroom. They bury them in their textbooks and websites, like the fine print in a credit card contract. Few investigators that I know have bothered to visit the Reid website, much less purchase and read their textbook. I have often equated interrogation training in the United States to a doctor being taught a medical procedure but receiving no instruction on the potential adverse side effects and how to recognize and deal with them. If you don't believe that a false confession can occur, you will never be on the lookout for the possibility.

Even when information on false confessions is offered in training classes, it is often contradictory, confusing, and in the example mentioned above, not completely bought into by the instructors. This includes even the basic premise behind why an investigator conducts an interrogation in the first place.

The Reid Institute insists that the only reason for an investigator to conduct an interrogation is not to obtain a confession, but to learn the truth.[49] If "the truth" is an admission to guilt, that would be correct; otherwise, this is definitely an exercise in semantic acrobatics.

The Reid Institute often contradicts itself on this. At one point in their text, they write: "The purpose of an interrogation is to learn the truth and persuade a suspect whom the interrogator believes to be lying about involvement in a crime to tell the truth about the crime that they committed."[50] I and others have heard Joseph Buckley, one of the authors of the fourth and fifth editions of the Reid textbook, say publically that "we do not interrogate innocent people."[51] In other words, the investigator has already determined that the suspect is guilty, and the only "truth" the investigator seeks is confirmation of what they believe.

Other interrogation schools and textbooks are much more honest. Wicklander-Zulawski & Associates, Inc., an interrogation school licensed to teach the Reid Technique, write in their textbook that "the purpose of the interview and interrogation process is to identify the guilty party and obtain a legally admissible confession. This outcome, without question, makes for the most satisfying of all interrogations; the case is satisfactorily resolved with a signed statement attesting to the suspect's involvement and perhaps the development of additional evidence."[52] Another textbook on interrogation tactics is very specific in stating that the purpose of an interview is to gather information, and the purpose of an interrogation is to get a confession to the crime the investigator believes they have committed.[53]

The use of threats and promises of leniency is another problem area with respect to training. The Reid Institute and others explicitly warn against direct threats of physical harm, threats of inevitable consequences (such as the surety of a conviction and long prison sentence), and any promise of relief or leniency from those consequences if they confess.

Where they waver is on the use of any *implied* threats or promises of leniency.

On even not-so-close examination, many of the suggested themes that investigators are trained to offer reek of the implication of leniency, some stronger than others. They are often combined with the implied threat that comes from the opposing side of the alternative questions—that the judge and jury will think the worse if you don't tell "your side of the story." (And we know what thinking the worst will bring—the implication here being life in prison or even the death penalty.) The Reid Institute argues that it cannot be proven that "innocent criminal suspects would be likely to interpret the investigator's statement [of an implied promise or threat] as such a significant incentive (i.e., a promise of leniency or threat of inevitable consequence or physical harm) as to support such a claim." They go on to say that the courts have accepted this theory of theirs. [54]

As I have said before, judges rule on admissibility of the evidence, not reliability. And consider how implied threats and promises are used in an interrogation. They are not just offered once, but multiple times as part of theme building and presenting alternative questions and forced choices. If they were offered once, I would tend to agree with Reid's argument. Instead, they are offered over and over, back to back, one variation or another. The interrogator is not tapping the nail lightly on the head but using a sledgehammer to drive that point home.

And yet again, the Reid Institute contradicts itself in its written material. An example can be found deep in the appendix of the workbook they distribute during their basic three-day class on interviewing and interrogation. [55]

"Appendix G, Maintaining the Integrity of a Confession" is an article reprinted from the Reid Institute publication titled *The Investigator's Anthology*. Its author, Brian C. Jayne, is a coauthor of the two most recent editions of the Reid Institute's textbook.

In the article, Jayne wrote about the issue of the use of improper interrogation tactics. Regarding the use of threats or promises, he wrote for the Reid Institute that "our position . . . is that even implying a threat or a promise of leniency should be considered impermissible as an interrogation technique." [56] He went on to say:

> Recognizing the psychological effectiveness of a threat to elicit confessions, some interrogators have used procedures which only imply

threats. By doing so, they hope to protect themselves from allegations that they threatened the suspect, yet hope to reap the same psychological gain as when using an actual threat.[57]

Implied promises of leniency fall into the same category as implied threats in that they could cause an innocent person to confess and, therefore, should not be permissible.[58]

The use of false evidence ploys and trickery is another topic in which conflicting information is given. The Reid Institute joins with the overwhelming majority of investigators who believe that techniques that involve deception "are not only helpful but frequently indispensable."[59] It is the "clear position" of the Reid Institute "that merely introducing fictitious evidence . . . would not cause an innocent person to confess." And on that point, I agree.[60]

Imagine an investigator walking into the interrogation room to confront the suspect. Looking down, he lies to the suspect, saying "We found your prints on the murder weapon," and then waits. That is "merely introducing" false evidence, but we know that this is not how interrogations work. Think about how, at the same time the investigator is lying about the evidence to maximize the severity of the situation, he is most likely following that up directly with telling the suspect there is no doubt as to their guilt, using a forced choice question and/or themes implying leniency if the suspect confesses.

Regarding that, the Reid "fine print" says that if the purpose of the evidence ploy was to convince the suspect that he would be found guilty, and if he confessed he will be given leniency, "it becomes much more plausible that an innocent person may decide to confess."[61] They also warn that the use of deception in the interrogation of a "youthful suspect with low social maturity" or "suspects with a diminished mental capacity" may lead to a false confession.[62] This, like all of the other warnings and safeguards, never makes it into the classroom.

YOU ARE ON YOUR OWN

If the investigator actually does go through formal interrogation training, once they finish they are pretty much on their own. As mentioned, few training schools offer any kind of final exam, and any formal follow-up designed to evaluate the investigator's performance is virtually nonexistent. This is why researchers who study interrogations and confessions often find such a hodgepodge of problematic tactics being used.

Not Just for Law Enforcement Anymore

Interrogation training is not restricted to law enforcement but open to anyone who is willing to pay for it. There are some specialty classes for the private sector, human resource personnel, or people who work in loss prevention. But these classes teach pretty much the same behavioral analysis and interrogation tactics taught to law enforcement. They just add a specialized twist or two in order to accommodate the needs of the private sector.

Often you will find people from professions outside of law enforcement sitting side by side with investigators as they take the training. As part of his research in interrogation practices and false confessions, associate professor of sociology David Gary took the Reid Institute course in 2015. Gary discovered that approximately half of the class consisted of business and school administrators.[63] Many find it disconcerting that Reid-style interrogation tactics are being used on students in schools. And when such interrogation tactics are used in the public sector such as for school disciplinary purposes, there are even fewer safeguards and oversight than with their use by law enforcement. Since the interrogator is not a law enforcement member and the student not formally accused of a crime, the rules of Miranda do not apply. The consequences of false confessions resulting from the use of these interrogation tactics by private citizens can be just as devastating. Besides unjust expulsion from school or the loss of a job, criminal charges could result if during the interrogation the suspect admits to criminal wrongdoing.

Giving Credit Where Credit Is Due

All this said, for many, the bottom line is that the interrogation tactics taught by the Reid Institute have been proven to be extremely effective in gathering true confessions from guilty suspects. Their use has resulted in untold numbers of crimes being solved. And the reality is that the use of even the most horrible and coercive of interrogation tactics does not automatically mean that the confession is false. Even if the judge ruled the confession to have been made involuntarily and is not admissible in court, that does not make it untrue.

Testing the truthfulness of the confession is Basic Investigations 101. Early on in any case, the investigator is at least mentally making up their hold-back information list, details about the crime that they believe to be true and would not be known to anyone outside of the investigation except the true perpetrator. If the confession contains these hold-back details, then you got the right guy. The problem is, confirmed false confessions contain those details as well. How that happens is the third step toward obtaining a false confession, and leads us to our next chapter.

6

CONTAMINATION

Sports analogies were never my strong point, but here goes anyway. Think of the interrogation as a football game. As we have seen, the home team (the interrogator) uses various tactics and plays to move the ball toward the goal (the confession). Some plays move the ball a little, others result in dramatic progress down the field. There may be setbacks, and you are not always successful. But when the ball goes over the goal, you've scored (and possibly won). Here, however, the analogy ends.

In football, crossing the goal line is where you make the most points. The field goal, if successful, is icing on the cake. When it comes to interrogations, crossing the goal line of obtaining an admission of "I did it" counts for only two points. The real score comes from the next step—getting the suspect to provide you with the details of the crime, those details that we love to refer to as ones that "only the true perpetrator would know." It is these details that truly confirm our belief in the suspect's guilt. They are the ones that will be used by the prosecutor to convince the jury to convict. After all, if the suspect didn't do it, how would they have known them?

This is a very powerful and convincing argument. It is rooted in a basic law enforcement practice of creating "hold-back details." These are details that the investigator has identified as those not known to the general public. Details that are kept from the media and other outside sources. Details that are used to check the validity of not only confessions but also witness statements, anonymous tips, and informant information. Details, which combined with the basic (and false) premise that someone would never confess to a crime that they did not commit, usually result in a guaranteed guilty verdict, if not a pretrial guilty plea from the suspect (more on plea bargains in chapter 12).

The reality is that the large majority of false confessions contain numerous such details. Not only details such as how many times the person was shot or stabbed, but even mundane ones, like the layout of the house, the color and type of furniture, or the type of clothing the victim was wearing. These details overwhelm the ones that are incorrect, and thus make the confession believable to even the most cynical of skeptics.

This paradox was brought home by the work of University of Virginia professor Brandon Garrett. Prof. Garrett studied thirty-eight false confession cases, cases in which the confession was confirmed to be false through DNA analysis. He discovered that in thirty-six of those cases (97 percent) the final confession contained numerous details about the crime that only the perpetrator should have known. The others were only admissions to the crime and contained no such details. [1]

How could this happen? Prof. Garrett was hampered in his research by the fact that the interrogations that he studied that resulted in such accurately detailed false confessions were not videotaped in their entirety, but were either documented in written statements signed by the suspect or by video or audio recordings of only the final version. In many cases, Prof. Garrett had to rely on the court testimony of the interrogator, who swore that the only way that the suspect could have known those details was by being there. And of course, good police work ensured that these details were not provided to the suspect by the interrogator or anyone else, a fact usually hammered into the jury during the prosecutor's closing arguments. [2]

The simple fact is that somehow, from someone, the innocent suspect learned those details. Somehow, the confession was contaminated.

The concept of contamination is well known to law enforcement (and through TV to everyone else as well) as far as it relates to physical evidence, and lengths are undertaken to mitigate this. For example, most law enforcement agencies maintain crime scene logs that document who enters a crime scene to help identify outside sources of trace evidence, such as hairs. Crime scene technicians wear gloves, changing them often to prevent the transfer of DNA evidence from one item to another. Laboratories will include in their analysis the DNA profiles of their employees, as well as law enforcement officers who handle evidence, in order to help detect unintentional contamination during the handling of evidence.

Law enforcement agencies also take pains to prevent the contamination of witness evidence. Witnesses are kept separated until they are interviewed to prevent them from sharing information and possibly incorporating what one witness believed that they saw into their own statement. Investigators are told not to ask leading questions, such as "Was the suspect wearing a blue shirt?" thus unintentionally providing the witness with information or suggesting what the answer should be. Care is taken to prevent the news media from photographing and broadcasting pictures of arrested persons if the investigator plans on having the witness try to identify them later in a line-up or through a photospread, which is a procedure whereby the witness is shown a series of photos, one of which is the suspect. Many law enforcement agencies have even changed the way that they perform line-ups and photospreads. They now have an investigator conduct the procedure who is totally unaware of which person in the line-up or photospread is the suspect. This is to prevent the allegation that the investigator may have intentionally or unintentionally provided clues to the witness as to whom the investigator believes they should choose.

So how does contamination play a part in confessions, especially false confessions? In order to fully understand, it is important that we remember what we learned about the basics of the interrogation process. Before an investigator begins an interrogation, they know at least the basic facts about the crime, and have already developed a theory as to what happened. When the investigator goes into "interrogation mode," they are supposed to believe that the suspect is guilty, and that their job is to get them to admit their role in the crime. The innocent suspect becomes convinced that their conviction is inevitable, and the only way to receive any help or to end the interrogation is to tell the investigator what they want to hear. As you will see, the final confession is a cooperative effort, in which the innocent subject and the investigator work together to create a story that at least resembles what the investigator believes to be true.

The same factors are in play with witnesses, informants, and even victims as well. Instead of believing that they are guilty of the crime, the investigator believes that they are "holding back" or in some way not being fully cooperative. Instead of the inevitability of a long incarceration, they believe that if their story does not confirm the investigator's belief, they will be charged as an accomplice, their children will be taken away from them, their parole will be revoked, or whatever other threat the investigator can think of that hits home to their individual circumstances. Their account then changes to resemble what the detective wants to hear.

But how does the innocent suspect know what to say that will, in their mind, get them out of this mess (or at least make it better)? Oftentimes, it is the investigator who tells them. And it happens in many ways.

QUESTION STRUCTURE: LEADING QUESTIONS

Any question that in itself suggests an answer is a leading question. These questions take more forms than we realize, but all provide the suspect, witness, or victim with direct information (or at least a suggestion) pertaining to where the investigator believes their story should go. And in spite of it being the main thing that investigators are told again and again to avoid when interviewing witnesses or interrogating suspects, it is the most common form of contamination.

For an innocent suspect trying to create an acceptable story for the interrogator, leading questions provide numerous clues. An example would be what is called a "forced choice" question, where the suspect is given options and asked to make a "yes" or "no" answer.

Let's say that the investigator is interrogating an innocent suspect who he believes was involved in the burglary of a house. By asking, "How did you get in, the back door or the basement window?" the investigator has essentially told the innocent suspect that the real burglar entered the home one of those two ways, eliminating all other possibilities. The innocent suspect has a 50/50 chance of getting it right, thus adding a detail to the narrative.

Leading questions can even cause a witness to "see" things that they never saw. In a typical research study, students were shown a video of a car accident and then asked to answer questions about what they saw. When asked the leading question, "Did you see the broken headlight?" many of the students answered that they had. In fact, there was no broken headlight. The structure of the question "told" the student that the broken headlight existed, and they adapted it into their account. [3]

Even the choice of words within the question can manipulate memory. In similar experiments in which the "witness" groups were shown a video of a car accident, one group was asked, "How fast was the car going when it hit the tree?" The second group was asked how fast it was going when it "smashed" into the tree. The word *smashed* implies that the car was traveling at a high rate of speed, and that inference was reflected when the second witness group estimated the car's speed to be much faster than the first group.[4]

INVESTIGATOR'S RESPONSE

While the investigator watches the suspect for signs of deception and guilt, the suspect is studying the investigator as well. The suspect is also looking for clues—clues to how the investigator is responding to their answers, clues to how well their story is going over. The innocent suspect uses these clues to pick up on bits and pieces of information that they will need to include in their final story if it is going to be acceptable to the investigator. These clues can be as subtle as the investigator's reaction to the innocent suspect's answers in the form of raised eyebrows, a quick look, or repetition of the question asked.

Take the earlier example of an innocent suspect attempting to convince the investigator that they burglarized a house. The investigator, who knows that the burglar entered by forcing open the back door, asked the leading forced choice question about how the suspect entered the house (back door or window). If the innocent suspect gives the incorrect answer (the window), and the investigator responds in a questioning or surprised tone, "The window?" that telegraphs to the innocent suspect that they got it wrong. When this happens during an interrogation that has been videotaped, you will often see the innocent suspect scrambling to change or explain away their answer. Of course, if they guess right, then they get a positive response from the investigator, and one more "hold back" fact is added to the story, thus reinforcing the suspect's guilt in the mind of the investigator.

Repeating a question can also provide "hold back" clues to an innocent suspect. If, in the above example, a few minutes after the innocent suspect told the investigator that they broke into the house through the window, the investigator asked, "How did you get in again?" this tells the innocent suspect that the first answer was wrong, and gives them a chance to change it. Juveniles are especially susceptible to this form of contamination.[5]

A more dramatic example of how the response of the investigator can mold the confession occurs when the innocent suspect is accused of lying when they give the "wrong" answer. If they give the "right" answer, then the investigator is happy, letting them know they are making "progress." Negative consequences might also be introduced into the investigator's responses, emphasizing the need for the suspect to adopt the "right" answer, especially when the investigator is using the "alternative question." As an example, let's use a case of sexual assault involving an elderly victim. The suspect denied the allegation, and when he refused to confirm the alleged details of the offense as given by the investigator, the investigator tells him in essence that if he failed "to remember" then that would mean that he was a sexual deviant, and that is how he would be perceived by the judge and jury.

In many ways, such an interrogation can resemble the child's game of "20 Questions." The innocent suspect, desperate to escape the inevitable consequence, slowly collects details that, in the end, will form a story that will be acceptable to the investigator.

SHARING THE EVIDENCE AND CRIME SCENE PHOTOS

To corrupt an old saying, crime scene photos are worth a thousand "hold back" details. Not only do they provide broad details about the crime but also supply lots of the minutia: the type of clothing the victim was wearing, the color and position of furniture, for example, all of which can help make the false confession even more believable. Though the practice has fallen out of favor, it is still frequently used with both suspects and witnesses. Some still advocate it through the creation of "war rooms," where interviews and interrogations are to take place. In a war room, crime scene and suspect photographs are displayed on the walls, and along with file cabinets (often empty), they are used to intimidate the suspect with the breadth of the investigation.

Contamination through the presentation of evidence is not confined to showing crime scene photographs to suspects and witnesses. Oftentimes, it is necessary to confront a suspect or witness with evidence when challenging their stories, but it must be done in a way that minimizes the contamination of the final narrative. It must be done carefully, and its use must be documented in order to later evaluate the reliability of the final statement. As you will see in chapter 11, law enforcement agencies in other countries have developed tactics in which the evidence is carefully presented to the suspect near the end of the interview, and only after any possible alternative explanation for it has been explored.

Presenting the suspect with the evidence is especially problematic when it is used to "correct" the suspect's account of the crime. As an example, consider Danial Williams's case. Before the autopsy of Michelle Bosko was completed, Danial confessed to the investigators that he had killed her by striking her with a shoe. When the investigator learned that she had been strangled and stabbed, they confronted Danial with the new information, and instead of asking him to account for why he originally claimed he had killed her with a shoe, they had him change his confession to fit the newly discovered facts.

Another tactic often used in conjunction with confronting the suspect with evidence is the investigator lying to the suspect. Even though courts condone both lying and confronting the suspect with false evidence, they can contribute to the contamination of the suspect's confession. For example, if an investigator decided to lie to the suspect about eyewitnesses, telling the suspect that an eyewitness saw him and his "buddy" going around to the back of the house about the time the burglary occurred, the innocent suspect would now know that there were two people involved, and he is going to have to name someone as his accomplice to make his confession believable. Additionally, the innocent suspect now knows that critical events that they need to include in their story took place in the rear of the premises.

THEME DEVELOPMENT

As discussed in the last chapter, theme development is the technique of "the investigator express[ing] a supposition about the reason for the crime's commission" and offering "a possible moral excuse for having committed the crime."[6] Often multiple themes are presented throughout the course of an interrogation and can be a source of contamination.

In the last chapter, we discussed how the Reid Institute published a book written by Louis C. Senese containing over two thousand theme suggestions for the investigator to use during their interrogations.[7] In theft cases, Senese suggests that the investigator minimize the seriousness of the suspect's criminal behavior by contrasting the theft of $1,000 (or whatever was the amount in question) with someone who stole ten times that much.[8] The point of this theme is to provide the suspect a moral excuse for the theft, but it also unintentionally provides the suspect with a crucial detail that he can then weave back into his confession: the amount of money actually stolen. For arson cases, a theme would be to suggest that the act must have been a "spur of the moment decision" because "no accelerant was used,"[9] thus providing both the excuse as well as information as to how the fire didn't start, thus narrowing down the list of "correct" answers that the suspect can give during the interrogation. When confronted with an auto theft suspect, Senese suggests that the investigator blame peer pressure, telling the suspect that they must have been tempted by the keys being left in the car or by certain valuable items in plain view. And for a burglary suspect, the investigator should blame the victim for:

- *leaving the doors or windows open.* Detail: Entry was made through an open door or window.
- *leaving the garage door open with valuables in sight.* Details: Items were stolen from the garage while the garage door was open.
- *leaving the house key where it could be found, such as under a mat.* Detail: There was no forced entry, and the homeowners kept a key under a mat.
- *not having an alarm, or not having the alarm activated.* Detail: The house either didn't have an alarm or it was not on at the time of the burglary.
- *having been away on vacation, and not taking precautions such as having someone take in the mail, and more.* Details: It was obvious from the outside appearance of the house that the homeowner was away.[10]

These are all themes that provide an innocent suspect with those supposedly "hold back" details that they can weave into a believable, but false, confession.

Since the suggested theme is one that is offered only as an excuse designed to get the suspect to admit to having committed the crime, once the admission is made, the investigator must then challenge the theme, often with evidence that contradicts the theme in order to get to the "truth." If not done carefully, the challenge can cause additional contamination. A great example taken from the Reid script was described in the last chapter. The case involved Jack, who had allegedly stabbed his wife to death. For our purposes, let's say that Jack is innocent but was convinced by the investigator that he would not only get convicted but also be sentenced to death unless he confessed. Jack bit on the investigator's theme that in a fit of rage he grabbed a knife off the table and used it to stab his wife. The investigator believed that the knife came from a drawer and needed Jack to include that into his narrative to make it "fit the facts." He uses the following theme to provide that information:

> Jack, you said earlier that the knife was on the table and not in the drawer. . . . We know the knife was not on the table. My concern is whether it was just in the drawer or if you brought it there with you, knowing all along that you were going to use it. Now, Jack, was the knife in the drawer or did you bring it with you? It was in the drawer, wasn't it?[11]

JUST OUT-AND-OUT TELLING THE SUSPECT WHAT HE SHOULD SAY

As we have seen, this form of contamination, when the suspect is handed details of the crime by the investigator, can creep in through the use of some interrogation tactics such as theme development or the use of false evidence ploys. But sometimes the contamination is blatant, especially in long interrogations where, blinded by tunnel vision and frustrated with the lack of progress, the investigator begins to push the envelope.

One fairly common example that occurs is when an investigator is attempting to challenge a suspect by confronting them with the strength of their case. The investigator will lead off with "Let me tell you what we know . . . " and then go on to outline the details of the crime or what the investigator believed was the role of the suspect.

Another example usually occurs when the investigator has obtained an admission by the innocent suspect but becomes frustrated when the suspect is unable to provide additional details or has difficulty remembering the details that were discussed in the interrogation. The investigator may

simply recite what they believe to be the correct story and ask the innocent suspect to accept or agree to the version as provided. An example
would be the following exchange between an investigator and a suspect:

Investigator: "Don't tell me you don't remember. You don't forget something like that. Listen, we know you shot him. You walked through that
door and shot him point blank in the head, didn't you?"
　　Suspect: "Yeah."
　　Investigator: "In fact you shot him three times in the head, didn't
you?"

This form of contamination seems to occur most commonly when the
investigator is totally convinced of the suspect's guilt and, after a long
interrogation, becomes frustrated at the suspect's refusal to confess, or if
they do confess, their "unexplainable" inability or resistance to provide
pertinent details in the correct order. Because it often occurs during the
"heat of the moment," the investigator may be unaware that this is even
happening, and may not realize it even in recollection until confronted
with a videotape that recorded the entire interrogation.
　　Even when the entire interrogation has not been videotaped, it is often
possible to observe this type of contamination in play. When the final
confession is all that is videotaped, or even in written statements, you will
see how the investigator provides portions of the story, and then asks the
suspect if he agreed. Like the example above, the confession basically
becomes an exchange of the investigator providing the narrative and the
suspect just agreeing with him.

STORY COLLABORATION AND "COLD READING"

While a false confession may be created by way of the investigator simply telling the innocent suspect what to say, there is usually more to it
than that. Surprisingly, in most cases, the final confession ends up being a
collaborative effort between the investigator and the suspect. To understand this phenomenon, it is good to remember the reason that people
falsely confess to begin with. The innocent suspect has been made to feel
that their conviction and imprisonment (and in some cases, death) is
inevitable. Desperate, the innocent suspect knows that the only person

who can help negate that inevitability is the investigator. In order for that to happen, the innocent suspect has to provide the investigator with a story that, to some degree, matches what the investigator has already concluded to be "the truth."

Though the innocent suspect may have obtained lots of hold-back details from the investigator and other sources, in most cases the investigator has tried to follow their training and to some extent to be careful not to tell them everything. Somehow, the innocent suspect must strive to gather as much of that information as possible. That "somehow" is through a tactic I call "reverse cold reading."

To understand "reverse cold reading," we must first understand "cold reading." I first learned of the cold-reading process when I was presenting a lecture on false confessions to a class of law students. As part of the lecture, I would present film clips of interrogations in confirmed false confession cases, during which I would ask the students to identify where any contamination occurred on the part of the investigator. One student pointed out that not only was the investigator unintentionally providing the suspect with details but that in turn the suspect was "cold reading" the investigator. The student went on to explain that he was an "entertainment psychic" and cold reading was the term used for the techniques that he used to make people think that he knew things that he didn't, just like the suspect was doing to the investigator.

At the student's suggestion, I purchased some books on how to be a psychic as well as watched some classes on YouTube. I learned that a successful cold reading relied on the psychic combining "very generalized statements . . . , the ability to read people . . . and a few tricks of guile."[12]

If you watch a psychic at work, you will notice that they will make a lot of vague generalizations. They also change their statements based on the verbal and nonverbal cues they receive from the person they're working on. You will also see this at play during an innocent person's confession. If being questioned about an alleged theft of merchandise from a drug store, and the innocent person is asked what was stolen, they may say something like "personal items," which of course is a common item found in drug stores. Like psychics, they will make several such statements, many of them guesses and just plain wrong. Confirmation bias will cause the investigator or the psychic's client to latch on to the "right" or close-to-right answers, and ignore the rest.

Another tactic is called "fishing." Here the psychic will phrase their statement as a question and listen to their client's response. If the response is a positive one, then the psychic turns it into a fact, and the client will usually respond with more information. [13] The way this works in the interrogation room is that the innocent suspect will insert a "qualifier," such as "maybe," "it could have been," or "I think" into their answer. If it is the correct answer, the investigator will accept it and rephrase it into the positive response. As an example, in one case involving an alleged sexual abuse, these exchanges took place:

Q: Did it go on your bed, down on the floor?
    A: I think it was on the bed.
    Q: It was on the bed, okay.

And a bit later:
    Q: Did you just—did you spit?
    A: Maybe.
    Q: Maybe you spit, okay.

The entire line of questioning went this way during the course of the interrogation. When the investigator wrote up his final report, each qualifying answer was presented as a definitive response to the question.

When psychics guess too much, or don't provide specific-enough information, they have excuses. They may say that the information is coming to them piecemeal, or that for some reason the psychic conditions are not good for that day. Investigators and suspects have their excuses as well. The suspect may say that they were drinking or using drugs as an excuse for their inability to remember exact details. The investigator may say that the suspect is being evasive or just trying to protect someone by not providing the desired level of detail. Whatever the excuse, the psychic's client and the investigator will work hard to fit the generalities to their specific circumstances or needs, and later give the psychic or suspect credit for providing much more detail than they actually did. "The good reader [or suspect] is the one who, deliberately or unwittingly, forces the subject [or investigator] to search his or her mind in order to make sense of . . . [the] . . . statements." [14]

Reading and interpreting a person's reactions to answers is important to both the psychic and the innocent suspect, as this will offer them many clues as to the "correctness" of their responses. A good example of this involves not a confession, but an interview of a cooperating witness, a topic covered more in chapter 9. It occurred in the 1970s following the rape and murder of several young girls who were kidnapped off the streets of Washington, DC. There was a lot of media attention given to this case, and the investigators were under a great deal of pressure to solve it.

A subject was arrested and charged along with several other men as having been a part of several rapes unrelated to the serial case in question. He told the investigators that in exchange for help with his pending cases he could solve for them the murders of the young girls. The subject said that he was not directly involved, but his codefendants were, and he was present during some of the rapes and murders. At the suspect's direction, the investigators took him to several different crime scenes, where he pointed out where specific events occurred.

Later, when he learned that he would not receive immunity for prosecution in the other rape cases, he refused to cooperate with investigators any further. [15] Family members told investigators that the suspect had told them that he knew the general details about the murders as well as the approximate locations of where their bodies were found from the media reports. He then used the cold-reading tactics that we discussed to "play" the investigators into giving him more details. When it came to the crime scenes, he just pointed the investigators in the general direction and carefully watched them, shaping his story based on their responses to his statements. [16]

OTHER SOURCES OF CONTAMINATION

As we saw in the previous case study involving the serial rapist attempting to help investigators solve a murder mystery, not all contamination comes from the investigator. Sometimes what the investigator considers their hold-back information just ain't all that is held back. These days, with twenty-four-hour news coverage, instant Internet news, social media posts, and neighborhood listservs, it is almost possible to know all that is public knowledge about the case. And there is still the old-fashioned way that such information spreads: through the neighborhood gossips and the rumor mill.

As such, the suspect may infer some hold-back information from the public details of the crime. This is known as "contamination by inference," and to further understand this let's look at a hypothetical case in which the body of a woman was discovered in an abandoned building. Based on the sex of the victim and the location where her body was found, it may be inferred by people hearing about the crime that a sexual assault had taken place. If information about a sexual assault was intentionally kept from the media by the investigator, they would believe that this is a detail that "only the killer would know." If, while interviewing a subject regarding an unrelated incident, the investigator asks if they know anything about the woman found in the building, and the subject replied, "Oh, the one who was raped?" the investigator may jump to the erroneous conclusion that this person had "insider knowledge" and must somehow be involved in the crime.

Contamination by inference can also occur in the interrogation room. An example can be found in the case discussed previously in chapter 5 of the young man who suffered frontal lobe brain damage at birth and suffered from severe cognitive problems. The investigator believed that he had been involved in a domestic fight with his lover, who he then forced off a thirteen-story-high balcony to his death. The autopsy revealed injuries to the decedent's neck, injuries that could have been caused by the fall but the investigators believed was the result of strangulation.

The investigators told the suspect that during the autopsy the medical examiner found some things that needed to be accounted for. The suspect was told that there was bruising and other injuries around the neck, including what looked like a thumbprint, all consistent with . . . . Two things happened at this point. The investigator paused, and though partially hidden behind the door, the video camera captured an upward motion of his hand as if going to his neck. The suspect filled in the blank with the most logical answer given all of the clues: strangulation.

During the trial, the prosecution harped repeatedly that it was the suspect who brought up that the decedent had been strangled, not the investigators. What was ignored was that the investigators painted the picture and left the suspect to infer the only possible thing that the picture depicted.

HEARING WHAT YOU WANT TO HEAR

Aside from the above means by which an investigator may provide the innocent suspect with the information needed to make a believable confession, the investigator may also "cherry pick" a suspect's innocuous statements, and through misinterpreting or restructuring them, create a confession where none exists. In this context, "seek and ye shall find" can be interpreted as "you see what you are looking for."

In 2015 in upstate New York, investigators believed that Angelika Graswald intentionally sabotaged her fiancé's kayak, causing it to sink and him to drown. Early in the interrogation, Graswald admitted that their relationship had been rocky. English was not the suspect's primary language, and she was unfortunate in her choice of phrases when she told the investigator that she wanted him "gone," which she later explained meant "away." The investigator twisted her words, repeatedly telling the woman that she had said that she wanted her fiancé dead and persisted in spite of her repeated attempts to correct him. [17]

In another exchange, Graswald had commented how before going out kayaking they had breakfast at Wendy's, and that she now wished that his last meal had been a better one. The investigator twisted this normal afterthought, much like a wife wishing she had not neglected to kiss her husband goodbye before he died in the traffic accident, and made it "evidence" of planning and premeditation.

Investigator: " . . . you said you wanted his last meal to be something good."
Graswald: "Yeah."
Investigator: "And I asked you, 'Well . . . '"
Graswald: "No, that's—that's what came to me after."
Interrogator: "Well, I—I said that—"
Graswald: "That's why I told it—"
Interrogator: " . . . but then he got Wendy's. Did you think that that might have been his last meal? And you said 'yes.' So you already had that in your mind is what I'm saying."

Another problem has been documented as occurring in interrogations of suspects for whom English is not their primary language, or who come from backgrounds or cultures where respect and deference for authority figures is the norm. If an investigator is asking leading questions, and especially when making statements with tags at the end like "okay?" or "right?" the suspect will generally respond with "yeah" or "yes." Called a "gratuitous concurrence,"[18] these responses are not made in agreement with what the investigator is saying. They are only acknowledging that the suspect is listening, and are meant as a sign of respect. When the investigator, unaware of this cultural nuance, interprets the concurrences as a sign of guilt, we have a big problem and are well on our way to a faulty interrogation and potential false confession.

As discussed in chapter 4, researchers have repeatedly observed that when an interrogator asks questions in a way that presumes that the suspect is guilty, the suspect often responds defensively. Defensive responses, taken out of context, might be interpreted by the investigator as signs of guilt. "Guilty" responses prompt more guilt-presumptive questions, and the downward spiral continues.

How something is said is just as important, if not more, than what is said. Inflections, pauses, and other parts of normal conversation usually don't make it into written statements, transcripts, or the investigator's summary of the confession. A left-out question mark in a transcript or a report can turn a protest of innocence into an admission. Bias on the part of the person creating the transcript can come into play as well. Research has found that if the person who is creating the transcript believes that the suspect who is being interrogated is guilty, they are more likely to interpret unintelligible responses as guilty answers.

In cases in which the entire interrogation is not electronically recorded, the way in which the interrogation and final confession are documented also affects what information is available and how it is interpreted. Here one has to rely on the ability of the individual investigator to thoroughly, accurately, and impartially document both the interview/interrogation and the subsequent confession. Such documentation can be slanted to reflect the individual investigator's personal observations and perceptions. In place of an electronic recording, conversations are condensed on paper, leaving out what may be crucial information, especially of the nonverbal or voice inflection sort. Things that at the time are not considered by the investigator to be important or relevant may be omitted. No matter how meticulous the documentation, what gets passed along is never the full and complete picture of the investigation or the interrogation, hence the strong need for videotaping confessions in their entirety.

The movie *My Cousin Vinny* portrays in a humorous but unfortunately all too accurate way in which this can happen.

While on a college road trip, Billy and Stan stop off at a convenience store in Alabama, where they unintentionally shoplift a can of tuna. After they leave the store, there is an attempted holdup, where the clerk is shot and killed.

Identified as being in the store around the time of the murder, Billy and Stan are arrested by the local sheriff. After Billy is interrogated, the two are charged with the murder.

On the stand at trial, the sheriff is asked what happened during the interrogation. The sheriff, reading from the "official file," testified, "I asked him if he did it, and he said, 'I shot the clerk.' I asked him again, and again he said, 'I shot the clerk.'"

Through the magic of film, the audience has the opportunity to see what really happened in the interrogation. Billy believes that he and Stan were picked up by the sheriff's office because they took the tuna fish without paying. The sheriff believes that he is interrogating a murder suspect. You can clearly see the disconnect between the two.

Sheriff: What about the tuna fish?
   Billy: Then I forgot about the can of tuna fish, and we left.
   Sheriff: Did he catch you with the tuna fish? Is that how it started?
   Billy: No, he didn't say anything.
   Sheriff: But he knew about it.
   Billy: I don't know.
   Sheriff: [throwing pen down and coming out from behind the desk to tower over Billy] Let's talk about that for a moment. You paid for the groceries. And then what?
   Billy: Went out to the car, and that's it.
   Sheriff: When did you shoot him?
   Billy: [clearly puzzled] What?
   Sheriff: At what point did you shoot the clerk?
   Billy: [even more puzzled] I shot the clerk?
   Sheriff: Yes, when you shot him?
   Billy: I shot the clerk?

At this moment in the movie, someone comes to the door and tells the sheriff that he is needed outside. The sheriff storms out, shouting, "I'm in the middle of a damned confession here," a definite indication of his mindset at the time.

The sheriff's mindset is even more evident during the trial when (as described above) he turned Billy's question into a confession. The sheriff heard only what he was listening for.

It is only a movie, but an example of where life imitates art.

MORE THAN "JUST THE FACTS"

Like a good novelist, the investigator knows that it takes more than details to make a story believable. As part of the shaping and contamination of the final confession, the investigator needs the suspect to weave in motive, emotions, remorse, and the perception of voluntariness into their narrative. Often this is done the same way that contamination about the details occurs. Through leading and suggestive questioning, the investigator suggests motive. Because the investigator tells the suspect directly or through inference that expressions of remorse play well to the judge or jury, the suspect becomes emotional and tells the investigator how sorry he is. In some cases, as the proverbial "icing on the cake," the investigator will even have the suspect write a letter of apology to the victim or their family. The letter adds an extra layer of credibility to the confession. Since most people have a hard time believing that someone would confess to a crime that they didn't commit, they have an even harder time believing that an innocent person would apologize as well.

The last and final touch is making the confession voluntary. During the confession phase, after having laid the "need to express remorse" groundwork, the investigator may ask the suspect why he is confessing. Complying with the investigator's suggestion, the innocent suspect will answer that they feel bad and regret what they did. And at the end of the confession, the investigator will invariably ask the suspect in an electronically recorded confession or add a paragraph at the end of a written one if the confession was voluntary, and whether or not they were threatened or received any promises. By this time the innocent suspect knows what the wrong answer will bring, so as in the rest of the confession they tell the investigator the answer that they want to hear.

THE DEAL IS DONE

The investigator has now fulfilled the three steps necessary to create a false confession. He identified an innocent person as a suspect. He subjected the innocent suspect to interrogation techniques that make him believe that, in spite of his innocence, his conviction is inevitable, and the only way out is to provide the investigator with what they want to hear. And the investigator then told the innocent suspect what to say.

Now it is time for the next stage, getting the false confession into the courtroom. The investigator does that by not doing what we will talk about next.

7

STATEMENT EVALUATION

Even with all of the advances in the tools available to investigators, from DNA to the almost overwhelming presence of surveillance cameras, a simple confession is still the most powerful piece of evidence that can be handed to a prosecutor. It is the gold standard of evidence, and, as we are seeing with Danial Williams, it will often trump all other evidence to the contrary. If a suspect gives a confession, they are more likely to be held in jail pending trial, plead guilty, be found guilty if they do go to trial, and receive a harsher sentence than someone who did not confess.

In this chapter we will see how false confessions can make their way past the numerous checks and balances that are in place in the criminal justice system. We will examine the process by which confessions, as well as witness statements, are supposed to be tested by the investigator to determine their reliability. It is a surprisingly commonsense process that you can use, whether you are critically evaluating a confession you read about in the news, see on a television show, or more importantly, are called upon to evaluate as a juror, when ultimately deciding on a person's guilt or innocence.

THE DIFFERENT DEGREES OF FALSENESS

You may have noticed that when talking about confessions and statements I often refer to their reliability rather than if they are false or not. When researchers study cases, they will usually only classify a confession as false based on the criteria listed in chapter 2 (i.e., no crime had been committed, it was physically impossible for the suspect to have committed the crime, etc.). In my work, both as an investigator and consultant, my initial concern is reliability. Is the confession or statement trustworthy enough for me to use it as evidence? False confessions and statements are inherently unreliable. However, depending on how the interrogation is conducted and the confession or statement evidence is obtained, true statements can be rendered unreliable. The methods by which false confessions are obtained and true statements made untrustworthy are the same. This is why I will sometimes use as case studies confessions that do not fall into the more restrictive "proven false" categories used by the researchers. Their study can be just as instructive as the study of "pure" false confession cases, as they both highlight the problems that lead to wrongful convictions and the truly guilty going unpunished.

Before going into the ways that both confession and statement evidence should be tested for its reliability, I want to go over what I call the "different degrees of falseness."

TOTALLY FALSE CONFESSIONS/STATEMENTS

These are statements and confessions that are factually false. The witness did not see what they said they saw. The suspect did not commit the crime.

TRUE CONFESSIONS/STATEMENTS WHERE CONTAMINATION NULLIFIES ITS RELIABILITY

Here the confession/statement is factually true, but using the criteria described below, it is impossible, or near impossible, to establish its reliability. The level of contamination is just too much. There were no details provided by the suspect or the witness that were not given to them first, either by the investigator or through outside sources. An extreme example would be someone who was the victim of a robbery committed by someone they did not know. The robbery occurred in broad daylight, the suspect did not wear a mask, and the suspect had a very distinct appearance.

Later, the suspect was arrested. The victim was called down to the police station and asked if they could pick out the person who robbed them from a line-up consisting of several individuals. As the victim was waiting to go into the line-up, the victim sees a news account of the suspect's arrest, in which the suspect is shown being walked down the hallway in handcuffs—what is known as a "perp walk." The victim then goes in and makes a positive identification of that person.

It is quite possible that the victim's identification of the suspect was made based purely on their memory from the time of the robbery. However, because she had been contaminated by seeing the news broadcast showing the suspect in handcuffs, we will never know.

STATEMENTS THAT CRIMINALIZE A NONCRIMINAL ACT OR INCIDENT

In order for this to happen, the investigator has to mistakenly believe that a crime was committed. Many so-called shaken baby cases fall into this category. These are cases in which an infant or small child comes into the emergency room or doctor's office with head injuries that the doctor diagnoses as having been caused by someone violently shaking the child by the shoulders. Recently the science behind the diagnosis of "shaken baby syndrome" (SBS) has been called into question, especially after in some cases the injury or death that was believed to have been caused by shaking was attributed to other, noncriminal causes.[1]

The infant is found unconscious and brought to the emergency room. The treating physical makes a mistaken diagnosis of SBS when in fact the infant is unconscious for a non-trauma-related medical reason. The investigators are notified and come in to start their investigation. After interviewing the parents, they discover that the child was in the care of the mother all day, and that is who found the child unconscious and called 911. The investigators interrogate the mother, telling her that the doctor, a medical expert, has concluded that the child had to have received those injuries from someone violently shaking them (not true). They have already locked her in to admitting that she was the only one with the child at the time, so it had to have been her. If she wants to help save her child (or not have the other children removed from the home), the investigators need to know what happened. The mother thinks, and comes up with a time when maybe she laid the baby down a bit harder than normal. "That could not be it," the investigators say. "You have to have done it harder than that." And so on, and no longer trusting her memory, and desperately trying to help in the medical treatment of her child, the mother and investigators concoct a narrative that included the required shaking. The mother confesses to a crime that is based on a mistaken medical diagnosis.

STATEMENTS THAT FALSELY INCREASE THE SUSPECT'S CRIMINAL CULPABILITY

These occur for two reasons. One is because the investigator has the facts wrong. The crime was committed and the suspect played a part, but not the role that the investigator believes. The investigator then creates a situation that in order for the suspect to escape the inevitable consequences and receive whatever benefit they think they are going to get, they have to change their story to match what the investigator perceives is the truth. The lookout suddenly becomes the shooter.

The second reason this occurs is because the investigator is not trying to determine the truth but to build a stronger case for the prosecution. It may have really been an accident, but there is a much greater likelihood of a conviction if the investigator is able to get the suspect to admit that there was some sort of intent to do harm. And as above, the suspect is willing to do so to receive the help, or whatever benefit they think they will get.

MOSTLY TRUE STATEMENTS THAT INCLUDE FACTUALLY INCORRECT DETAILS

There are many reasons why a true confession or statement may contain information that can be proven to be factually incorrect, most of which have to do with the interrogation itself. Those reasons, and how to evaluate the incorrect details, are discussed in more detail below. Why this type of confession or statement is included in this list is because I have seen those factually incorrect details included at the insistence of the investigator. It is much like what was covered regarding increasing the suspect's culpability. The investigator is mistaken about some detail;

maybe they misread the crime scene report and thought the victim was tied with an electrical cord rather than a clothesline. They got the suspect to the point where they believe that confessing is the only option, and they are willing to give it up, but the investigator is frustrated because in the confession they keep getting the type of bindings wrong. The investigator finally gets them to come around and give the "correct" answer. Of course, this becomes problematic in court for the prosecutor when the defense attorney is able to raise doubt about the confession because his client "didn't even know what the victim was tied with."

Now that I have talked about all the different ways a confession or statement can be false or otherwise unreliable, we will move on to how the investigators are supposed to sort the wheat from the chaff.

THE MISSING INVESTIGATIVE STEP

It is one thing for an investigator to get a false confession, it is another for that false confession to result in a wrongful conviction. There is a whole system of checks and balances in place, the purpose of which is to prevent such miscarriages of justice. Several parties representing all sides are involved. First, the investigator has to convince the prosecutor that the confession is a good one. In cases in which the prosecutor needs to present the evidence before a grand jury in order to get an indictment, the grand jury members must be convinced of its reliability as well. Then there is the defense attorney who is tasked with fighting the confession tooth and nail. At some point a judge will determine if the final confession was made "voluntarily." Then, if the suspect does not accept a plea offer, the confession is put in front of a trial jury, which is the ultimate judge of its truth.

It takes a lot for a false confession to result in a wrongful conviction, and in examining cases in which this has occurred, there is plenty of blame to go around. As we have discussed, many people still take a confession at face value. For the investigator, prosecutor, and judge, it is often a godsend. Because a confession on the surface is such powerful evidence, the investigator and the prosecutor are reluctant to look a gift horse in the mouth. To the judge, it indicates a higher chance for a plea bargain, therefore one less case on his docket. For the defense attorney, who often has a huge caseload himself, the confession is an immense headache. Most don't have the investigative or financial resources necessary to do the required follow-up or to hire the experts needed to fight a false confession case. Many defense attorneys also don't believe that people would confess to a crime that they did not commit, and fall victim to the same tunnel vision that has affected the investigator and the prosecutor. Often the end result is a guilty plea by the innocent suspect (more on this in chapter 10).

If a case involving a false confession goes to trial, there is usually little hope for the innocent suspect. Many jurors share the perception that any confession must be true. Studies have shown that in spite of overwhelming evidence of innocence, including DNA evidence, jurors are reluctant not to convict if the suspect has confessed. [2]

Earlier we talked about the steps the investigator must take to obtain a false confession. They must first incorrectly identify an innocent person as a suspect. Second, they use coercive tactics during their interrogation, and third, contaminate the confession evidence. One commonality found in all of the steps is tunnel vision. And it is tunnel vision that leads investigators and prosecutors to fail to take what I call the fourth step—not property evaluating the reliability of the information given by the suspect during the confession.

IMPORTANCE OF THE CRITICAL EVALUATION OF CONFESSION EVIDENCE

A good investigation involves the gathering of information, critically fact-checking that information, and the investigator properly documenting their actions and findings along the way. For example, if a victim tells an investigator that they were beaten about the face with a belt, the investigator examines the victim's face for injuries consistent with such a beating. They attempt to find the belt that was used. The investigator tries to find witnesses to the attack, and they photograph the injuries on the victim's face. They may even have the victim examined by a medical doctor who is experienced in treating such injuries to confirm that they are consistent with the attack as described by the victim.

To use another example of gathering and testing investigative information, if a suspect's DNA is found on the crime scene, it is also not taken at its face value. The investigator wants to know the source of the

DNA (blood, semen, skin cells) and the location where it was found in context to the crime. The investigator questions how the evidence was collected. Was there any chance of unintentional contamination during the collection, and what are all of the possible explanations for why the DNA might have been left there? The laboratory will not take their findings at face value either. A second DNA scientist will check the work of the first to be absolutely positive that the DNA match was correct. Nothing can be taken for granted.

Confession evidence should be no different. Its reliability must be questioned and tested just like all other evidence before it can be accepted as fact. Unfortunately, this is too often not the case. Instead of being the beginning of the next phase of the investigation (the testing phase), the confession marks the end. Blinded by the words "I did it," the investigator feels whatever comes after that must be the truth.

Several times I have made the following point when discussing with my co-workers the validity of a confession that they had obtained. If the suspect had come into the police station saying that they were a witness to the crime and gave you the same "facts" that you got during the confession, knowing what you know about the crime and crime scene, you would have called them a liar and thrown them out on their rear. Why should a confession be treated with any less skepticism?

The critical evaluation of confession evidence serves the same purpose as the critical evaluation of any evidence. It prevents mistakes from occurring and strengthens the quality of the investigation. Like any other evidence, if an interrogation and confession are obtained correctly, properly documented, with adequate fact-checking performed, there is little any defense attorney will be able to do to attack it.

THE PROPER INVESTIGATIVE MINDSET

To conduct quality investigations and ensure the reliability of evidence, the investigator must have a "proper investigative mindset." This term was coined in the United Kingdom, and as we will see more in chapter 11, it is a key point hammered into their investigators during their training on how to conduct interviews. It basically boils down to the ABC of investigations:

Assume nothing

Believe nothing
Challenge everything[3]

This philosophy is applied across the board, to all aspects of the investigation. Investigators are taught that "whatever appears to accurate, reliable, and sometimes incontrovertible evidence . . . [may] . . . turn out to
be less than reliable. . . . Information should never be accepted without
question."

In the United Kingdom, investigators are taught that when applying
the investigative mindset to consider that not all the details collected
during an investigation are considered equal. They break it down into
categories: information and facts.[4] Their definitions will be useful to us to
consider as we discuss the proper evaluation of confession evidence.

Information consists of details that have yet to undergo the test of
validity to determine if they are accurate or real. In addition to the information itself, the reliability of the source of the information must be
examined.[5] An example would be a witness who said that they saw the
crime while standing at a specific location. One way to help establish the
reliability of the witness would be to confirm through video surveillance
cameras in the area that they were actually there, and to go to the exact
spot where they said they were to see if they could see what they said they
saw.

Facts are details whose accuracy and reliability have been established.
The most accurate facts, called "hard facts," are ones that can be physically confirmed.[6] An example would be that the victim was shot three
times in the chest, a fact confirmed by the autopsy report, or that a call
was placed on a cell phone at a specific time, a fact confirmed by the
telephone records.

"Soft facts" are the majority of facts that the investigator has to deal
with, and must be constantly evaluated as new information becomes
available. Such facts include multiple witness statements that appear to
corroborate each other. Investigators are cautioned against treating soft
facts with the same consideration as hard ones.[7] An especially compelling
eyewitness identification may not be as reliable as first thought if questionable procedures were used to obtain the identification.

Even details that were considered to be hard facts may, under additional scrutiny, find themselves on shaky ground. We saw an example of
this in the last chapter, where the time stamp on the ATM machine was
later discovered to be several minutes off from the time stamp on the

video camera. This resulted in the arrest of women who were believed to be using the victim's card when they were actually using their own.

Many of the things that investigators use to turn information into hard facts are faulty, outdated, or can be unintentionally manipulated. As discussed in chapters 2 and 4, polygraph examinations should not be used as the final arbitrator of the reliability of a witness. Many of the so-called forensic sciences, such as bite-mark analysis and the fire sciences used in arson investigations, have been discredited, although they are still being used. And as we will see more in the next chapter, even fingerprint and DNA results can be made unreliable through the improper interpretation of the evidence by the examiners. Gregg McCrary, a retired FBI behavioral analyst who conducts crime scene analysis and teaches law enforcement personnel on the topic, says it all boils down to the question, "How do we know what we think we know?"

A follow-up question to McCrary's is, "Who should be asking?" As we have repeatedly seen, tunnel vision and verification bias plays a huge role in obtaining false confessions, and the original investigator is often personally invested in the outcome of the case. The use of a "devil's advocate" role is ideal here. Using someone who is outside of the investigation to review the facts and evidence, asking questions and challenging assumptions, would elevate the investigation to a higher level. Though this approach is slowly becoming more widespread, as we will see in this and in other chapters, this is not something that is easily embraced by the law enforcement culture.

Now that we have our investigative mindset in place, let's move on to the evaluation of the confession.

A CRITICAL PRELIMINARY STEP

Let's use an analogy that many of us can relate to either in our own extended families or friend networks. When people talk about addiction, they say that the first step in treating the problem is acknowledging that one exists. The same principal applies to false confessions, and the reasons behind them. When doctors are taught how to conduct a medical procedure, they also learn what can go wrong, the signs and symptoms of problems, and how to take preventive measures. If you are not looking for something, you will never see it.

Compared to most investigators, you are now ahead of the game. You know that not only do false confessions occur, but how. As we have discussed, though the Reid Institute discusses some of these issues in their textbook and on their website, this topic barely makes it into the classroom. When it does, it is dismissively downplayed. Like the majority of interrogation instructors, they offer virtually no training on the different ways that confession contamination may occur, and provide no advice except "avoid asking leading questions."

When it comes to much of what will be covered next in this chapter, a lot of methodology and concepts are actually covered in Reid's textbook. But again, none of it is considered by them to be of enough importance to take a prominent place in their classroom training.[8]

CRIME SCENE FACT BASELINE

The first step of the evaluation of any confession should have begun long beforehand. Using the proper investigative mindset and what we now know about information versus facts, the investigator would have conducted a crime scene analysis or reconstruction. In the field, the words *analysis* and *reconstruction* are used interchangeably. It is defined by the Association of Crime Scene Reconstruction as "the use of scientific methods, physical evidence, deductive and inductive reasoning and their interrelationships to gain explicit knowledge of the series of events that surround the commission of a crime."[9] More simply put, this is where the investigator separates information from facts, and hard facts from soft, and develops a probable scenario of the crime and their list of "hold back" details. This information can now be used to test and evaluate not only incoming tips, witness statements, and confessions but also the investigators' theories as well.

In any investigation, new evidence and information are coming to light all the time. Because of that, the crime scene analysis must be a fluid hypothesis, open to change as new evidence and test results become available. This is why anyone whose job it is to review the confession for accuracy and reliability needs to revisit the investigation that led up to the interrogation and confession. They must determine if the original facts, theories, and assumptions still hold true.

GOAL OF THE EVALUATION

Similar to the way a coach can best analyze his teams when their practice sessions and games are videotaped, a confession can be best analyzed when recorded in its entirety. That is the only way that the development of the confession during the interrogation and the reliability of much of the evidence provided by the suspect can be critically and thoroughly evaluated. The issue of videotaping interrogations and even interviews of witnesses and others will be discussed more in chapter 12, but for now, there is absolutely no justifiable reason why law enforcement agencies are not routinely videotaping interrogations as a matter of policy. But whether there is no videotape of the entire interrogation, a video of the final version of the confession, a written confession, or what the investigator alleges the suspect said, the basic principles of confession evidence evaluation still apply.

The evaluation of confession evidence for reliability begins with a couple of simple and obvious concepts: (1) for a confession to be considered trustworthy, it must be factual, and (2) the details contained in the confession must be subjected to the same accuracy and reliability tests as any other information obtained during the investigation.

Before going further, let's go back over an issue that was brought up in chapter 2 and discuss how it relates to the evaluation of confession evidence. Innocent suspects give false confessions; however, absolute proof of their innocence may be difficult to obtain. Examples of absolute proof of innocence would be that it was later discovered that the crime to which they confessed never happened, the suspect was physically incapable of committing the crime, and more. It's worth bearing in mind that partially false and otherwise unreliable confessions can be given by guilty suspects. An example is the confession of Jay Wilds regarding the 1999 murder of Hae Min Lee in Baltimore, Maryland, that was featured on the NPR podcast *Serial*.[10] Wilds told investigators that he had helped Lee's ex-boyfriend, Adnan Syed, bury Lee's body after Syed had allegedly murdered her. Wilds's confession contained numerous inconsistencies and what were later determined to be outright lies. One piece of information that Wilds did provide was the location of Lee's car, which had been missing since her disappearance and murder, a detail that was previously unknown to the investigators. So while at least one critical detail in Wilds's confession was found to be reliable, many of them were not.[11]

It is the goal of any critical review of confession or statement evidence to test its accuracy and reliability. Can the confession be considered factual? What weight should be given to it? Is the confession or statement trustworthy enough to send a person to jail?

JUST THE "FACTS"

One step in determining the reliability of a confession is the examination of the details provided by the suspect. Like any other evidence, they cannot be taken at face value, but must undergo the test of corroboration. There are primarily two different types of corroboration, often referred to as *independent* and *dependent* corroboration.

Independent Corroboration

Independent corroboration occurs when the suspect tells the investigator something about the crime that the investigator did not know before going into the interrogation room, a detail that the investigator can then go out and corroborate. This type of information should be the goal of every interview and interrogation conducted by the investigator. Independent corroboration is always preferable over dependent corroboration because the chances of the information being contaminated by the investigator, while still present, are far smaller than with dependently corroborated details. The best type of independent corroboration comes from physical evidence. An example would be if a suspect confesses to killing a convenience store clerk during a robbery and then hiding the gun in his attic behind the Christmas decorations. If the investigator then goes and finds a gun at that location and a forensic examination proves that it was the murder weapon, that is pretty strong evidence. However, the investigator must be careful not to read too much into it. What that actually proves is that the suspect knew where the gun used in the murder was located. Like with Jay Wilds's confession, his knowledge of where Lee's car was located doesn't automatically erase the problems caused by the other inconsistent and incorrect details that he gave.

Investigators must use caution when using witnesses, victims, informants, and even forensic experts to seek independent corroboration of confession details due to the danger of "postconfession contamination."

This is discussed more in subsequent chapters, but basically, the fact that these people are told that a person confessed might influence their findings. As an example, let's say that a victim reported that her attacker was armed with a knife and used an extension cord to tie her up. During the interrogation of an innocent suspect, the investigator unintentionally contaminated the interrogation by telling the suspect those details. Convinced by the investigator of the inevitability of his being convicted and sentenced to life in prison unless he confesses, the innocent suspect includes those details to make the confession acceptable to the investigator. In addition, the innocent suspect tells the investigator that he also punched the victim several times in the face. This was a detail that was unknown to the investigator as it was not included in the victim's original statement (because it didn't happen). The investigator goes back to reinterview the victim and tells about the innocent suspect's confession. The investigator tells the victim that the innocent suspect also admitted that he punched her several times during the assault, and asks her if that is correct. Because she was told that the innocent suspect confessed (so of course he must be the right guy), she says "yes," thinking that maybe it was just a detail that she forgot or just to help make the case stronger.

Dependent Corroboration

Dependent corroboration is when the details provided during the confession by the suspect match those hold-back details known to the investigator. The trick is confirming who said it first, the suspect or the investigator. Professor Garrett's study of confirmed false confession cases that contained numerous hold-back details, discussed in chapter 6, shows that a large number of investigators do not understand how such contamination can occur. Even those who do understand are usually unaware of when it happens, which is why a recording of the entire interrogation is critical in helping to determine reliability. But even when the entire interrogation was not recorded, clues can often be found in the recorded final confessions. One such clue can be when the investigator has to correct or remind the suspect of specific details that they either got wrong or left out of the final confession.

Details That Just Don't Fit

Many times confessions and statements contain missing details, details that just don't fit, or details that don't make any sense. Instead of ignoring or explaining them away as is so often done, they should be closely examined, as they may offer valuable clues, bolstering or raising red flags concerning the confession's reliability. Sometimes such statements are indicators that there are things not yet uncovered in the investigation, point to the possible misinterpretation of evidence, or even that a witness or informant might not have been totally forthcoming with their information.

One thing to consider is the weight of the questionable statement when compared to other details that passed the independent/dependent corroboration tests. Another consideration is whether or not a missing detail might be something that would increase the criminal culpability of the suspect or link them to other crimes. An example of this would be if the suspect confessed to the murder of a child but would not admit to sexually assaulting them as well. Another example might be if a suspect lied about how they disposed of the stolen property, knowing that if they are honest and provide its location then the investigator would also locate additional items stolen in other crimes.

A red flag that a confession might not be reliable is when it becomes apparent that the suspect could not provide specific details because they were not provided to them first. The Marty Tankleff case, discussed in earlier chapters, is an excellent example of this. Tankleff only confessed to the details about his parents' murder that were known to the investigators at the time of his interrogation. Tankleff failed to provide any of the facts and details that were being uncovered at the time of his interrogation by other investigators and had not yet been passed on to his interrogators.

A suspect admitting to aspects of the crime that never occurred is another flag of unreliability. Take the earlier example of the case in which a child was murdered. If there was no evidence that the child had been sexually assaulted, yet the suspect confesses that he committed sexual acts that would have left evidence behind, that should raise red flags with the investigator.

Additionally, if the suspect is unable to accurately provide mundane, neutral details about the crime, especially when specifically asked, one should raise their eyebrows. Such details may include things like the layout of a room where the crime occurred, what the victim was wearing, or if a violent storm was taking place at the time of the crime.

BREAKING DOWN THE CONFESSION

Spreadsheets

It is often difficult to see things in context simply by reading a confession transcript or statement or watching a video. Breaking down the interrogation and confession helps the evaluator visualize how the confession developed. The interrogation should be charted out like a timeline, and almost line for line. This allows the evaluator to see exactly what interrogation tactics were used and when, the suspect's response to those tactics, the number of denials by the suspect, and who first introduced the hold-back details of the crime. The spreadsheet (an example of which can be found in Table 7.1) essentially lets the evaluator see who is telling the story. Is it the suspect's or the investigator's confession?

This approach works well if the interrogation was video or audio recorded in its entirety. I have found it especially helpful with extremely long interrogations as it is easier to flag specific examples of contamination early on and then see if and how that information is adopted by the suspect later on.

Spreadsheets can also help counter the investigator "cherry picking" the suspect's statements. A single, apparently damning comment may be defused or take on an entirely different meaning when reviewed by the evaluator in context with the rest of the interrogation.

Don't Trust the Transcript

In cases of long, recorded interrogations it is often tempting for the evaluator to rely primarily on a written transcript. Unfortunately, most interrogations take place under less-than-ideal recording situations. The investigator and suspect may not always speak clearly, and oftentimes they talk over each other. In law enforcement agencies where electronically recording interrogations was not their highest priority, the sound equipment is often of bargain-basement quality, and soundproofing of the rooms is often minimal or nonexistent. It has been joked that electronically re-

Table 7.1. Sample Interrogation Spreadsheet

Detective	Suspect	Observations
So if you think you are going to sit here and tell me you don't know any more information [on the suspects] . . . you're just putting yourself back in that same old boat of not being helpful.	I can go out and try to find out more. I haven't been seeing these people. I will do this so you can just leave me alone. I will find this out for you if you let me go . . .	
I don't feel that you've extended yourself far enough at this point . . . because you certainly aren't being quite honest with me.		
Let me share this with you. I've got four or five of y'all . . . bum rushing into the apartment . . .		Contamination: four to five people involved in the murder.
I've got you being the . . . number-two man through the door . . . participating much more than what you've given yourself.		Contamination: detective believes suspect was second through the door.
Now you left out about the confusion about the folks next door.	The who?	Contamination: something happened with the neighbors of the victim.
I think you were in that hallway when they were arguing back and forth with those neighbors that live next door where this happened . . .	But in that hallway. It was a lot of people in that building that night . . . 'cause he was selling crack . . . all them crackheads.	Contamination: provides details as to above.
You are not helping. You are not being honest about what really transpired, when y'all pushed your way in that apartment.	How am I not being honest? I just told you.	Contamination: suspects pushed their way into the apartment.
You gave me a story. It's not the right story.	What is? What is the right story?	
The one that happened.	Could you tell me please? Just be honest with me and I will say it. . . . What did you hear that I did?	Suspect pleading for detective to provide the details so that he can incorporate them into the narrative.

Detective	Suspect	Observations
I'm not going that way with you. . . . I worked hard to get this information . . .	And I'm working hard to tell you the information.	

corded interrogations are supposed to have lousy sound, that is so they can act as audio Rorschach or inkblot tests: the person listening is left on their own to interpret what they hear.

Misinterpretations often occur. Even when done by trained and experienced professionals, transcripts are often inaccurate. Pauses, voice tones, and inflections are often left out, and can radically change the interpretation of the written transcript. The transcript also does not capture the physical actions of the participants. Is the investigator shouting and poking their finger into the suspect's chest, or talking calmly while seated?

Bias can also play a role. If the transcriber believes in the guilt of the suspect, sections of the tape that someone else may determine are unintelligible may get "filled in" with guilt-presumptive words or statements.

Cross-cultural interrogations, especially when a translator is used, can be especially problematic. We discussed in chapter 6 about how sometimes, through gratuitous concurrence, some people might seem as if they are agreeing with the investigator's statements by saying "yeah" or "yes" when they are actually only acknowledging that they are listening.[12] And if a translator is needed, many law enforcement agencies rely on their own people, and this can create a guilt-presumptive filter through which the suspect's answers are interpreted.

Comparing the transcript to the electronic recording of the interrogation is critical. In cases in which there is a cultural difference or a translator is used, additional experts are often required to review the interrogation and offer their interpretations of what is actually going on.

Getting Down to Brass Tacks

The sole purpose of the above is to help determine the accuracy and reliability of the confession. Part of that will include examining the interrogation tactics that were used; what, if any, real or implied threats or promises were made that led the suspect to believe that it was a good idea to confess. But as we know, even the most improper and coercive of interrogations can result in accurate and reliable confessions. The focus now is on the details that were (or in some cases were not) provided by the suspect.

The evaluator would identify the details about the crime that were provided by the suspect and break them down into a list. Which ones are known to be accurate, and which ones are not? Of the accurate details, which ones were previously unknown to the investigators? Could those be corroborated, and if so, then how? If not, then why not?

Of the accurate details that were already known or believed to be true, who provided the detail first, the investigator or the suspect? Could the suspect have possibly learned them from any other source other than by being there? In general, if there was a way that the suspect was, or could have been, made aware of the detail before they provided it during the interrogation, then that detail should not be used in determining the reliability of the overall confession.

Regarding any inaccurate details, or details that the suspect was questioned about but could not provide any answer, what are all of the possible explanations for this inaccuracy or apparent lack of knowledge?

Though the evaluator can best answer these questions if the interrogation was electronically recorded in its entirety, it is possible to do the same for confessions in which only the final version was captured by an electronic recording, written statement, or through the notes and memory of the investigator.

There are other approaches open to the evaluator that can be used in conjunction with the above questions. One is to break down the details provided by the suspect about the crime and their actions. The evaluator then asks, If these details are true, what would be expected to be found at the crime scene?

A witness statement that was part of a case I once reviewed is a good example of what this can reveal. This woman was the prosecutor's star witness at trial. She claimed that she was in the front bedroom of their row house getting ready for work when she heard multiple gunshots fired outside of her house. The witness said she looked out her window and saw a pickup truck driving toward her house being chased by two gunmen. Both gunmen were firing their handguns multiple times at the truck, which ended up crashing into a parked car and tree in front of her house. The witness said she saw one of the gunmen, who she identified as a man that she knew from her neighborhood, run up to the driver's side door and fire several more times into the driver's side of the car.

After breaking down the individual details of the witness's statements, the following is what I expected to find when I visited the crime scene and examined the crime scene photographs and other reports:

- The windows in the front bedroom should provide a clear view of the scene.
- If one or both of the gunmen were firing semiautomatic handguns (the type that eject the shell casings once the bullet is fired), then shell casings should be found up and down the street.
- The location of damage to other cars and property from bullets that missed the pickup truck should reflect the gunmen firing from multiple positions as they ran down the street.
- There should be multiple bullet holes in the passenger side of the car and likely in the left side of the victim.

Crime scene photographs of the pickup truck revealed that it had been struck only once, and that was through the back window of the cab. The only injury to the victim came from that gunshot, which struck him in the back of the head. The photos showed that the passenger side window was rolled up when the police arrived, and there were no bullet holes in the passenger door or window.

The only gunshot damage to any other vehicle or property was to a couple of cars parked far down the street at the intersection. The only shell casings that were found were found in the street near that intersection.

When I visited the crime scene, it was obvious from the position of the witness's bedroom windows that though she had a clear view of where the pickup crashed and came to rest, her view down the street was limited and there was no way she could have seen the location where the shell casings were found.

Though this may seem like an extreme example, it is actually not uncommon, especially when it comes to false and unreliable confessions. Consider a similar comparison of the details provided by Danial Williams (Table 7.2).

Another tactic that the evaluator can use when conducting a preliminary review of a confession is to listen to what the investigator says during the interrogation and make a list of the details that they learned or could infer about the crime based on the investigator's questions and

Table 7.2.   Comparison of Danial's Statements with the Physical Evidence

Danial's Statement to the Police During His Interrogation	Physical Evidence Found at the Crime Scene or During the Autopsy
Danial said he did not ejaculate	Semen was found on vaginal swabs from Ms. Bosko's body and on the blanket found near her body
Danial said that he did not use any weapons	Ms. Bosko was stabbed with a knife
Danial said that he did not choke Ms. Bosko	Ms. Bosko was strangled
Danial said that he did not touch the blanket	Semen stains on the blanket matched the semen found on the vaginal swabs from Ms. Bosko's body
Danial said he hit Ms. Bosko a couple of times, maybe in the head, and said that he hit her three times on the side of her head with his fist	Ms. Bosko had no bruises on her face or head
Danial said the underwear he was wearing during his interrogation was the underwear he wore before and after raping Ms. Bosko	Ms. Bosko's DNA was not found on Danial's underwear, but a mixture of her DNA and Ballard's was found on the blanket near her body
Danial said he went to Ms. Bosko's apartment in his bare feet	Bare footprints from Ms. Bosko and her husband, but not from Danial, were found on the floor of the bedroom
Danial said he tossed Ms. Bosko to the floor and said Ms. Bosko was resisting while he pushed her to the back bedroom and during the rape	Ms. Bosko had no bruises or other injuries from being tossed on the floor and had no defensive or scrimmage wounds or bruises anywhere on her body
Danial said Ms. Bosko was not wearing any panties	Ms. Bosko's panties were found turned inside out on the bedroom floor near her body
Danial said he hit Ms. Bosko once on the head with a hard, flat-soled shoe	Ms. Bosko had no bruises or injuries to the side of her head
Danial said he tossed the shoe away after hitting Ms. Bosko in the head	The police found no shoe near Ms. Bosko's body in the bedroom and did not seize any shoes from the apartment
Danial said he did not stab Ms. Bosko	Ms. Bosko had three penetrating stab wounds to her chest and multiple hesitation stab wounds that did not penetrate deeply into her chest
Danial said he did not see any blood when he left Ms. Bosko	Ms. Bosko was stabbed, her shirt was bloodstained, blood pooled on the floor beneath and next to her body, and blood covered her face

Danial's Statement to the Police During His Interrogation	Physical Evidence Found at the Crime Scene or During the Autopsy
Danial said he pushed Ms. Bosko from the living room to the bedroom	None of the papers hanging from a shelf and protruding into the narrow hallway between the two rooms were disturbed
Danial said he used his hands to restrain Ms. Bosko's hands while raping her	Ms. Bosko had no bruises or injuries to her hands or wrists

Source: "Comparison of Danial's Statements with the Physical Evidence," Norfolk Four; A Miscarriage of Justice, http://www.norfolkfour.com/images/uploads/pdf_files/Williams_Confession_Comparison.pdf. Accessed March 21, 2016.

statements. The evaluator then compares the investigator's statements to the crime scene photos and reports. If during that review of the interrogation the evaluator is able to come up with a pretty accurate picture of what happened simply by listening to the investigator's questions, there is a good chance that quite a bit of contamination was present.

At the end of all this, the evaluator, whether it be the investigator, prosecutor (who should have done the evaluation as a matter of course), defense attorney, or devil's advocate, should have a much clearer picture of the strengths and deficits of both the interrogation and the confession (or in the case of a witness or victim, their statement). The evaluation may raise more questions than it answers. Unfortunately, there is no scoring chart or checklist that can be applied to come up with a definitive answer as to the final accuracy and reliability of the confession. That, too, is often a subjective conclusion, but one that is in a better position to be defended than before the evaluation.

Looking at the Big Picture

One additional thing for the examiner to consider when evaluating the confession, or in fact any other statement evidence, is the "big picture" of the investigation. We know that the first step to obtaining a false confession is mistakenly identifying an innocent person as a suspect. Looking at the overall investigation will provide the evaluator with information as to how the subject turned, in the minds of the investigator, into a suspect.

Once again we turn to the United Kingdom for ideas. Their investigators are taught that each investigation is to be thoroughly documented so that anyone coming behind them has an audit trail of their decision-making processes. Key decision points in the investigation are entered into a "decision log," along with the information that was used to make that decision. Throughout the case, the investigator and their supervisors are supposed to go back and reevaluate earlier decisions, and especially consider them in light of whatever new evidence has been developed.

Since this is not a normal practice in most law enforcement agencies in the United States, it will be up to the evaluator to develop the audit trail, which is usually done in the form of an investigative timeline. The investigative timeline needs to include not only the events surrounding the crime itself but also how the investigation progressed, who was interviewed and reinterviewed and when, and at what point facts were uncovered and made known to the investigators during the case. [13]

A timeline of the investigation achieves the same goals as the spreadsheet does for the confession—it allows the evaluator to visualize the flow of the investigation and helps them identify how and why the suspect became the suspect, the possible impact of biases such as tunnel vision, and the presence of potential contamination in witness and victim statements.

The timeline provides the evaluator with the basis to perform a good test for the presence of tunnel vision. They will be able to see when specific facts became known to the investigator, and how those facts were used to make major decisions, such as when to interrogate the suspect. They will also see what facts became known to the investigator after that major decision point and how they were interpreted by the investigation. The evaluator then switches the order in which the various facts were discovered, maybe placing the "postinterrogation facts" first. The evaluator then considers if the same decision would have been reached if the later-discovered facts were known first. They would also ask themselves if the investigator would have been interpreted the later-discovered facts in the same way if they had been discovered earlier.

Let's again use Danial Williams's case as an example. During the first hours into their investigation into the murder of Michelle Bosko, the investigators determined that Bosko was raped and killed by a single perpetrator who was known to her. They based this on observations they made about the crime scene, including the fact that there were no signs of forced entry to the apartment.

The key decision point where Williams was identified as a suspect occurred when a friend of Bosko's told the investigators that she believed that Williams, Bosko's next-door neighbor, had a creepy fixation on her, and had in the past come over to use her telephone at night.

Investigators viewed everything from that point onward through a guilt-presumptive lens. They considered it suspicious that Williams was being "too cooperative" when, at their request, he agreed to come down to the police station to assist them in the investigation. Information that should have caused them pause, such as Williams passing the lie detector test, was ignored. They pushed the interrogation for hours, until Williams confessed and provided a narrative consistent with their theory: that he talked his way into Bosko's apartment and raped and killed her by himself.

Evidence that was developed after the key decision point and confession was that the DNA profile from the sperm found on and around Bosko's body came from a single subject, and that subject was not Williams. Rather than view this as exculpatory for Williams, the investigators interpreted that fact to mean that, contrary to their initial crime scene analysis and Williams's confession, he still committed the crime, just not alone. As you remember, this caused the investigator and prosecutor to continually embellish and expand their theory of the case to include a total of seven sailors and Omar Ballard, whose DNA it turned out to be.

So let's switch things around. The first part remains the same: the investigators' initial theory is a single perpetrator who Bosko knew. But this time, the investigators obtained the DNA results back from the laboratory before interviewing Bosko's friend, who pointed them to Williams. So far the facts are matching their theory.

With the DNA results available to them, the investigators now talk to Bosko's friend. She tells them her suspicions about Williams, but at the same time she told them that they should also consider Omar Ballard as a possible suspect.

This time, now having two suspects, as well as physical evidence that could definitively identify the true perpetrator, would the investigators have followed the same path? Or would they have done a bit more background on their suspects, thus learning of Ballard's criminal past and his assault on another woman in the area? Would they have had Williams's and Ballard's DNA tested first, thus allowing them to use the test results during any interrogation that followed? And if in this scenario, as Ballard did when he was actually interrogated, he confessed to having committed the crime alone, would the investigators have assumed that he was lying and seek out additional suspects?

Aside from suspects, timelines can help identify witnesses whose information may have been influenced by contamination. Discussed in more detail in the following chapter, witnesses and victims are often interviewed several times during the course of an investigation. Many times new or different information is developed during these interviews. A timeline can be used to compare these witness interviews and the information that they contain to when new information becomes known to the investigators. The same principal can be used if a suspect gives multiple confessions to the investigators over a period of time. If the witness's or suspect's information changes in concert with the new information coming to light, then the details surrounding their interviews deserves a closer look.

So far the emphasis of the book has been on suspects, with passing mentions of unreliable witness statements as well. In the next chapters we will explore how police interrogation practices can contribute to bad statements from witnesses, informants, and even victims as well.

8

WITNESSES

They are scenes familiar to all of us—the highlight of any trial. The witness takes the stand, swears to tell nothing but the truth, and in relating what they remember, they confidentially point to the defendant as the person who they saw commit the crime. The jailhouse informant describes to the jury the late-night discussions with his cellmate, in which he confessed to having committed murder in chilling detail. The forensic scientist who positively links the defendant to the crime scene through bite marks, hairs, or other trace evidence. Their testimony is compelling. It is often wrong.

Mistaken witnesses, especially eyewitness testimony, lying informants, and misinterpretation of forensic evidence, result in more wrongful convictions and other miscarriages of justice than false confessions. Though they are usually the result of many factors, oftentimes their roots can actually be traced back to the same things that can cause an innocent person to give a false confession. In many cases involving witnesses and forensic experts, their errors are usually not malicious ones. They honestly believe in what they are saying, and their sincerity comes across to the jury. Other witnesses know they are lying, but because of tunnel vision and the improper use of interrogation tactics and contamination, they, like the innocent suspect who has provided a false confession, have become trapped in a story that they must stick to or suffer the consequences.

We will be breaking down the types of witnesses into two categories. The first category includes the witnesses (coerced and uncoerced), victims, and forensic experts discussed above. This chapter will discuss how interview and interrogation tactics can adversely influence the reliability of their testimony. The next chapter will deal with the other category: the informants, "cooperating" witnesses, and jailhouse snitches who fully expect to be compensated for providing what law enforcement decides is their "truthful" testimony.

MALLEABLE MEMORY

Many of us think that memory is captured and retained like a camera capturing a video. In some ways it is, especially when it comes to the limitations. Perceptions are based on what we see, much like the camera only captures what it is pointed at. Unlike the camera, our mind tries to fill in the voids. We often do so by inference, or by searching for clues from others. Like a false confession, false and altered memories are often shaped by the way we are questioned about the event. Memory is easily contaminated.

Hugo Munsterberg, a professor of psychology at Harvard University, was vacationing with his family at the beach when he got a call from back home, telling him that his house had been burglarized. He rushed home and made a superficial survey to help the investigators determine what was stolen. Later, after a man was caught with some of the stolen property, Munsterberg testified at his trial. Under oath, he told the jury with absolute certainty that two burglars broke into his house at night, entering through a cellar window. Munsterberg listed the items that had been stolen from his house, and provided other details that helped to lead to the man's conviction. Later, Munsterberg discovered that much of what he had said was wrong.[1]

Some of the details were honest mistakes of memory. The items Munsterberg said were stolen by the thieves included ones that he had forgotten that he had put into long-term storage. Others, he realized, such as the detail that there were two burglars and their point of entry into the house "clearly rose through the influence of suggestion" by the police.[2]

Munsterberg used his experience as a case study in his 1908 groundbreaking book *On the Witness Stand: Essays on Psychology and Crime*.[3] The use of the scientific method to study human behavior was in its infancy then, and researchers were just beginning to understand the limits of memory and how easily it can be contaminated and altered by outside influences.

One experiment used by researchers back then is often repeated in different formats during the training of recruits in police academies today. During the normal course of a class, a "crime" is suddenly committed in front of the students. In Munsterberg's day, the "crime" was enacted during a scholarly conference attended by judges, lawyers, physicians, and psychologists. During the meeting, the door to the room flew open. A man dressed in a clown outfit ran in, chased by another man carrying a gun. There was shouting between the two, a fight, shots fired, and the two fled the room. The whole event lasted about twenty seconds. The "witnesses," all scientifically trained observers, were then asked to write a detailed account of what they saw. Needless to say, their accounts differed wildly. Munsterberg wrote that "the majority of the observers omitted or falsified about half of the processes which occurred completely in their field of vision." Additionally, Munsterberg noted that "the judgement as to the time duration of the act varied between a few seconds and several minutes."[4]

This quirk of human nature is the bane of investigators and prosecutors. While discrepancies between memory and facts are not the fault of the investigator, many of the methods by which they attempt to extract reliable memories from witnesses actually contribute to making those memories even more unreliable. Munsterberg identified many problematic tactics and other issues, including tunnel vision, faulty methods of detecting deception, the use of leading questions, and the suggestibility of the young—all factors that contribute to both false confessions and unreliable witness statements today.

THE WILLING WITNESS

As we have seen from Munsterberg's work and other research, even the most cooperative of victims, or the most willing of witnesses, can provide unreliable information. Besides the natural problems caused by memory limitations and perception, the willing witness and victim often look for clues from the investigator to fill in the blanks and shape their narratives. These clues are often provided in the same way as they are to innocent suspects under interrogation—through contamination. Leading and suggestive questions, sharing accounts between witnesses, and other methods of statement contamination can all influence what the victim or witness thinks happened. As with false confessions, those who are young, suffering from mental or cognitive issues, suggestible, physically exhausted, traumatized, or under the influence of alcohol or drugs are susceptible to providing inaccurate information.

Law enforcement is becoming more and more aware of this danger. Many agencies have adopted "double-blind" eyewitness identification procedures, where the investigator showing the photospread or conducting the live suspect line-up with the victim or witness is totally unaware of which photo is of the suspect, or where the suspect is standing in the line-up. The procedure has been proven to eliminate any chance that the case investigator may unintentionally, through word or action, "tip off" the witness to whom the investigator believes they should pick.

Another age-old tactic is when there are multiple witnesses to a crime, investigators take great pains to keep them separate. They take them into the police station in separate vehicles and keep them isolated in separate rooms so that they not be able to share what they saw or heard. However, it is when the witnesses are interviewed that contamination is likely to take place. Investigators receive little to no training on both how to prevent unintentional contamination during the interview and how to most accurately extract the information that the witnesses do have. Often, investigators will eliminate the benefit of the early separation of witnesses by comparing their statements with other investigators, then reinterviewing the witnesses to "address" any contradictions.

Such "cross-contamination" can occur when investigators attempt to corroborate information that they receive later in the investigation from other witnesses, informants, and especially following the confession of a suspect, as discussed in chapter 7. A witness may have reported that "A" and "B" occurred during the offense. During their confession, the suspect admitted to "A" and "B," but also provided detail "C," a detail previously unknown to the investigators. If during their reinterview of the witness, the investigators tell them that the suspect confessed, and also admitted to detail "C," the witness may then "remember" and incorporate detail "C" into their account of the crime. They may do this because detail "C" actually happened and they simply forgot, or it was just not included in their original statement. However, especially in the case of an innocent suspect who gave a false confession, the witness may believe that since the suspect confessed that detail "C" must be true. They then include it as part of their testimony, either to help ensure a conviction or because it is now implanted as a false memory by the investigators.

The more a witness is reinterviewed by investigators, the greater the potential for contamination and memory manipulation. An example can be found in the Supreme Court's decision in the case of *Strickler v. Green*,[5] a 1999 kidnapping and murder case in Virginia. In that case, a key witness initially told the investigators that her memory of the events that she witnessed were "muddled." At trial, the key witness's memory was no longer muddled, and she was able to provide an immense amount of detailed information about the crime, saying that she had "an excellent memory." Through the reports prepared by the investigators who had conducted multiple interviews of the witness, it was evident that her memory improved with each of the interviews. The witness agreed that her memory became better because of "the associations that [the investigator] helped me make" during those interviews.[6]

Investigators have unintentionally contaminated a witness's or victim's memory simply by trying to be supportive. While a student at the University of North Carolina, Chapel Hill, Jennifer Thompson-Cannino was raped by a man who broke into her off-campus apartment. Based on a composite drawing created from her description of the suspect, Ronald Cotton was developed as a suspect. When shown a series of photographs that included one of Cotton, Thompson-Cannino picked him out, saying, "I think this is the guy." Pushed by the investigators, Thompson-Cannino became "positive," but then asked the investigators if she "did OK." "You did great," they answered. From that point on, bolstered by the comments made by the investigators, Thompson-Cannino was 100 percent positive that Cotton was the man who raped her. Her testimony to that effect sent him to jail in spite of an alibi that put him elsewhere. Years later, DNA evidence proved her wrong.[7]

Cotton won his freedom not only because of DNA but also because both Thompson-Cannino and the investigators were later able to examine and acknowledge their mistakes. Others are not so fortunate. Since the videotaping of eyewitness and victim interviews is not common practice, such subtle contamination goes unknown. The lack of documentation could be unintentional or part of institutional practices. I once watched a class on the documentation of witness interviews conducted by an investigative supervisor during a basic investigator's class. The supervisor told the new investigators that they should not document any statement made by a witness or victim in which they said that they didn't think they could make an identification of the suspect. The supervisor said that if they did so, it would only be used to discredit the witness if later on they did make an identification.

OUTSIDE SOURCE CONTAMINATION

Like innocent suspects, the statements of witnesses and victims can be unintentionally influenced by sources other than law enforcement. A victim, who previously could not identify a suspect, suddenly "recognized" him when seeing a person on the news who had allegedly committed a similar crime. Therapists working with patients who they believed have repressed memories of traumatic events have helped them "remember" in detail their abduction by UFOs, participation in satanic cult practices, and ritualistic childhood sex abuse by parents, teachers, day care providers, and others.[8] This is not to say that a witness's or victim's memory cannot be "jogged" through proper therapeutic techniques or other outside sources; however, this new evidence must also undergo the same critical corroboration as any other statement evidence.

THE "HELPFUL" FORENSIC EXPERTS

Contamination of the evidence provided by witnesses and victims has also been seen to impact the work of forensic scientists and experts, especially in the more subjective fields of hair, fingerprints, and bite-mark analysis. Being inappropriately provided with case details, confession evidence, and the theories of the investigators has been shown to bias the experts in their analysis.[9]

As an example, in one study that has been duplicated numerous times, six fingerprint examiners from around the world were given a set of latent crime scene prints and were asked to compare these prints to sets of elimination prints taken from known subjects. The examiners were not aware that they had conducted previous examinations on the latent prints.[10]

Before they conducted their examination, the examiners were falsely told that the elimination prints were from suspects who had been eliminated from the investigation or who the investigators believed to be the true perpetrator.[11]

In this experiment, four of the six examiners came to a different conclusion about the latent prints than they had previously reported. One examiner was reported to have changed his mind three times.[12]

THE "UNWILLING" WITNESS

When investigating a crime, an investigator must deal with the cards he is dealt. When prosecuting a drug murder that occurred in a known prostitution area at 3:00 am, your witnesses tend not to be, as one prosecutor I know would always say in her closing argument, members of the local church choir. Witnesses and victims come from all walks of life. Like suspects, they may be young, suggestible, have cognitive or mental health issues, substance abuse problems, or suffer from lack of sleep. They may be traumatized by what they saw or what happened to them. They may have reasons not to be fully forthcoming, as they were the victim of or witnessed the crime because they were in the area to purchase drugs. They may wish not to be cooperative at all, maybe because of lack of trust in the police, don't want the hassle, not wanting to be perceived as a "snitch," or a desire to "take care of it" themselves.

Just about every investigator will tell you that in their experience the unwilling witness is the norm. Some are uncooperative through apathy, some fear, some because of distrust of the system, and some because they are involved in criminal activity themselves. David Simon, a *Baltimore Sun* reporter who was imbedded in the Baltimore Homicide Unit for a year, wrote that for investigators, the "God-given truth . . . [is that] . . . everyone lies. Witnesses . . . lie because they think they have to. Everyone else lies for the sheer joy of it, and to uphold a general principal that under no circumstances do you provide accurate information to a cop."[13]

I can personally attest that it seems as if the majority of the time I spent on any investigation was in an attempt to convince people that it was a good idea to tell me what they knew. Patience and persistence is the key here. Developing the evidence and the rapport to convince the person that you are someone they can trust takes time. And time is not something that investigators usually have a lot of.

As in false confession cases, the problem begins when the investigator has it wrong. The investigator incorrectly believes that the witness is lying or holding back information. It is this witness who is even more susceptible to providing false or misleading statements and testimony. In these cases the investigator will go into "interrogation mode," using the real or implied threats of inevitable consequences and real or implied promises of leniency. The tactics that have been found to induce an innocent suspect to give a statement that could result in their loss of freedom, or even exposure to the death penalty, can be even more effective with someone who is only being asked to "cooperate" with law enforcement. [14]

The Reid Technique recommends that if a witness persists in not "telling the truth," then they should be accused of committing the crime themselves, and interrogated as if a suspect. [15] Other threats that are often used by investigators include the possibility of losing custody of their children, eviction from public housing, and the notification of their parole or probation officer of their lack of "cooperation." Because a witness is not a suspect and they are not officially in police custody, they do not have to be advised of any rights not to talk to the investigator or have an attorney present during the interview. The conditions under which they are interviewed are usually not subjected to the same scrutiny as a suspect's, especially if in the end they break and decide to "cooperate" with the investigator and prosecutor.

Unlike a suspect, with whom the investigator usually has only one crack, the uncooperative witness can be susceptible to repeated interrogations. The investigator can stop by the job or home, at all times of the day or night. The investigator may make use of the power of the grand jury, if it is available to them. The witness is served with a subpoena and compelled to come down to testify under oath. Where in many jurisdictions a witness cannot be compelled to talk to an investigator, they can be forced to talk and answer questions before a grand jury, unless they can convincingly assert that such testimony will incriminate themselves. If they still refuse, the witness can be subjected to jail time, and they can be charged with the crime of perjury if the investigator or prosecutor does not believe their account.

One example of the abuse of the grand Jury used to occur regularly in the District of Columbia until it was stopped by a court order. A witness would be served a grand jury subpoena to appear on a certain date. Once they appeared, they were ushered into the office of the prosecutor or conference room. There, the prosecutor or investigator, or both, would interrogate them. If the witness refused to talk, or did not provide a statement that was acceptable to the prosecutor or attorney, they would receive another subpoena to return the next day. The process would repeat itself. On some days, the witness would be told to wait in the waiting room. At the end of the day, the witness was asked if they were ready to talk and/or "tell the truth." If a satisfactory answer was not forthcoming, the witness was served with yet another subpoena.

Once a formally "uncooperative" witness finally agreed to "tell the truth," they were taken to the grand jury to testify. The grand jury is a secretive proceeding. No one is allowed inside except the prosecutor, witness, or the grand jury members themselves. The witness is placed under oath and led through their testimony by questions from the prosecutor. Often, as is the case when an investigator takes a written statement or an electronic recording of the final version of a confession, the prosecutor will ask the witness if anyone threatened or coerced them into testifying to the facts as they did. The witness, like the suspect making the confession, usually answers "no." They know that answering otherwise may subject them to additional interrogation when all they want is for it all to end.

A suspect's alibi witnesses are especially likely to be subjected to coercive interrogation tactics in cases in which tunnel vision has taken hold. Rather than be open-minded and through a thorough interview of the witness obtain details that can later lead to confirmation or rebuttal of the alibi, the investigator will interrogate. The goal of the interrogation, as in the interrogation of suspects, is not to obtain the truth but to discredit the alibi witness.

THE PROSECUTOR'S ROLE

One of the most critical responsibilities of the prosecutor is the critical evaluation of the evidence brought to them by the investigator. But like the investigator, this role can be hampered by tunnel vision, lack of information, the prosecutor's personal investment in the investigation, their lack of training, and/or the desire to win. Like an investigator being judged by the number of arrests they make, prosecutors are judged by their conviction rate.

Few prosecutors receive any formal training in how to properly interview witnesses. Many take their cue from the investigators with whom they work, and like the investigators, they have a poor understanding of how statement evidence contamination can occur. As discussed above, many times, especially in more serious cases, the prosecutor and investigator work hand in hand in "cracking" uncooperative witnesses. The prosecutor is even more involved when the witness is a "cooperator," someone who is testifying in order to receive assistance with their own criminal case, a topic that will be covered more in the next chapter.

Even without the influence of the investigator, prosecutors can contaminate and mold witness testimony on their own. In most cases, prosecutors meet with witnesses before trial to go over their testimony. This is an important step in preparation for any trial. For the majority of witnesses, this may be their first exposure to the courtroom. Courtroom procedures are explained, and the witness is told what questions to expect from both the prosecutor and the defense attorney. Sometimes the witness may be cautioned about saying certain things during their testimony that the judge had determined should not be heard by the jury. An example would be if the witness was able to identify the defendant at the time of the crime because they knew each other from before when they were in prison together. If the jury heard that the defendant has been previously convicted of a crime, that might unfairly bias them in the current case.

While such "coaching" of the witness is permissible, it can sometimes go too far.

In an effort to eliminate discrepancies, avoid problematic details, and otherwise "smooth out" a witness's testimony, the prosecutor may fall into the same contamination traps as the investigator. The use of leading questions, sharing evidence and other witness statements, and highlighting specific facts can all help to reshape the witness's testimony to make it stronger for the jury. When interviewed, "several former prosecutors found it 'disturbing' and 'dangerous' that so many prosecutors gave facts to cooperating witnesses in the course of eliciting information from them."[16] Having sat in on untold numbers of witness conferences, I always noted that when the prosecutor of another investigator said, "I don't want to put words in your mouth, but . . . ", it was usually too late. As these sessions are usually unrecorded or undocumented, such contamination usually goes undiscovered.

In the case of witnesses who were previously "uncooperative," and especially those that are again wavering, the prosecutor may remind them of the earlier threats that were made to gain their cooperation. If the witness had testified before the grand jury, the prosecutor may remind them that when they testified to what the prosecutor and investigator believed was "the truth," they were under oath. Any deviation from that earlier testimony carries the possibility of the witness being criminally charged with perjury.

When it comes to all evidence, including witness evidence, the prosecutor has a legal and ethical duty to turn over any information that might be of assistance to the defense attorney. This not only includes the use of any real or implied threats or promises made by law enforcement to the witness but also any discrepancies in the witness's accounts. Such information is commonly referred to as Brady, after the Supreme Court case *Brady v. Maryland*.[17] In that case, John Brady and Donald Boblit were arrested in connection with a carjacking during which the car's owner had been killed in the attempt. Brady confessed to his part in the crime but said that Boblit was responsible for killing the victim. Boblit gave five different confessions. In the first four, he blamed Brady for killing the victim. In the last confession, Boblit said that he was the one who killed the victim.[18]

Brady and Boblit had separate trials. Brady's attorney asked for copies of all of Boblit's confessions; however, the prosecutor turned over only the ones where Boblit said that Brady did the murder. Brady took the stand and testified that Boblit was the one who killed the man, and he was convicted. The Supreme Court ruled that this selective release of Boblit's confession denied Brady's attorney of evidence that pointed to his innocence (at least to having committed the actual murder) was unlawful.[19]

Because many of the encounters that investigators and prosecutors have with witnesses are unrecorded or minimally (if at all) documented, Brady evidence often goes undiscovered. Many times it is not intentional, but sometimes, as in the case above where the lieutenant told new investigators not to document a witness's initial statement regarding the possibility of making a later eyewitness identification, it is.

CREDIT WHERE CREDIT IS DUE

An important point that I make often is that, like in the interrogation of guilty suspects, the tactics discussed in this chapter can also result in a witness providing factual and reliable information. Many guilty people are in prison because of the aggressiveness and perseverance of an investigator or prosecutor. However, when this aggressiveness and perseverance is combined with tunnel vision, improper interrogation tactics, contamination, lack of investigative corroboration, and poor documentation, justice is not done.

9

COOPERATORS AND INFORMANTS

The use of informants to solve crimes and prosecute criminals is as old as law enforcement itself. In ancient Rome, they were called delatores, and were paid either based on the value of the information or a percentage of the estate of the accused. In the 1600s, England began a formalized system that paid "blood money" for information. This led to organized rings of informants, usually criminals themselves, some of whom made handsome livings off snitching on their cohorts. Eugene Francois Vidocq, the notorious French criminal who later became what many considered to be the world's first detective, agreed to inform on his fellow prison inmates in exchange for his incarceration in the prison of his choice. [1] Vidocq's name lives on in the Vidocq Society, a Philadelphia-based organization dedicated to helping law enforcement agencies across the United States solve cold cases. [2]

Just as old as law enforcement's use of informants is the problems that they bring. Mercenaries working for money or some other consideration, informants have always had the reputation of being generally untrustworthy. As much as they are "worked" by law enforcement, they work the system to benefit themselves. There are thousands of documented cases throughout the ages of informants making up crimes that didn't happen, falsifying evidence, entrapping people, and inventing false confessions from innocent subjects. Untold numbers of innocent people have been arrested, convicted, and sometimes put to death because of dishonest snitches.

The problem of dishonest informants increased in the United States through the imposition of mandatory minimum sentencing. Faced with decades, if not life in prison with no chance of parole, the only escape is for the defendant to provide significant amounts of information of value to law enforcement. This would allow the judge to depart from the set sentencing guidelines and give the defendant a reduced sentence. Jails and prisons are referred to as "cheese factories" because they generate so many "rats" willing to inform on others.[3]

The problem for many caught in this trap, especially when it came to drug offenses, was that they were the "small fry." Criminal organizations compartmentalize. Drug couriers and small-time dealers, facing life in prison, didn't have the inside knowledge that is necessary to bargain with the prosecutor. The incentive to come up with something, anything, that will make them valuable to law enforcement is pretty high.

In spite of the inherent dangers, informants are considered to be one of, if not the most, valuable tool of law enforcement. Many crimes would go unsolved without their information. In many cases, they are the only way that law enforcement can penetrate drug gangs and other organized crime organizations.

Many in the so-called stop snitching movement say that their focus is on informants who themselves are criminals, or as they say, "are in the game," and snitch in order to avoid jail time, obtain protection for their own criminal activities, or receive other compensation. In their mind, the "little old lady" down the street who just happens to witness a crime does not fall into the "snitch" category. The real snitches, as the term defined by many in the movement, are generally broken down by law enforcement into two basic categories: informants and cooperators. The lines between the two are often blurred.[4]

Informants

Informants, also called *confidential informants* or *CIs*, are persons who are, have been involved, or are associated with criminal activity, and are providing information to law enforcement for some form of compensation or assistance. They are usually not incarcerated at the time that they are "working" (incarcerated or "in-custody" informants are discussed below). Generally, they are not expected to testify in court, so their identities never become known.

People become informants usually in only a couple of ways. One is by being charged with a crime themselves. The subject is offered a deal. Working as an informant will get the charge dropped, lessened, or let the prosecutor recommend that they receive a less severe sentence. When a prosecutor is part of the mix, a plea deal (discussed more in the next chapter) is usually involved. However, law enforcement officers, especially in cases involving drugs, often handle the negotiations themselves. If the informant provides them with enough information that they feel is of value, they will simply ask the prosecutor to dismiss the case.

Sometimes law enforcement will recruit an informant with only the threat of an arrest. The investigator will develop a criminal case against the subject, and then approach them with an offer—snitch or get arrested. This is often done in an effort to protect an ongoing investigation, and it allows the informant to continue their activities without raising the suspicions of their cohorts by getting arrested.

Another way to recruit an informant is through personal relationships. Through contacts over time, the law enforcement officer and informant get to know each other, and the suggestion is made that becoming an informant would be a lucrative proposition for both of them. The informant is offered money or some other form of compensation, such as help getting into public housing or assistance in dealing with a "problem" (which sometimes turns out to be a criminal competitor). Often they believe that by being an informant, law enforcement will turn a blind eye to their minor infractions of the law.

Subjects who became informants after they had been arrested in order to "work off charge" sometimes continue the relationship afterward, except this time in exchange for money or other compensation.

Snitching for money can be relatively lucrative for the informant. The US Drug Enforcement Agency's "super snitch" Andrew Chambers made as much as $4 million working for various federal agencies over the years.[5] But for those living on the fringes of society, even fifty bucks a tip is a significant amount of money.

Informants have been known to "cop shop," offering their services to multiple law enforcement agencies, even to multiple investigators and units within the same agency. Often, the agencies and investigators are unaware that the informant is "working" for someone else, making it impossible to track the reliability of their information. Or, if the informant is discovered to be unreliable by one agency or investigator, they simply go find another that is unaware of their track record.

In the context of false confessions, informants are problematic in many ways. They can be what is behind the identification of an innocent person as a suspect. Through improper questioning and contamination, they may provide false evidence "confirming" a confession or witness statement. And in some cases, they may step out from behind their veil of secrecy and offer false testimony as a witness. Such was the case in the wrongful conviction of Donald Gates.[6]

On June 22, 1981, at approximately 9:00 pm, twenty-one-year-old Catherine Schilling left her job at a law office in the Watergate Office Building in Washington, DC. She was walking to the Georgetown home that she shared with friends, and had made plans to go out dancing that evening. Schilling never made it.[7]

The next day, Schilling's nude body was found in Rock Creek Park, a park that bordered her Georgetown neighborhood and would have been part of her walk home. She had been raped and shot five times in the head.[8]

The case went unsolved until longtime police informant Gerald Mack Smith came forward with a tip. Smith said that he had been drinking in a park with Gates when Gates confessed to him that he had robbed and killed Schilling. The investigators paid Smith $50 for the initial tip, and an extra $250 when he picked Gates out of a series of photographs. Based on the tip, the investigators arrested Gates on an unrelated outstanding arrest warrant and obtained a sample of his hair.[9]

An FBI hair examiner examined the hair, and later testified that it was a match when compared to a hair found on Schilling's body. Gates was charged with the murder, and both the FBI expert and Smith testified against him at trial. On September 16, Gates was convicted and sentenced to twenty years to life in prison.[10]

In 1997, an internal review of the FBI laboratory revealed that the hair examiner had been giving false and misleading testimony that was not supported by their lab results.

In 2000, a DNA test that was performed on semen recovered from Schilling's body eliminated Gates as the contributor. Gates was set free on December 19, 2009.

It had since been discovered that Smith's credibility as an informat was at the time under serious question by some of the investigators who knew him.[11] When he first snitched on Gates, he had just been indicted on his third felony charge. In exchange for his testimony at trial, the prosecutor dropped the indictment against Smith. Gates's attorney did not know this at the time.[12]

Cooperators

Often referred to as *cooperating witnesses* or *CWs*, these are people who were caught up in a criminal investigation, have been charged with a crime, or are already serving a prison sentence and hope to obtain leniency through testifying against others.

The prosecutor and the CW's defense attorney are usually both involved in this process. Plea deals, discussed in detail in the next chapter, have to be negotiated. As part of the plea deal, the CW may seek to be charged with a lesser crime, the protection of family members and associates from prosecution, to prevent or minimize the seizure of assists, reduced prison time, to be sent to a specific prison, or some other benefit. In addition to testifying in court about their own criminal activities and those of others, the CW may be directed to help progress the investigation by gathering additional information, wearing a wire, or other activities. The more the CW is willing to do, and the more information that they can provide, the better the chance they have of escaping prison time and protecting those important to them.

Even more than informants, CWs are highly incentivized to provide information that law enforcement wants to hear. The deal negotiations and debriefings can resemble interrogations, except that prosecutors are not restricted by the same rules as investigators when they interrogate a suspect or witnesses. While investigators are not supposed to make real or implied threats of inevitable consequences or real or implied promises of leniency, prosecutors often do. That is because they can. They, not the investigator, have the power to make those things happen. And because negotiations and debriefings may require several meetings and those discussions are not recorded, it is often difficult to determine the level of coercion and the amount of contamination that was used to obtain the account that is acceptable to the prosecutor. And just like when an investigator is conducting an interrogation of a suspect, that account has to match law enforcement's theory of the case in order for the CW to get their deal.

Jailhouse Snitches

Jailhouse snitch is the term used for an inmate of a jail or prison who, in exchange for some benefit, agrees to testify against another inmate. They are different from CWs in that their testimony does not involve information about their own criminal activities. Usually their testimony centers around an alleged confession made by a fellow inmate to them.

There are numerous cases in which reliable information from a jailhouse snitch has proven critical to a case. The infamous 1969 California murders of actress Sharon Tate and three others, followed by the double murder the next night of Leo and Rosemary LaBianca, is such a case. The murders had been orchestrated by cult leader Charles Manson and committed by several of his followers in hopes of creating a race war that Manson referred to as Helter Skelter. A major break came after one of Manson's followers who had participated in the murder was arrested on another crime. She confessed to her participation in the murder to a cellmate, who then called the police. [13]

As valuable as the jailhouse snitch proved in the Manson case, federal prosecutors are taught that they are considered to be the most dangerous type of cooperating witness when it comes to providing false or misleading information. [14] They are highly incentivized because for many, snitching is their last hope of getting a charge dismissed or reducing a long prison sentence.

Jailhouse snitches can be found in all different types of cases, but they seem to proliferate in high-profile cases. During O. J. Simpson's murder trial, his attorneys requested that he be housed in a cell by himself, knowing that any inmate that comes in contact with him might claim that he confessed or made other incriminating statements to them. [15]

There are many reasons why a jailhouse snitch would want to cooperate with law enforcement. Some come forward in hopes of getting a deal on their pending case, or having their current sentences reduced. Others do so for whatever extra benefits that the jail or prison might have to offer, such as extra phone calls, special foods, and additional family visits. Any request by the jailhouse snitch for such assistance and any deal made by the prosecutor is supposed to be made public, so that the jury can use that information to help judge the veracity of the jailhouse snitch's testimony. This naturally weakens the strength of their testimony, and jailhouse snitches know that. Many jailhouse snitches will avoid asking for help up front, saying that they are coming forward because they are troubled by the nature of the crime, have a relative who was the victim of a similar crime, or other "good citizen" justification. It is only after they testify that they then began to bombard the prosecutor with their requests for assistance, assistance that is then often provided.

Jailhouse snitches are sometimes actively recruited by law enforcement. A suspect's cellmate may be pulled out and interviewed by investigators, asking what the suspect is saying about the crime they are alleged to have committed. Real or inferred offers of assistance may be offered during these discussions if the cellmate agrees to "keep their ears open." In other cases, the investigator may recruit the services of a prior informant or jailhouse snitch. The investigator might be able to make arrangements, formally or informally, with the jail or prison administration to house the informant with the suspect, and then direct the informant to see what information they can obtain.

Crooked jailhouse snitches can be extremely creative in how they obtain the details that they need to convince investigators and prosecutors that the suspect confessed to them. A simple trick is just to talk to the suspect, asking them what the cops allege they did. The jailhouse snitch may present themselves as the local "jailhouse lawyer," someone who is knowledgeable of the law and wants to offer the suspect their advice. A naïve suspect may share details of what is alleged by law enforcement, which is then turned from "They claim I did . . . " To "I did . . . "

Another simple trick is for the jailhouse informant to get their hands on any court documents or other papers that the suspect might have in their cell to allow them to assist their attorney in their defense. These papers often contain numerous details that can be crafted into a false, but believable, confession.

Some jailhouse snitches have become masters of the craft. In the 1990s, prosecutors and investigators in the Pennsylvania/Jersey area became enamored with career criminal John Hall. [16]

Hall was a career criminal in his own way. He was constantly being incarcerated for forging prescriptions, car thefts, and illegal drug use, crimes that would sometimes lead to high-speed car chases and more serious things. But almost as soon as he was in jail, he was out. Hall had a system. He got confessions from his fellow inmates, confessions that he would trade to investigators and prosecutors for favors or reduced sentences. And not just any old confessions. Hall specialized in cases in which the prosecutors knew they were in trouble. Hall's information was just what they needed.

Hall became known as "The Monsignor" because of all of the confessions that he had allegedly heard. In 1995 alone, "he snitched out defendants in five murder cases and sent one defendant to death row." Hall became so busy that he had to start farming out his information to other inmates, allowing them to negotiate the same benefits he was getting for himself.[17]

Hall's system was simple. He ingratiated himself with inmates by helping them write letters and legal briefs, acting as what is commonly referred to as a jailhouse lawyer. From those conversations he learned the basic details about their cases.

Hall then contacted his people on the outside. They would then go to the library and research the newspaper archives. On occasion, he would have them visit the neighborhoods where the crimes occurred, picking up details to help make the confessions believable. On at least one occasion, he had his cohort visit the home where the crime scene occurred, where she was able to talk her way in to see how the inside was laid out. He even had them help plant evidence for investigators to find.[18]

Hall would then reach out to the prosecutors or the investigators to let him know what he had. Through his conversations and meetings with them, Hall was able to pick up even more details that he could incorporate into his narrative. Hall knew enough not to try to trade his information for favors outright. His story was always that he was outraged about the crime or some similar motive, and that he just wanted to do the right thing. It was only after he testified that he and his attorney approached the prosecutor or investigator for help, which they always received.[19]

Not every prosecutor or investigator was taken in by Hall's charm. Many recognized him for the con artist that he was, but this did not deter others from using him and vouching for his reliability.[20] They were guilty of breaking the cardinal rule of working informants: they had personally become too close to their informant.

Hall's "research assistants" eventually turned on him, turning over to the authorities letters that he had written outlining his request and plans. In spite of being exposed, several of Hall's victims remain incarcerated, some on death row.

Hall is not an anomaly. In 1989, a grand jury was convened in Los Angeles County, California, to investigate the involvement of jailhouse informants in criminal investigations.[21] The grand jury discovered that in many cases, phony secondhand confessions that had been allegedly made to jailhouse snitches were created in the same way that false confessions are created in the interrogation room. In order to receive their benefit, the jailhouse snitch knows they must provide a "confession" that fits the facts of the case as they are believed to be true by the investigator or prosecutor. In many cases, the grand jury found that investigators and prosecutors shared investigative documents and crime scene photographs with the jailhouse snitch. In others, the same forms of contamination that occur during suspect interrogations occur during jailhouse snitch interviews.[22] The best jailhouse snitches are con artists, using their skills of manipulation and cold-reading tactics to gain the trust of investigators and prosecutors and draw information from them, just as they did the victims of their crimes. "Federal agents and detectives alike are constantly being outwitted by streetwise jailhouse informants."[23]

Anonymous Tipsters

The problem of false information from anonymous tipsters is one not often considered by law enforcement. Many law enforcement agencies have tip lines, set up to allow people with information about a crime to provide that information anonymously. Most, if not all, of these tip lines offer cash rewards if the tip leads to an arrest. The tipster is given a number or other form of identification that allows them to receive payment and still remain anonymous if their tip leads to an arrest.

Some of the rewards are quite substantial. The Metropolitan Police Department (MPD) of Washington, DC, offers a reward of up to $25,000 for information on homicide cases. MPD makes the payment of any reward money conditional upon conviction.[24] Where the tipster is still able to remain anonymous, many do not, knowing that testifying in trial increases their chance of obtaining the maximum amount of the reward. Like with informants, the temptation is to modify their testimony to fit the investigator's and prosecutor's theory of the case, thus increasing the chance of conviction. Many times, a witness will testify on the stand that they were not testifying in order to obtain the reward money, or that they did not know that they were even aware of the reward, only to have some or all of the money paid to them afterward.

I have worked cases in which an informant's, jailhouse snitch's, or CW's information was corroborated by the information provided by an anonymous tipster, only to later discover that the tipster was the informant themselves. The informant called in the information either to boost their own credibility, double-dip on the reward money, or both. I have also had cases in which I have spoken with an anonymous tipster who has attempted to "pump" me for information to help boost the credibility of their information.

THE NEED FOR CORROBORATION

Because the same, if not enhanced, conditions that can lead to false confessions from an innocent suspect can create false information or testimony from informants, CWs, and jailhouse snitches, the need for the proper corroboration of their information is just as great, if not greater. Tunnel vision and verification bias plays a huge role in the lack of such corroboration by investigators and prosecutors. These people are highly motivated to provide information confirmation of what the investigators and prosecutors believe to be true. And unlike in the case of suspects, investigators and prosecutors tend to develop long-term relationships with their informants, CWs, and jailhouse snitches. There is a well-known phenomenon of investigators and prosecutors "falling in love with . . . [their] . . . rat."[25] Perhaps this contributes to the reason, as the Los Angeles grand jury discovered, that so few informants, CWs, and jailhouse snitches are never charged with perjury, even when the proof of their lies becomes indisputable.

Though we have touched on it a bit here, the next chapter will talk about the process that some believe has generated more false confessions than has ever occurred in any interrogation room—the plea deal.

10

PLEA BARGAINING

Those who are wrongfully arrested and charged with a crime usually have two shots at the false confession apple. The first is when the police interrogate them. The second is when they are offered the chance to take a plea deal and plead guilty.

Before the Civil War, plea deals were an extremely rare occurrence (as they were intended to be).[1] Our original justice system was designed to have all sorts of checks and balances so that no one person or party had too much power. The police could investigate and arrest, but the decision to formally charge someone with a crime rested with the prosecutor. In felony cases (usually cases in which, if convicted, the suspect faced more than a year in prison), a grand jury consisting of local citizens was tasked with hearing the evidence and deciding whether or not a crime was committed and if there was enough evidence to take the suspect to trial. The suspect had their own attorney, who was on their side, presenting alternative explanations to the evidence that the prosecutor and police believed pointed toward the suspect's guilt. The judge was the impartial referee, making sure that both the prosecutor and defense attorney played within the rules. And finally, both sides had an equal opportunity to present their side of the story to an impartial jury of twelve citizens, who were to be the final arbitrators of the case.

It is because of all of these hoops and hurdles that many people find it hard to believe that wrongful convictions can occur. This mindset was especially true in the days prior to DNA-related exonerations. When I was working homicides as an investigator, several of us were toying with the idea of coming up with a board game that reflected this attitude. As each player/investigator moved around the board, they had to maneuver around or cope with multiple obstacles, including things such as no cars available to conduct a neighborhood canvas, uncooperative witnesses, laboratory screwups, and judges throwing out confessions. These hurdles, combined with the ones we felt were built into the criminal justice system (which are actually intended to act as checks and balances) seemed to make it almost impossible for a guilty person to be convicted, much less an innocent one. Giving in to our cynicism, we created an "Act of God" card, and drawing that card was the only way the player could get their case before a jury and obtain a guilty verdict.

The reality is that these days, for 95 percent of those accused and charged with a crime, these safeguards don't come into play. They opt instead to cut out the middleman and go straight to the end game. They plead guilty.[2]

But why? A guilty plea is nothing more than a confession, and it is being achieved at a much higher success rate than the investigators can claim occurs in the interrogation room. In addition, guilty plea/confessions occur while the suspect has an attorney by their side, something that every investigator knows would doom the outcome of a police station interrogation from the start. So what is going on here? Why are guilty pleas so common?

Let's go back and look once again at the primary reasons that suspects confess to an investigator in the interrogation room. First, the investigator sets up the suspect to believe that they are facing an undesirable inevitable consequence, and in order to escape or lessen that consequence, they must confess to what the investigator believes to be the truth. Second, the suspect is just worn down and wants the interrogation to end. Is this same dynamic at play during plea-bargaining sessions?

The answer is absolutely, but with two very important exceptions. First, whereas the interrogator is not supposed to make even implied threats of an inevitable consequence, the prosecutor can make real threats with almost total impunity. Second, the prosecutor can make—and keep—real promises of future benefit to the suspect, some of which include:

- The prosecutor will dismiss some of the charges and/or reduce the charges to less serious ones than they believe are supported by the evidence at hand.[3]
- If the suspect does not confess and instead goes to trial and is found guilty, their sentence will be greater (often much greater) than if they plea/confess.[4]
- If they are currently being held without bail, or are in jail because they cannot afford to post the bail they have, they will be released immediately.[5]
- Certain assets will not be seized.
- Family members and/or associates will not be charged with a crime, or if they are charged the charges will be reduced or dropped.

Item one on the list above is significant because the potential for a suspect to be facing an enormous amount of prison time can be the result of the prosecutor stacking on as many charges as possible on top of the original charge, with each new charge carrying its own jail time. As an example, if the suspect was arrested after committing a robbery inside of someone's home in Washington, DC, in which a gun was used, they could, depending on all of the events that took place, potentially be charged with Burglary in the First Degree while Armed, Robbery while Armed, Receiving Stolen Property, Carrying a Pistol without a License, Possession of a Firearm during a Crime of Violence, Unregistered Firearm, and Unregistered Ammunition. If the victim was over sixty, that can increase the penalty, as can any prior gun offense.

Furthermore, the crime that the suspect is alleged to have committed might fall under mandatory minimum sentencing policies. These policies can impose sentences for nonviolent and seemingly minor crimes that some call "so excessively severe, they take your breath away." The increased jail time and other penalties that the suspect faces if they choose to go to trial are sometimes referred to behind closed doors as the "trial tax," something as much a "part of the courthouse as its limestone columns."[6] And of course, in jurisdictions where the death penalty is on the table, that is the ultimate bargaining chip.

Often, with minor crimes, the suspect pleads because they just want to get on with their life. Attorney fees may be more than they can afford, and if they are being held in jail because they cannot make bail, they may be at risk of losing their job or disrupting their family lives. They may also tell themselves at the time that having the conviction on their record is something they can live with anyway.

Like the investigator in the interrogation room, the prosecutor often makes use of the high-pressure sales tactic of adding a deadline to the plea offer. Or the offer may not have a definite cut-off date but the benefits that the prosecutor is willing to offer decrease significantly as time goes on. This inhibits the ability of a defense attorney to do their own investigation, if they even have enough information on hand to conduct one. Many jurisdictions restrict the information that a prosecutor is required to hand over to the defense attorney, so the defense attorney often has to take the prosecutor's word as to the strengths of the case against their client. Even though the prosecutor is required via the Brady laws to turn over information to the defense attorney that is helpful to their client, that information might not have yet been uncovered or fully explored, and won't be if the suspect agrees to plead guilty.

As discussed in the last chapter, plea deals are the hammer by which law enforcement creates cooperating witnesses and informants. With crimes that involve multiple suspects, conspiracies, or criminal enterprises, the suspect might have any potential benefit from the plea withheld contingent upon their cooperation. It is up to the prosecutors, often in conjunction with the investigators, to determine whether or not a suspect's level of cooperation is sufficient and whether their information is reliable enough to receive any break. This places the suspect under a huge amount of pressure to deliver to the prosecutors and investigators information that matches what the prosecutors and investigators believe to be "the truth." In some cases, the plea deal is contingent upon the suspect testifying in court. If the suspect reneges and does not testify in the way that the prosecutor wishes, the deal is off. Insight as to the type of coercion and contamination that prosecutors can interject during such negotiations can be found in the investigation into the murder of twenty-two-year-old Stephanie Swipe.

STEPHANIE SWIPE MURDER

It was at approximately 10:38 pm on the night of July 23, 2001, when the Harrisonburg, Virginia, Police Department received a 911 call for a possible suicide at the apartment of Stephanie Swipe. When they arrived,

Swipe's mother, Pam Woods, met them, and said she had come by to check on her because Stephanie had not been answering her phone. Woods had used her own key to enter the apartment, where she found Swipe collapsed behind the front door and bleeding. Woods quickly went through the apartment to look for her twenty-one-month-old grandson, who she found safe and sound, locked in the bathroom.

Investigators quickly determined that Swipe's death was not a suicide. She had been stabbed multiple times in what appeared to have been a violent struggle with her attacker. Blood samples were collected from the apartment. While most of them were linked to Swipe through DNA testing, some were determined to have come from an unknown male subject. Since investigators knew that knife attacks frequently resulted in the suspect cutting themselves, they felt they had good reason to believe that the male blood came from the killer.

During their investigation into the victim's background, the investigators discovered that the father of Swipe's child was a man named Ivan Teleguz. Teleguz was separated from Swipe and was paying her child support and, according to Swipe's family, the relationship between the two was not good.

The investigators traveled 233 miles to Teleguz's hometown of Ephrata, Pennsylvania, where he was interviewed and his alibi obtained. When the investigators learned from the laboratory about the unidentified male blood found on the murder scene, they returned with a search warrant to obtain a sample of Teleguz's blood. The laboratory determined that the DNA from Teleguz's blood did not match the unknown male DNA from the blood on the scene, so Teleguz was put on the back burner as a suspect.

The investigation went on to examine other aspects of Swipe's life, which led to other suspects, all of whom were eliminated through DNA testing. Things were at a standstill until, through a convoluted route, investigators identified Michael Hetrick as a possible suspect.

As they looked more and more into Hetrick as a suspect, the better he became. The investigators learned that he had received a cut to his hand about the time of the murder, a cut that he had a hard time explaining. The investigators and the prosecutor had developed a theory that Hetrick had killed Swipe at the request of Teleguz, and they set out to prove it.

The investigators got a search warrant authorizing them to obtain a sample of Hetrick's blood for comparison to the unidentified male blood found on the crime scene. They then went to Hetrick's home to interview him, an interview that rapidly turned into an interrogation. The interrogation was captured by the investigators on audiotape.

The investigators told Hetrick they were there to interview him about the murder of Stephanie Swipe. They informed him about the unidentified blood on the scene, and asked him if he knew anyone named Ivan Teleguz. Hetrick said he didn't. They went on to tell Hetrick about Teleguz and his criminal past.

The investigators gave Hetrick a copy of the affidavit for the blood sample search warrant for him to read. The affidavit spelled out in minute detail the investigator's case, including their theory that Teleguz paid Hetrick to commit the crime for him.

The investigators then told Hetrick that the prosecutor in the case was "young and aggressive" and had "authorized" the investigator to tell Hetrick that

> if you are connected and you are the contributor to the blood we found, and you cooperate with us, she would not seek the death penalty for you. . . . If you're involved, you don't cooperate, she'll go after the death penalty. We're a very conservative community; it would be a good case. . . . You get one opportunity at this, OK?[7]

The investigators refused to listen to Hetrick's repeated requests that he be allowed to talk to a lawyer before he said any more. They continued to tell Hetrick what a "bad guy" they believed Teleguz was.

Frustrated with Hetrick's unwillingness to talk, especially without having consulted with an attorney, the investigators reached out to the prosecutor by telephone. After Hetrick spoke with her on the phone for several minutes, the prosecutor asked the investigators to put her on speakerphone so she could describe her conversation with Hetrick on tape. The prosecutor said that she had identified herself to Hetrick and told him

> what I will tell him, and this applies only, um, before you leave the interview room. This deal will not be offered in the future. And if he determines, uh, if you determine that he is not willing to accept the terms of this offer, that no further communication will be given regarding any future cooperation. If indeed he is able to provide substantial assistance, as well as his role and the role of Mr. Teleguz in regarding the murder of Ms. Swipe, then, and only then, will I agree not to seek

the death penalty against him if he cooperates fully. In the event that he should change substantially his version of the events he gives you today, or if he refuses to testify, then certainly I would be able to seek the death penalty. . . . But, if you decide to cooperate, I will agree not to seek the death penalty so long as you cooperate truthfully, and cooperate fully . . . and this offer will only be good today, and only at this time, and I'm not going to entertain any future offers.[8]

The investigators continued to emphasize that in order to avoid the death penalty that Hetrick would have to say that Teleguz was involved in the murder of Swipe. Toward the end, Hetrick asked:

Hetrick: "So you guys want Ivan."
   Investigator: "We want Ivan."[9]

Hetrick then began to give them Teleguz, following the script provided for him in the search warrant affidavit. The DNA test later confirmed that it was Hetrick's blood in the victim's apartment.

The Snipe case highlights the ability of prosecutors to make absolute threats and promises that investigators are taught are improper (though it should be noted that in this case, the investigators were making the same threats and promises at the direction of and on behalf of the prosecutor). It could be possible that Teleguz was involved somehow in the murder of Swipe. However, instead of following a more ethical investigative route, the investigator and prosecutor chose a shortcut. The tactics used by the investigators and the prosecutor along with the subsequent contamination rendered Hetrick's information unreliable according to standard corroboration practices. It is interesting to note that though Hetrick's final testimony did differ significantly from his original statement, the prosecutor did not withdraw her offer because it still included the basics that she wanted—Teleguz hired Hetrick to murder Swipe.

Plea deals may be offered for many reasons besides to quickly dispose of cases and lessen the workload of the investigators and prosecutors. Some motives are benign or benevolent, such as when the prosecutor tries to spare a victim or a victim's family from the trauma of a long, drawn-out court proceeding and provide them with some finality to the case. Some motives are murkier, as when a plea is offered to cover up problems with the case such as the hint of some misconduct by the investigator or the discovery that the informant or cooperating witness was not as reliable as previously thought. The acceptance of a plea deal by the suspect makes any such problem go away. And since plea negotiations are not subject to public scrutiny, these problems do not see the light of day.

While there are many excellent defense attorneys out there who will fight tirelessly for their clients, they too are usually behind the eight ball when it comes to plea negations because of the lack of information. Other defense attorneys may be under the additional burden of an extremely high caseload and/or no money for investigative work. They have to take the prosecutor's word at face value. Sometimes, especially in minor cases, they only have the chance to talk with their client once or twice before the client has to decide whether to take a plea deal or not.

By law, the defense attorney has to tell their client that a plea deal has been offered. They have to tell the client their options, what they are facing if they go to trial and lose, and how they would benefit from what the prosecutor is offering. In the end, it is up to the client to make the final decision, no matter what the defense attorney thinks about the deal.

RECO COATES CASE STUDY

On November 12, 2007, Irving Williams (named changed to protect the privacy of the witness) had just returned to his apartment after forgetting to bring some bleach down to the basement laundromat where he was washing clothes. Suddenly, Anthony Collins, a small-time drug dealer who frequently sold drugs in the apartment building, rushed in through Williams's open apartment door, followed by four masked suspects, one of whom had a knife and began stabbing Collins. Williams attempted to hide in the bedroom but was dragged out by one of the suspects, who hit him with a frying pan. All four of the suspects then fled the apartment. Collins later died of his injuries.

Almost a year later, using rumors, secondhand "death bed statements," memories "enhanced" with time, and a witness of questionable reliability, eighteen-year-old Reco Coates was identified as a suspect.

After investigators had come by his house looking for him, Coates came into the police station to find out what was going on and was first interrogated by investigators on October 25, 2008. He was not advised of his Miranda rights.

Investigators told Coates that they believed that he was one of the subjects who had participated in Collins's murder. Coates adamantly denied any involvement. Investigators repeatedly told him that he had two choices: either confess and cooperate or be charged with murder and go to jail for as long as thirty years. The investigators suggested that they had physical evidence that would connect Coates to the crime, though no such evidence existed. They suggested the usual themes, such as that the situation got out of control and he acted in self-defense.

The investigators suggested that if Coates was not involved, then he knew who was. In desperation, Coates tried but became frustrated when he could not get details from the investigators, at one point pleading:

> So what was involved in the, in the crime? What . . . I need to know
> what did y'all find so I can know who to say had what, 'cause y'all
> ain't helping me. [10]

Frustrated, the investigators gave up.

Eight months later, the investigators came under pressure from their supervisors to close out the crime. On July 14, 2009, Coates underwent his second interrogation by the investigators. After being advised of his Miranda rights, the investigators raised the pressure several notches. They advised Coates that they had enough probable cause to arrest him and he was going to prison unless he cooperated. The investigators began to suggest names of possible codefendants to Coates, and again, he tried to confirm what they were saying, but complained that they were not giving him enough information so he could help them. The investigators began to feed Coates information about the crime, continuing to threaten him if he did not "get it right." Coates tried to fit the bits and pieces into an acceptable narrative. As he made mistakes, they corrected him. At one point the investigator complained that Coates wasn't giving them the "right story."

Investigator: You gave me a story. It's not the right story.
    Coates: What is the right story?
    Investigator: The one that happened.
    Coates: Just be honest with me and I'll say it. [11]

In the end, Coates confessed to being part of the crime. The confession came slowly, with Coates giving different versions, leaving out some of the details that he had included before. The investigator would tell Coates that he wasn't helping himself "'cause we got to keep reminding you of stuff every time you say something . . . and you keep leaving things out." The end result was a confession, but a confession where the only facts that had not been fed to Coates multiple times by the investigators turned out to be grossly inaccurate.

Coates was arrested, charged with the murder, and held in jail without bond. What little follow-up investigative work was done based on the confession yielded no new information, and none of the persons who Coates named as accomplices were ever arrested. The grand jury handed down an indictment, charging Coates with:

- First Degree Murder while Armed—Felony Murder
- Murder 1 while Armed—Premediated Murder
- Armed Robbery
- Burglary 1 while Armed
- Assault with a Dangerous Weapon
- Possession of a Firearm during a Crime of Violence
- Carrying a Dangerous Weapon

Coates's defense attorneys fought hard to suppress the confession because of the extreme level of coercion the investigators used, but they failed. The case kept getting continued time and time again. In 2011, I was asked by the defense attorneys to review the interrogation and confession.

I applied the methodology discussed in chapter 7. When I charted out the interrogation and confession, it became painfully obvious that Coates could not provide the investigators with any accurate details about the crime unless they told him first, and that they had to continually remind him of those details so he could put them into their final narrative.

In June 2012 I testified about my findings in a hearing before a judge in the Washington, DC, Superior Court. The prosecutor and judge shifted the focus of the hearing from the accepted methodology that I used to test for contamination and reliability to unrelated matters, such as base rates for false confessions and if I was going to testify that the confession was false (which is not allowed, as that is up to the jury to decide). Following the hearing, the judge ruled that my testimony would not be admitted before the jury.

The case was reassigned to another judge. The defense attorneys argued that I should be allowed to testify regarding the contents of the interrogation and confession. They were helped immensely by the investigator's "inability" to remember numerous details of the interrogation, such as who brought up what detail first. The defense attorneys planned on using my testimony and charts to show that the confession was created by the investigator and reluctantly and under great pressure adopted by Coates.

Very soon after that, the prosecutors approached the defense attorneys with a plea offer. They offered to drop all of the charges, which could have led to Coates spending the rest of his life in prison, to one charge of voluntary manslaughter, with a total sentence of eight years. That meant with the time that Coates had already spent in prison, he would only have to serve just over four more years.

The deal was made that Coates couldn't refuse. And the prosecutors got their closure statistic without having to fight what had suddenly become a very problematic and potentially embarrassing case.

THE ROLE OF THE JUDGE IN PLEA BARGAINING

In the large majority of jurisdictions, judges have no official role in the plea negotiation process. They have the option not to follow the prosecutor's recommendations, but that occurs rarely. In many locales, the defense attorneys know which judges have a tendency to inflict a higher "trial tax" if a suspect refuses to take what they would consider a "reasonable" plea. The judge, like everyone else, has a vested interest in getting cases off their dockets. Like investigators and prosecutors, judges are often evaluated by how many cases they can move through their courtroom.

There are several reasons why the courts have been so overwhelmed with cases in the past several decades. There has been a marked increase in crime during that time, which probably goes hand in hand with the increase of things that are crimes or are now considered more serious crimes than before—the result of the war on crime and drugs. "Zero tolerance" policies have removed some of the discretion able to be exercised by law enforcement, possibly causing more arrests. All of this has helped to overwhelm the courts so that if the ability to plea bargain cases didn't exist and every case went to trial, the judicial system would come to even more of a crawl than it is today.

Once the prosecutor and defense attorney have reached an agreement, it is up to the judge to seal the deal by "taking the plea" from the suspect in a court of law. This is usually the only aspect of the plea negotiations visible to the public, except in cases in which it is necessary to keep it temporarily secret in order to protect an ongoing investigation.

When finalizing the plea, the suspect is first placed under oath. The judge then asks the suspect a series of question to ensure, on the official record, that the plea is "voluntary" and "factual." These questions include whether the suspect was threatened or promised anything to make them plead (outside of the terms of the agreement) and whether or not the suspect understands which constitutional rights are being given up by pleading guilty (such as the right to a trial, the right to confront and cross-examine witnesses, and in most places, the right to an appeal). The judge will ask if the suspect has conferred with his defense attorney and is satisfied with their services. The judge will review with the suspect the terms of the plea agreement, such as the agreed-upon sentence and any other conditions, but the judge will remind the suspect that the final sentence is left up to his discretion.

The judge will ask that the prosecutor state the facts of the case to which the suspect is pleading guilty. These "facts" are carefully constructed to fit the "elements" or acts that the suspect must have performed to meet the requirements of the crime to which he is pleading guilty. The list of facts may leave out information that the prosecutor believed to be true in order to "qualify" the suspect to plea to a less serious crime. Using our earlier robbery suspect as an example, the "statement of facts" may not include that a gun was used or that the victim was a senior citizen, so that the suspect can plead to simple robbery without the enhanced penalty for robbing a senior citizen. At the end, the judge will ask the suspect if the facts are true and if the suspect is pleading guilty because they are in fact guilty.

If the suspect wavers on any of the questions, answers "no," or challenges any of the details in the statement of facts, the plea is in danger of "falling through." The defense attorney is usually given a chance to talk with his client and "iron out" any issues. If the suspect challenges some specific detail in the "statement of facts," the judge may rule that that detail might not have any impact on the overall confession, and go on and take the plea.

In some places, a plea deal can be negotiated whereby the suspect does not have to confess to having committed the crime. The suspect can still insist on their innocence; they are only admitting that they believe that the prosecutor has enough evidence in all likelihood to convince a judge or jury to convict them. This is known as an Alford plea from the Supreme Court case of *North Carolina v. Alford.*[12]

PLEA BARGAINS AND FALSE CONFESSIONS

While the benefits of plea bargaining in clearing up case backlogs and infiltrating organized drugs gangs are obvious, so are the dangers. Plea negotiations contain all of the problematic issues that can lead to both false confessions and outright lies from informants and cooperating witnesses. Because unlike the investigator's threats and promises, the prosecutor's are real. Plea negotiations can be like police interrogations on steroids. And unlike confessions obtained during police interrogations, plea deals rarely undergo anything but the most superficial of scrutiny by the courts or the public.

But do the statistics back up the assentation that plea negotiations contribute significantly to the wrongful conviction problem? Of the 1,700 confirmed wrongful conviction cases listed in the National Registry of Exonerations, 15 percent (261) were cases in which the suspect entered a false guilty plea.[13] Like false confession cases, this is probably only the tip of the iceberg, and for many of the same reasons.

First, this number is only the number of confirmed wrongful convictions in which the innocent suspect entered a guilty plea. It does not at all reflect the number of innocent persons who were convicted because a witness or codefendant, through a coercive plea negotiation, was convinced to perjure themselves and lie to get their own deal. The National Registry does give us a hint at the potential extent of that problem. In the 1,700 confirmed wrongful convictions, 55 percent (940) had perjury or false accusation as a contributing factor, though the Registry does not break the figure down any further.[14]

Additionally, many people look upon guilty pleas like confessions. Not understanding the dynamics of how both work, they can't believe that someone would do either if they had not committed a crime. And remember, when a suspect agrees to plead guilty, they usually forfeit any right to appeal, thus limiting their ability to claim their innocence later on.

The exoneration process for a wrongful conviction is long, labor intensive, and expensive. Organizations doing that sort of work, such as the Innocence Project, have to prioritize their limited resources. This means that the innocent person who pled guilty on a minor charge, resulting in them being released from jail and/or getting probation or a small fine, will never have their wrongful conviction undertaken by such organizations.

Last but not least, plea negotiations have often been used to prevent innocent persons from obtaining full exonerations. Such was the case of Aaron Michael Howard.

HOWARD CASE STUDY

In 1988, Bobby Parker was driving his car in the southeast section of Washington, DC, when he stopped at a stoplight. While waiting for the light to turn green, a car pulled up behind him, and several men got out and began shooting at Parker, killing him.

Investigators developed strong cases against three suspects, with numerous witnesses identifying them as the shooters. In contrast, only one of the witnesses identified Aaron Michael Howard as one of the shooters. That witness, a man with confirmed psychiatric problems, whose own mother said she would never believe a word he said, came forward only after he had been charged with drug possession. Wanting to make a deal, he told the investigators that he had witnessed the shooting, gave details that contradicted all of the other witnesses, and named Howard as one of the shooters. To support his story, the witness said that his sister had been with him at the time. The investigators located the sister, who at first denied having been there with her brother at all. The investigators put the two in a room alone together to "work it out." After a time, the sister came out with a different story, now saying that she was at the crime scene when the shooting occurred. At trial, when asked to identify Howard as the man who she saw shooting at Parker, the sister picked out the wrong man in the courtroom. Howard was convicted and sentenced to twenty-one years to life in prison.

In 2002, Howard filed a motion under the (then) relatively new DC Innocence Protection Act, and his case was reopened in 2006. In 2007, I was supervising a project that was performing a comprehensive review of Washington, DC, homicide cases when I was asked by the Appellate Division of the US Attorney's Office to assist in their reinvestigation into Howard's case. Working with an Assistant US Attorney, we met with Howard's attorneys, reviewed the documents, and conducted our own series of interviews. The two witnesses against Howard had died, but I was able to interview their mother, as well as the alibi witnesses for Howard who, along with numerous other defense witnesses, were never called by his attorney to testify. Fortunately, we were able to locate the original investigator's notes, which gave us a much clearer picture than normal of how the investigation progressed and on what information important decisions were made. Being able to locate original documents from a fifteen-year-old case was a welcome rarity.

After several months of review and investigation, both the Assistant US Attorney and I agreed with Howard's attorneys that Howard was innocent of the murder. A memorandum was filed to that effect; however, the US Attorney for the District of Columbia decided against recommending the exoneration of Howard (as was dictated by the evidence of the case) and instead offered him a "compromise." They told Howard's attorneys that he might have a valid claim, but that he would have to wait months to have it heard in court, with no guarantee of success. The other option would be for Howard to agree to plead guilty to voluntary manslaughter, at which point they would drop all of his other convictions, he would be released from prison immediately, and would not have to serve any time on probation or under any other government supervision. Rather than face months more in jail with an uncertain outcome, Howard decided to accept the offer and was released after spending twenty years behind bars. As such, Howard's case cannot be counted as a confirmed wrongful conviction, and he is unable to obtain any compensation for his time spent behind bars.

In short, plea negotiations are often less about true justice and more like business deals, with the majority of the cards on the side of the prosecutor. Like police interrogations, plea negotiations often limit not only the choices that a suspect has but also the information available to them to make those choices. The upside is that during a plea negotiation, unlike a police interrogation, the suspect is supposed to have their defense attorney on their side. But what if the attorney isn't committed to the defense of their client or comes with his or her own set of biases against false confessions?

DANIAL WILLIAMS PLEA NEGOTIATIONS

Following his confession to the murder of Michelle Bosko, Williams appeared before a judge to be formally arraigned. Since he could not afford an attorney, he was appointed Dan Shipley, an experienced attorney who had represented people facing the death penalty in the past. He was to be assisted by an ex-prosecutor named Bob Frank.

Defense attorneys, like everyone else, are influenced by the cognitive biases of tunnel vision and verification bias, as well as by their past experiences (both good and bad). A few years before, Shipley had lost a death penalty case that deeply affected him. Frank's experience as a prosecutor left him with the belief that people don't confess to crimes that they did not commit.

The first time Williams met Shipley was at his initial arraignment. He had not even had a chance to go over the facts of the case before; according to Williams's parents, he came out of the courtroom and told them that Williams "did it." Cocounsel Frank also believed that Williams was guilty, both having a hard time understanding why someone would confess to a crime that they didn't commit.

Like many attorneys who represent clients who are facing the death penalty, Williams's attorneys believed that their primary responsibility was getting that option taken off the table. Though they believed that the only evidence that the prosecutor had was the confession, they did not focus on that aspect of the investigation for quite some time to come, preoccupied as they were with the death penalty facet of the case.

As is typical in confession cases, the investigators figured that Williams was a done deal. For all practical intents and purposes, the investigation stopped. They never even bothered searching Williams's apartment, which, if Williams had committed the crime, should have yielded all sorts of forensic evidence from the clothing Williams had allegedly worn during the attack.

Williams tried to convince his attorneys of the absurdity of his confession. He obtained a copy and identified several key issues and discrepancies. On a play of Williams's first name, his attorneys began to call him "Denial." When time came for a hearing to attempt to suppress the confession, the attorneys never raised any of the issues that Williams had pointed out, nor did they raise the possibility that the confession might be false.

Needless to say, they lost this suppression hearing. Soon after, Williams's attorneys were offered a plea deal that would result in Williams spending his life in prison. The death penalty was off the table, and Williams's attorneys wanted him to jump on the chance. When he refused, they tried to use his parents to persuade him.

Williams and his family believed that his attorneys were doing nothing to investigate his claim of innocence. They did not hire an investigator, and did not attempt to get a formal statement from his key alibi witness, his wife, though they knew she was terminally ill with cancer. Such a statement could have been used as evidence in trial after her death.

Things changed for the investigators and prosecutors when the DNA test results from the semen recovered from Bosko and around her body came back. Williams was not the person who left the semen behind. Williams was ecstatic, believing that this would prove his innocence. But instead of considering that their initial theory of a single perpetrator was right and that Williams had falsely confessed, the investigators and prosecutors took the usual tact of assuming that someone else had to have been part of the murder along with Williams.

The investigators didn't have far to go to find their next victim. They latched on to Joe Dick, another sailor who was living with the Williamses at the time. Dick had cognitive issues that interfered with his thought and speaking processes. He had been interviewed earlier concerning what he knew about Williams, and had actually told the investigators that he had been on duty at the night of the murder. Contrary to best practices that dictate that a suspect's alibi should always be checked before they are subjected to an interrogation, investigators proceeded without confirming his duty schedule. The same detective who interrogated Williams also interrogated Dick.

Dick denied any involvement or knowledge about Bosko's murder, as did Williams. And as during Williams's interrogation, Dick took a polygraph and passed. The investigators chose to ignore this and plowed ahead. In the end, Dick confessed, saying that he had participated in the murder along with Williams. And as with Williams, many of Dick's details did not match the crime scene facts.

The investigators and prosecutor thought that they were done, until the lab reported once again that the DNA from the crime scene matched neither of their suspects. The investigators and prosecutor changed their theory once again, believing that a third person must also be involved. They went back at Dick, who had no support from his attorney or family as they all believed he was guilty. Dick began giving up more names, more interrogations took place, more confessions that didn't make sense were given, and none of the newly identified suspects matched the DNA found on the scene.

Dick and another codefendant decided that in order to escape the death penalty that they would not only plead guilty but also agree to testify against Williams. At this point, Williams had to deal with his confession, two cooperating witnesses who would testify against him, and defense attorneys who did not believe him and wanted him to plea. To save his life, Williams decided to accept the plea deal.

SUMMARY

Though police interrogations and plea deals are purported to be tools by which the truth is learned and justice is furthered, they have the ability to do quite the opposite. But is there a better and safer way? While interrogations and plea negotiations are similar in very many ways, many of the unique problems associated with plea negotiations require that they be addressed separately. But when it comes to the ability of investigators and prosecutors to obtain admissible, accurate, and reliable information from suspects, witnesses, informants, and cooperating witnesses, is interrogation the only way? Next we will see what happens when an entire law enforcement system rejects every interrogation tactic that we hold near and dear to our hearts here in the United States.

11

IS THERE A BETTER WAY?

This is a study of contrasts, a tale of two countries. What happened when two similar places shared a common problem, and how did each decide to deal with it?

Beginning in the 1970s, the public in both the United States and the United Kingdom were becoming more and more aware of high-profile wrongful convictions that were the result of false confessions. The television crime drama series *Kojak* premiered in 1973 with the pilot called "The Marcus-Nelson Murders."[1] This was a dramatization of the 1963 murders of Janice Wylie and Emily Hoffert, who had been found in their New York apartment, sexually assaulted and murdered. The case was closed when the investigators obtained a false confession from George Whitmore, not only to this but also another unrelated crime. He was exonerated in 1972.[2]

The United Kingdom had false confessions of their own. The "Birmingham Six," a case involving six men wrongfully convicted after they falsely confessed to the police that they were responsible for the 1974 bombing of a Birmingham pub, is one example. The "Guildford Four," who were convicted of various charges including the bombing of two pubs and the murder of a British soldier in 1974 following their false confessions, is another.

The law enforcement agencies in both countries shared many similarities and some major differences. The American law enforcement system was originally modeled on the British concept, the major difference being that the British law enforcement agencies are under central control, while in the United States each agency has a great deal of autonomy and does not answer to any one person or agency.

Law enforcement agencies in both countries were using the same interrogation tactics, tactics that were conducted in private interrogation rooms out of the public view. And they both had their own form of preinterrogation warnings. American agencies used Miranda warnings, advising the suspect both that they had the right not to speak to the police and if they decided to exercise that right that the refusal itself *could not* be used against them in court as evidence of their guilt. In the United Kingdom, the warning is similar, with the caveat that, if later, they decide to say something in court (such as provide an alibi) that they could have provided to the investigator at the time of their interrogation but chose not to, that earlier refusal *could* be used against them.

So how did these two similar countries, which spoke the same language, had similar approaches to law enforcement, and used the same interrogation tactics, respond to the apparent problem of false confessions leading to wrongful convictions? In the United States, the response was a split between the academic community and law enforcement, and though consensus is gradually building, largely it remains split to this day.

THE US RESPONSES

The responses to the problem of wrongful convictions stemming from false confession in the United States was split was between two camps: the psychologists and social science researchers who were trying to study police interrogation tactics and the phenomenon of false confessions, and law enforcement agencies themselves along with the interrogation schools who were training them. The researchers were severely hampered by their lack of access to material with which to analyze this topic. Across the board, law enforcement agencies were not recording interrogations in their entirety, and with a few exceptions, law enforcement agencies were closing the door to any researcher who wanted a peek inside. In spite of this, researchers, using the available interrogation manuals, laboratory experiments, court transcripts, final confession statements, and other means were able to begin to show that the interrogation tactics that were being used by investigators were not all that benign.

Law enforcement personnel, on the other hand, didn't want anything to do with what the research was saying. They were just happy with the way things were. Already smarting from the belief that the relatively recent *Miranda* decision had already impacted their ability to "do their job" enough, they resisted anything else that they thought might make their job more difficult.

The interrogation schools were none too happy about the rise in interest from researchers either. Law enforcement training is big business. For decades they had taught that the use of their tactics, tactics developed only through experience and based on no actual science, actually prevented false confessions and wrongful convictions, and here were these upstarts using "research" to try to say otherwise.

Then came a spate of court orders and local legislation responding to the increase of questionable and/or confirmed false confessions obtained by law enforcement investigators. Because of this, more and more agencies began video or audiotaping interrogations in their entirety. These tapes became material that researchers could formally request and obtain, allowing unprecedented access into the interrogation room and the chance to actually study methods and outcomes.

Though individual law enforcement agencies fought the electronic recording requirement tooth and nail (and those that are not currently in compliance still do), this unprecedented access to what really went on in the interrogation room was a boon to both the researchers and reformers. Now they could study the interactions between the investigator and the suspect and see what tactics were used and how they impacted the interrogation. The recordings were also showing the level of tunnel vision and verification bias present in the interrogations and the amount of contamination being committed by the investigators. Additional reviews revealed that investigators were routinely and blindly accepting confessions as fact, performing little to no follow-up or corroboration into the suspect's statements. The ever-increasing number of DNA-based exonerations of wrongful convictions involving false confessions bolstered all of these findings.

The response to this new information by law enforcement and the interrogation schools was mixed. Prosecutors fought, and have been many times successful, in keeping the researchers' findings about the relationship between false confessions, interrogation tactics, and confession evidence contamination out of the courtroom and away from the jury. The curricula used by the interrogation schools changed little, and though the Reid Institute was more willing than others to accept that false confessions were possible, they still contended that they were the result of investigators who were not using their technique properly rather than acknowledging that the techniques themselves might be flawed.

On the flip side, the fourth and fifth editions of the Reid textbook, *Criminal Interrogation and Confession*,[3] published in 2001 and 2013, respectively, practically doubled in size from its earlier editions. In this edition, as well as on their website (www.reid.com), the Reid Institute included a lot of new material on the issue of false confessions, including chapters on the types of false confessions and the need to corroborate the information obtained during an interrogation. They have also dropped their earlier resistance to videotaping interrogations in their entirety. Unfortunately, as discussed in earlier chapters, little to none of this new information makes it into the classroom instruction.

When faced with confirmed wrongful convictions, some jurisdictions attempt to honestly face the problem and find real solutions. Unfortunately, sometimes these solutions are what can be referred to as "single fixes," where one fix is believed to solve the problem but in reality fails to address the root causes. A typical example can be found in the findings of an ad hoc committee created by District of Columbia Superior Court judge Lee Satterfield in response to several confirmed wrongful conviction cases that had recently been uncovered in Washington, DC. At that time, the Metropolitan Police Department had been, as a result of legislative action by the DC City Council, videotaping interrogations for several years.

When the commission released its findings in 2011, they reported that since the Metropolitan Police Department was already videotaping interrogations that best practices were being followed and made "further reform unnecessary at this time."[4] Though the issue of tunnel vision, problematic interrogation techniques, and lack of follow-up investigations of confession evidence were brought up to the committee at that time, those issues were ignored.[5] It seemed as if videotaping was considered a one-stop solution to all issues stemming from problematic interrogation techniques.

This is not to say that videotaping isn't a very valuable practice. Before and after the committee findings were published, several confessions obtained by Metropolitan Police Department investigators were ruled inadmissible by trial judges or disregarded by juries, primarily because of the tactics captured on videotape. In other cases, such as the Reco Coates case (discussed in chapter 10), the prosecutors offered low plea offers or dismissed cases outright because of problematic interrogations that were only able to be reviewed because of videotaping. On November 12, 2015, the DC Court of Appeals threw out the conviction of then eighteen-year-old Jalonte Little, who was convicted largely because of his confession to a carjacking that occurred in 2008. During the interrogation, investigators who were trained in the Reid Technique made numerous threats, including the insinuation that he would be raped in jail, as well as promises of leniency. While videotaping as a best practice did result in his improperly obtained confession being overturned on appeal, it did nothing to prevent the tactics from being used in the first place, getting past the investigator's supervision, and then being blessed by a prosecutor and the original trial judge.[6]

For us in the United States, the last several decades has brought little reform in the area of improving police interview and interrogation tactics, and what reform had been brought has been piecemeal.

UNITED KINGDOM'S RESPONSE

Law enforcement's response to the wrongful conviction problem in the United Kingdom was quite different from that of the Americans. Forensic psychologist Barrie L. Irving observed sixty police interviews of suspects and in 1980 reported his findings to the Royal Commission on Criminal Procedure, which had been set up in the 1970s following the wrongful conviction of two juveniles, ages fourteen and fifteen, and an eighteen-year-old adult with learning disabilities. All three had been interrogated by the police and confessed to having set a house on fire, resulting in the death of one of the occupants.[7]

Irving discovered that the primary focus of the observed interrogations was not to obtain information, but to get a confession. To achieve this goal, Irving said that during their interrogations, the investigators made use of several coercive tactics, including minimizing the seriousness of the offense, using false evidence ploys, stating inevitable consequences, and emphasizing that it was in the suspect's best interest to confess. Unlike in the United States, the Royal Commission found those tactics to be unacceptable, and recommended that investigators receive better train-ing in the psychology of interviewing. In 1986, the commission mandated that all police interviews with suspects be audio recorded in their entirety and that special procedures be put into place to protect juvenile suspects and others who might be more susceptible to police pressure. [8]

While this new requirement was initially met with resistance, police in the United Kingdom, like the majority of their counterparts in the United States who have been forced to videotape interrogations, soon discovered that this was a good thing. This new order also gave researchers a wealth of raw material with which to study how police interrogations work.

Researchers reviewed several hundred audio recordings of suspect interrogations, and their findings were not surprising. Though the investi-gators had stopped using many of the Reid-style approaches that had been observed in the earlier study, they still continued to use confrontational tactics. Prior to beginning the interrogation, the overwhelming majority of the investigators reported that they were already convinced of the suspect's guilt. The investigators began the interrogation by confronting the suspect with their belief in the suspect's guilt, often blitzing them with the evidence against them to hopefully get them to confess (by this time, investigators were no longer permitted to lie to the suspect about the evidence in the case the way they were prior to these reforms). The suspect was given little chance to provide their side of the story, including any alibis that could later be checked out. In some cases, the researchers noted that if the suspect was reluctant to confess, the investigators be-came more verbally abusive in their repeated accusations. [9]

In short, investigators were more focused on getting confessions than information. If the case was strong and the investigators had good evi-dence, the suspect was more likely to confess. But what was the most surprising was that in the overwhelming majority of the interrogations, if the person was going to talk they talked, and if they were going to con-fess, they confessed pretty quickly. Only about 3 percent confessed later on in the interrogation because of the actions of the investigator. [10] So the current confrontational interrogation approach was not only not working, it encouraged tunnel vision and verification bias in the investigators, and the chance to obtain an awful lot of helpful information was being lost in the process.

In addition to the above issues, both the researchers and the police were also concerned about how the interrogation process impacted the public's perception of law enforcement. They did not buy into the Reid philosophy that it was necessary to treat suspects on a "lower moral plane" in order to obtain the truth.[11] The United Kingdom realized that today's suspects might be tomorrow's witnesses, or even tomorrow's jurors. Harsh and verbally abusive interrogation tactics that focused solely on obtaining confessions was not the fair and impartial image that the United Kingdom wanted to project. And the use of such tactics on vulnerable suspects, such as juveniles and those with cognitive or mental disorders, not only contributed to false confessions but also to the negative perception of law enforcement by the public.

Fortunately, at the same time, extensive research had been underway examining how to properly interview victims of child sexual abuse as well as juvenile witnesses to crime. Many of the recommendations that came out of these studies were based on decades of research into how people remember events and the best ways to get them to relate those memories to others. These were combined with many of the approaches that psychologists and psychotherapists used when interviewing uncooperative or hostile patients. For these patients, just like suspects of a crime, the honest disclosure of information could impact them in at least what they believed to be an adverse manner, such as an involuntary commitment to a hospital.[12] Unlike investigators, the psychologist doesn't have the "power of the badge" to help persuade the patient.

The result of this research and collaboration was a major review in the 1990s of not only interrogation practices but also how investigations were conducted in general. Interrogation as Britons knew it was out. New principals of interviewing were established. The new goal of an interview was not to obtain a confession but accurate information, as much of it as possible. Interviews were structured as to not be guilt presumptive, but were to be approached by the investigator with an open mind using the "investigative mindset" (discussed in chapter 7). Corroboration of what the suspect says was emphasized. Fairness for all was emphasized, and juveniles and others who were considered to be vulnerable subjects were to be evaluated and treated with special consideration. Even the word *interrogation* was replaced with a less combative one: P.E.A.C.E. was born.

Actually, P.E.A.C.E. is not the name of the process but only the best known of several acronyms that were created to help investigators break down the stages of the process. The process itself is called investigative interviewing and, with some minor differences, it is used when interviewing witnesses, victims, and suspects alike. The process is no more combative or confrontational whether the subject is a victim or perpetrator. After its success in the United Kingdom, law enforcement agencies in other countries, such as Australia, New Zealand, Norway, Sweden, Denmark, and others, adopted the investigative interviewing approach. Because the development of the investigative interviewing process was, and still is, driven by research, it has undergone various changes over time, as well as adaptations to local laws and individual agency needs. The basic principles remain the same. To explain them, I will be relying heavily on Eric Shepherd and Andy Griffith's 2013 book *Investigative Interviewing: The Conversation Management Approach* [13] considered by many to be the bible of investigative interviewing and investigation. I am going to loosely use the individual stages of P.E.A.C.E., focusing primarily on the interview of suspects, and include how some other law enforcement agencies have modified them for their use. I will also briefly offer a comparative analysis of the different stages to law enforcement practices in the United States.

P IS FOR PLANNING AND PREPARATION

Knowing your evidence, your suspect, and what information you hope to obtain is basic to the success of any interview. The investigator's knowledge of the crime and the evidence allows them to apply their investigative mindset to compare what the suspect is saying to what information has been developed during the investigation. This knowledge and case expertise will be used later on when exploring with the suspect any contradictions that come up in their story.

Investigators in the Nordic countries specifically identify what they believe is the incriminating evidence against the suspect and then come up with as many alternative explanations for that evidence as possible. For example, if a suspect's cell phone was found at the scene of a burglary, one explanation could be that the suspect dropped the phone while committing the burglary itself. Another explanation might be that it was lost earlier while shopping, they had loaned it to a friend, or the cell phone had been stolen from the suspect sometime before. All of these possible alternatives would be explored later with the suspect, as we will see. [14]

Knowing everything about the suspect will help the investigator not only develop their interview approach but also identify any special issues that need to be addressed both before and during the interview. The investigator will delve into the suspect's background, including past contacts with the law, education, his employment situation, medical background, and relationships. If the suspect was interviewed in connection with another crime, can the investigator in that case offer any insight? What is the suspect's primary language? Will an interpreter be required? Is the primary investigator the best person to conduct the interview, or would another member of the team be more suitable? If the suspect is a juvenile, or has cognitive or mental health issues, what precautions must be taken to ensure that their rights are protected and that they understand the process? In the United Kingdom, such "vulnerable individuals" are appointed an "appropriate adult," who is separate from their attorney and whose job it is to act as a neutral observer to ensure that the suspect comprehends what is happening. [15]

Knowing what information that the investigator needs to or hopes to obtain is not the same as going into the interview hoping to obtain a confession. More accurately, it means that the investigator has identified what they don't know, or information that they need to confirm or discredit. They will determine the specific "elements" or acts that the law requires to have taken place to make the alleged act a crime. By developing this "wish list" of information, the investigator is less likely to miss an opportunity to explore that area before the interview is over.

Part of the preparation stage is making contingency plans for any possibility. If during the interview the suspect provides an alibi or other information that can be corroborated, the investigator must be sure that other investigators can check it out immediately.

I will be the first to say that many times the ability to plan and prepare in the manner suggested above is a luxury. Events can unfold quickly, and the suspect is in front of you before you know it. Even so, extremely rare are the occasions in which the investigator has to walk into the interrogation room without the time to at least do the basic background work. In one of my cases, I was called to the scene of a murder where the victim had been beaten to death by a hammer. The first police officer on the scene had received an assignment for an "unknown disturbance."

When they arrived on the scene, the suspect was out front, covered with blood. The first thing he said was "He's inside, I killed him." The officer immediately placed him under arrest and advised him of his Miranda warnings.

Before going to the patrol car to talk to the suspect, I did a quick survey of the scene. The victim, a younger man, was on the floor of the apartment surrounded by a huge amount of blood spatter. A long-handed hammer was lying next to his battered head. When I got in the patrol car, the suspect began telling me how he had acted in self-defense. I knew nothing about him, nothing about the victim, and had no time to digest what the crime scene was saying. I calmed down the suspect, made sure that he understood and waived his Mirada warnings, and obtained his narrative statement as to what happened. Because I knew so little, I was behind the eight ball when it came to evaluating his statement, so I decided not to question him at that point. The suspect had told me that he had to hit the victim with a hammer because the victim had poked him in the face with a knife.

This was my opportunity. I wanted to have any injury on the suspect evaluated and documented, and I also needed time to prepare for a real interview. Since the departmental policy was that any injury to any prisoner required that the prisoner undergo a medical evaluation and treatment, I had the patrol car transport him to the hospital. That gave me a good eight hours to process the crime scene and do the background that I needed. Once the suspect was released from the emergency room, I was ready for him.

This critical step is one that is often skipped by investigators not trained in the P.E.A.C.E. technique. They are not looking for information, but a confession, so they feel that all of this preparation is unnecessary.

Ben Franklin said, "By failing to prepare, you are preparing to fail." Det. Adam Mason of the Troy, New York, Police Department is but one example of how disastrous the attitude that you don't need to prepare can be. He was one of the investigators who, during the investigation into a mistakenly diagnosed "shaken baby" case, got a false confession from Adrian Thomas. During an interview for the film *Scenes of a Crime* that documented Thomas's interrogation, Mason said:

> They do offer seminars here and there on interviewing suspects, and I did attend a one-day seminar a few years back and, ah, I—you pick up

some pointers here and there. But to be honest with you, when I go into an interview, I don't even refer to those pointers. I just kind of go with the flow of the interview. And I don't even plan ahead of time what my approach is going to be. I just do it. [16]

E IS FOR ENGAGE AND EXPLAIN

Two separate actions, engaging and explaining, are interwoven during this stage of the interview. The initial engagement takes place the first few minutes of the investigator's interactions with the suspect and when the investigator "sets the stage" for the rest of the interview. This usually begins with an introduction, the investigator introducing himself by name and offering his hand to shake. The title that the investigators use for themselves help to establish the relationship—"Investigator so-and-so-" is more formal than using just first name and last. The planning stage would have helped to determine which one is more appropriate in the given situation.

The introduction is also the beginning of developing reciprocity with the suspect. It is an unconscious response that if someone gives us something, we give something back. By the investigator giving their name and offering their hand, the suspect will usually offer their name and their hand in return.

The investigator can build upon the reciprocity by simply sharing small things with the suspect as well as providing them with small creature comforts. As an example:

Investigator: "It's kind of cold in here. I'm going to get something hot to drink before we get started. Would you like something?"
Suspect: "Yeah. Some coffee."
Investigator: "How do you like it?"
Suspect: "Black . . . with a couple of sugars."
Investigator: "I will take care of that and be right back."

Sounds deceptively simple, but it is highly effective. Small gestures like that help set the stage and build rapport, making the suspect more likely to talk. It is an approach that is effective across cultures. It has been used effectively by intelligence officers to build relationships and obtain information from hardcore terrorist prisoners. And it was a technique used by Hanns Scharff, the master interrogator of the aerial branch of the German army during World War II (the *Luftwaffe*). Scharff was famous for his ability to obtain high-quality information from downed US pilots during World War II without resorting to the tactics such as torture usually associated with the Germans. [17] It all began with a simple introduction.

In explaining the process, the investigator will tell the suspect why he is being interviewed. The investigator will go over the main topics that they would like to cover, as well as various procedural things (i.e., videotaping the interview, the investigator will be taking notes, the role of a second investigator if there is one, etc.). Lastly, the investigator will lay out the "ground rules." The suspect is told that they will be given as much time as they need to answer the question, and they are asked to go into as much detail as possible. There is no need for the suspect to rush. The investigator will listen and not interrupt, and in return the suspect is expected not to interrupt the investigator when it is their turn to talk. At times the investigator will rephrase things that the suspect says, and may go over the same topic more than once, but that is only to make sure that the investigator understands what the suspect is saying. And the investigator expects the suspect to tell the truth and the investigator will do the same.

In the United Kingdom, this is the period during which they will advise the suspect of their "Caution," which is similar to Miranda warnings in the United States. During the interaction in the engage and explaining stage, the investigator will be able to obtain a better idea of the suspect's current cognitive state and command of the language. If need be, the investigator can modify how they explain the "Caution" to ensure that it is understood by the suspect.

This list is only an example of what might be included in this stage. The explaining process seeks to accomplish exactly the opposite of what a US interrogation seeks. Where the US investigator wants to increase the suspect's anxiety level, the P.E.A.C.E. investigator wants to lower it. By explaining what is happening, and presenting themselves as not only having an open mind but also being genuinely interested in the suspect's side, the investigator follows a higher moral principle, showing respect, which is more likely to lead to a cooperative suspect.

A IS FOR ACCOUNT . . . CLARIFY AND CHALLENGE

Here the investigator gets into the meat of the matter. The first part of the interview is called the interviewee's (or suspect's) area. The suspect will be asked to give their side of the story, but first they are asked if they "did it." They are not accused of having committed the crime, just asked to provide their account as to what happened. There are many ways the investigator may do this, depending on the circumstances under which the suspect is in the interrogation room.

If they have been arrested, the investigator may say, "You have been arrested for . . . " and tell them the offense. The investigator goes on to say, "We want to understand what happened, so please tell us what you know about this." The exact wording would depend on what the investigator has learned about the suspect and the offense during the P and E stages of the interview.

The suspect may not be under arrest but only under investigation for an allegation because they were believed to have been seen leaving the scene of the crime, or for some other reason. The opening sentence might be the investigator asking the suspect to explain where they were on a certain day.

If the suspect chooses to admit to the offense, then the investigator will continue to allow them to provide their own account, and afterward proceed to ask appropriate follow-up questions, the style of which will be discussed in more detail below.

Even if the suspect does not admit guilt up front, they are encouraged to provide as detailed an account as they can, without interruption from the investigator. During this time, the investigator will take notes, from which they will be able to identify the portions of the suspect's account that need additional clarification. It is only after the suspect has finished providing their story that the investigator moves to the second phase, which is called the "interviewer's (or investigator's) area." This area is further divided into two parts, the clarification phase and the challenge phase.

First is the clarification phase. Using notes taken during the suspect's area, the investigator will go through and provide the suspect with an overview of what the suspect had just said. This ensures that the investigator understood the suspect, and it will also lock the suspect into the account that they just provided. The investigator then picks one point that he feels requires additional detail, and then asks the suspect to provide that detail. For example, if the suspect said that after leaving the bar, they drove home, the investigator would ask the suspect to explain the route that he took to get home. After the suspect explains the route, the investigator would summarize the suspect's answer, ask if the summary was correct, and then ask a follow-up detail, such as more information about the suspect's car or things they saw on the way home. The questioning continues until the investigator has wrung out every single detail possible from that line of questioning. The investigator would then go back to the suspect's original account, pick another issue that needs clarification, and start again. The process continues until each issue has been thoroughly explored and the suspect has committed to the story that they provided for each point.

P.E.A.C.E.-trained investigators are taught what types of questions to ask and what to avoid. They are very well versed on the need to ask open-ended questions, and to avoid leading questions that suggest an answer. In a proper P.E.A.C.E. interview, the types of contamination created by the investigators' style of questioning often seen in interviews in the United States and interrogations practically do not exist. The resulting information is more pure and much more reliable.

The second part of the "interviewer's area" and the last stage of the account phase is the challenge. Here the suspect is asked to account for any inconsistencies in their own account, but especially for any inconsistencies between their story and the evidence. This is not done in an accusatory way, or in a "gotcha" fashion. Instead, the problem is laid out on the table and the suspect is asked for their explanation.

As an example, say the suspect gave a full account of where they were the day of the murder in question. At the time the murder occurred, the suspect said he was across town at a bar. Through his clarification questions, the investigator learned that the suspect drove his car, a yellow Volkswagen with tag number JQX546H, to the bar and parked it in the back parking lot. Additional questions revealed that the suspect was the only one who had keys to the car, that the suspect saw three acquaintances inside, that he could provide the name of the bartender, and recall the amount of the tab and that it was paid by credit card.

The investigator has reason to doubt this, as the investigator's initial corroboration of the suspect's account revealed that a traffic speed camera captured a photo of the suspect's Volkswagen two blocks from the scene of the murder at the time the suspect claimed he was miles away in the bar. In his challenge, the investigator would simply ask the suspect to account for the fact that the camera captured a picture of his Volkswagen near the crime scene.

You see how through careful questioning and probing the investigator has allowed the suspect to box himself in. And instead of launching in to an accusatory interrogation, the suspect is asked to explain the discrepancy. One reason that this is important is because the suspect might actually have a legitimate explanation that was not uncovered during the investigator's questioning. This method of questioning, with the philosophy of keeping an open mind, keeps the investigator from jumping to conclusions and going down the wrong path.

Once the investigator has confronted the suspect with the discrepancy, then one or more of the following is likely to occur: (1) the suspect will try to backpedal on his original accounts that he has repeatedly verified throughout the interview as true, (2) the suspect will stick to his original story, which, using the detailed information obtained through questioning, the investigator can either verify or blow out of the water, (3) the suspect will choose to remain silent, in which case the investigator can conduct the same follow-up as mentioned in (2), or (4), the suspect will make a full or partial incriminating statement or confession. Any which way this goes is good for the investigation. If the suspect is innocent, this gives him an opportunity to prove it. If he is guilty, then the photo evidence of his car being near the scene was just made a whole lot stronger.

C IS FOR CLOSURE

For the P.E.A.C.E.-trained investigator, how the interview is concluded is as important as how it starts. The suspect needs to be afforded an opportunity to provide any additional information or make any statements that they feel are important or might not have been covered in the interview. The investigator will also explain what will happen next, and what the suspect can expect. The interview needs to end on a civil note, as the investigator may have the need or opportunity to conduct additional follow-up interviews at a later date and therefore is invested in maintaining a positive rapport. Even if no further interviews are needed, the investigator or another law enforcement officer might need to talk with the suspect in connection with another matter, and by ending the interview this way, their future cooperation is much more likely.

E IS FOR EVALUATION

This is an all-important stage that is too often skipped by US investigators. As discussed in chapter 7, the investigator must now evaluate the information provided by the suspect and test it for its reliability. Have any new details been learned that can be corroborated? Did the suspect provide details that were known to the investigator, and were they provided absent of any contamination? What other follow-up work needs to be done?

The P.E.A.C.E.-trained investigator must also evaluate the status of the suspect at the end of the interview, not only their demeanor but their physical well-being as well. Has their mental or physical state changed in such a way that special considerations, such as a suicide watch, need to be implemented?

Finally, the P.E.A.C.E.-trained investigator must evaluate their own performance, often with the help of co-workers and supervisors. The performance of the investigator is then rated and their actions critiqued to help them improve their skills in preparation for the next interview.

INVESTIGATIVE INTERVIEWING TRAINING

Becoming a good interviewer is not something that comes naturally for most people, and it cannot be achieved overnight. Not only must investigators be taught the basics of the process, but also, as mentioned in the evaluation section, they must continually hone their skills.

Unlike interrogation training in the United States, P.E.A.C.E. training addresses the root cause of problematic confessions and statements. The training includes segments on the ethics of interviewing and investigations, the causes of false confessions, the problems caused by cognitive biases such as tunnel vision, development of the proper investigative mindset, and how to evaluate the reliability of evidence.

P.E.A.C.E. training is provided in a system of five "tiers." The first tier is taught to the frontline officer. It is usually a three-day course that teaches the officer the basics on how memory works, memory enhancement techniques, and how to avoid the most common errors of interviewing (e.g., asking leading questions, interrupting). The training gives the officers the basics on how to obtain accurate information through their interviews.[18]

The second tier is an introduction to the P.E.A.C.E. method of interviewing and is given to all members working in investigative units. This tier is a two-week course that goes into more detail about the P.E.A.C.E. process. Investigators learn more about the different techniques used to interview witnesses and suspects (including uncooperative ones).

Investigators working serious crimes such as murder are trained at the third tier level. In some places, the third tier is broken down further and includes separate training for investigators who conduct child interviews, advanced training in witness and victim interviewing, and advanced suspect interview training. The third tier training is several weeks in duration. Often the investigator must first prove that they are proficient in the basics of P.E.A.C.E. interviewing before being accepted into third tier training, and before graduating, they must pass a postcourse exam and provide copies of interviews to prove they have mastered the material.

Tier four is for the highly skilled investigators who are recruited into this final stage of training and learn how to supervise and evaluate investigators and their interview skills. Tier five personnel are trained to oversee it all, from the training to the supervisor of the investigators to keeping up to date with the latest research and developments. They help develop new training and new policies for the agency.

For law enforcement agencies that have embraced the investigative interviewing model, the training never stops. Investigators are expected to continue to improve their skills through critical self-evaluation as well as peer and supervisory review of their work. Many agencies hold monthly meetings to review the latest updates as well as conduct feedback sessions on the prior month's interviews.

"P.E.A.C.E.? WE DON'T NEED NO STINKING P.E.A.C.E."

"What we are doing now works, and the courts say it's OK, so why change?" This is the sentiment that I usually encounter when I discuss bringing investigative interviewing and specifically the P.E.A.C.E. concept to the United States. The other objection is usually based on its name. If it were called CRUSH or ENFORCE, it would be a much easier sell. But that's a matter for another discussion.

Let's look at the first objection. Yes, current US interrogation tactics such as Reid work, and as we have seen, ironically, they can work too well, allowing investigators to obtain confessions to crimes the suspect did not commit. The courts may say that the tactics are okay, but that does not make them less problematic when it comes to obtaining reliable statements and confessions. And as I have said before, the courts are concerned about the admissibility of a confession, not the reliability. That leaves "So why change?" Maybe because P.E.A.C.E. is better? I personally believe it is.

The P.E.A.C.E. model virtually eliminates all of the problems created by the current interrogation practices in the United States. The coerciveness is gone, thus ensuring the admissibility of the statement by the courts. The potential for contamination is minimized, thus increasing the reliability of the statement. The investigator will most likely obtain a ton more information from the suspect, information that even if it does not result in a confession will usually strengthen the case against them. And because of the overall training, the investigator will conduct better and more thorough investigations.

MYTHS AND MISCONCEPTIONS

Law enforcement personnel tend to hate both the way things are and change. Of these, the latter tends to be the most despised. Despite complaints, the love of the status quo is deeply entrenched, and anything new is usually countered with objections based on myths and misconceptions. The same attitudes are true about incorporating some concepts found in investigative interviewing into current practices.

Brent Snook has faced these issues for years. A professor in psychology at Memorial University of Newfoundland, he also teaches the

P.E.A.C.E. model of investigative interviewing and has been working for years to help bring it to Canadian law enforcement. Snook coauthored an article addressing the myths and misconceptions that many in US and Canadian law enforcement have about P.E.A.C.E., and which are going to be discussed here.[19]

WE ALREADY DO P.E.A.C.E. WE CALL IT THE BEHAVIORAL ANALYSIS INTERVIEW

The Reid Institute and other interrogation schools have countered the investigative interviewing movement by insisting that we have actually been using this method all along. They say that the preinterrogation Behavioral Analysis Interview (BAI) does the same thing as P.E.A.C.E. Remember, this is the nonaccusatorial interview in which the suspect's account is obtained and explored, and only then is the investigator supposed to move into the interrogation phase.

In actuality, nothing could be further from the truth. If you put aside the differences in the length, type, and quality of training it takes to learn to do a P.E.A.C.E. interview versus a BAI, the focus of the two is quite different. With the BAI, the investigator receives little to no training on how to properly conduct an interview to obtain the maximum amount of information. Where a properly conducted P.E.A.C.E. interview might take hours, the estimated time to complete the BAI is approximately thirty-five minutes.[20]

Furthermore, the primary purpose of the BAI is to use pseudoscience such as body language analysis to determine if the suspect is being deceptive in their response to the investigator's questions and to decide whether or not to go on to the interrogation stage. There is no attempt to use these disputed and disavowed techniques such as the amount of eye contact made to detect deception or determine guilt in a P.E.A.C.E. interview. Instead, the P.E.A.C.E. interview focuses on gathering and comparing information and details in order to assess the suspect's reliability and guilt.

WE WILL NEVER GET ANOTHER CONFESSION!

They said this when the courts outlawed the third degree. They said this decades later when the Supreme Court made investigators advise suspects of their Miranda warnings. And the same type of people who said those things are the same ones who, like the Reid Institute and other interrogation schools, believe that law enforcement "must deal with criminal suspects on a somewhat lower moral plane."[21] It's true that P.E.A.C.E. interviewing requires that the investigator treat the suspect ethically, with respect, and to keep an open mind. And it is true that unlike the goal of a US interrogation, the goal of the P.E.A.C.E.-trained investigator is not to obtain a confession, but accurate, reliable, and admissible information. More like a search for the truth.

It is because P.E.A.C.E. makes no overt attempt to persuade a resistant suspect to confess that many consider it to be a "soft" interviewing approach. Then again, I have heard many US investigators complain that their Reid training is too soft. They say that it is okay for white-collar criminals but it doesn't work on the hardcore "gang bangers" that they have as witnesses and suspects. One has to wonder what techniques *are* "working" for those investigators when it comes to their "gang bangers," how often those techniques make it into the public eye, and what the blowback is when it comes to the reputation of the law enforcement agency within that community.

Currently, research suggests that confession rates for countries that use Reid-style interrogation techniques and those that use investigative interviewing are about the same.[22] Even if later research shows that Reid-style techniques produce higher rates, the question still remains as to the admissibility and reliability of those confessions. To be honest, if I am going to go through all of that work to get information from a suspect, I want the end result to be both reliable and admissible. And if I use a method that might not result in a confession but instead helps me get an intimately detailed alibi that through a follow-up investigation I can destroy, that is as good as a confession any day.

P.E.A.C.E. WON'T WORK BECAUSE OUR LAWS ARE DIFFERENT THAN IN THE UNITED KINGDOM.

It's true that there are some differences in the laws of the United States and the United Kingdom, but there are also differences between the laws of the US federal government, state governments, and local jurisdictions. Law enforcement practices in one state are often modified and adopted to work within the boundaries of another state.

P.E.A.C.E. is no different, and in fact, several countries such as Denmark and Norway have adopted the overall approach with appropriate changes to address their specific legal issues.

Another objection pointed to as a reason that P.E.A.C.E. will not work here is that in the United Kingdom, a suspect's refusal to answer questions posed to them by law enforcement can be used against them, especially if later on they give the jury an alibi that they could have provided the investigator at the time of the interview. In the United States, a suspect's choice to talk or not to talk cannot be used against them in court, thus necessitating the more manipulative tactics used by US investigators.

However, the suspect's right to remain silent in the United States is hardly an impediment to the implementation of the P.E.A.C.E. model of interviewing. Outside of the large number of people who would go on and waive their Miranda rights without any persuasion, investigators are very good at getting past this speed bump. Additionally, the engage and explain stage of P.E.A.C.E. is designed to foster an environment in which the suspect wants to talk without the trickery and manipulation that some investigators use to get past Miranda.

CURRENT OBSTACLES TO INVESTIGATIVE INTERVIEWING IN THE UNITED STATES

Despite the objections listed and answered above, there are two major logistical obstacles to bringing investigative interviewing to the United States as a sweeping change. The first is that, unlike in the United Kingdom, we have no central agency overseeing or controlling all law enforcement entities in the United States. While the US Department of Justice might implement some standards for federal law enforcement agencies and individual states have some in place for law enforcement agencies within their borders, changes and reform are almost always an agency-by-agency thing, making uniform implementation of new procedures and techniques difficult. The requirement that interrogations be videotaped from start to finish is a good example of the difficulty of implementation. Some law enforcement agencies videotape because of court decisions, some because of local legislation, and some because the agency itself chooses to. Many law enforcement agencies just don't do it at all, and they give the same, disproven reasons for not doing so. And among those that do, there is no real consistency as to when, how, or where it is required.

The second biggest obstacle to the successful implementation of investigative interviewing in the United States is the level of commitment it would require. US law enforcement agencies like things quick, cheap, and easy, as long as the perception of the public is good. Most interrogation training in the United States fits that bill. In less than a week, with no real effort, an investigator becomes a certified interrogator. There is no test, no follow-up to ensure that the investigator is correctly using what they learned. It is just a box to check.

To become good at investigative interviewing requires weeks of training, not only of the investigator but for their supervisors as well. This is followed by constant refresher training and peer-supervisor reviews. All of this requires time, money, and a huge commitment from the investigator, their supervisor, and upper management.

It also requires a new look at the existing culture. The confession can no longer be considered an investigative shortcut. Interviews can no longer be done "on the fly." And for some it is hard to keep an open mind and treat a suspect with respect, especially if the crime under investigation is an especially heinous one. Seeking truth rather than confirmation is harder, but the end result will be a more accurate and fair one.

12

SAFEGUARDS AND REFORM

One of the best bosses I ever had told me to never complain about a problem unless at the same time I could at least suggest a solution. But when it comes to the problems that result from the way investigators interview and interrogate suspects, witnesses, and others in the United States, there is no one fix. As you have seen, the problems do not only rest with the techniques and tactics used but also are multifaceted in nature and require a multifaceted approach to reform. And though false confessions and bad statement evidence starts with the investigator, there are many other individuals and organizations that allow them to result in wrongful arrests and convictions.

In spite of the critics who continue to minimize the impact that false confessions have, law enforcement officials at the highest levels have begun to attempt to address the problem. In 2010, the Center for American and International Law in Plano, Texas, began holding well-attended seminars for local law enforcement personnel on best practices in investigations, which included presentations on the issues of false confessions and their prevention. Also in 2010, the National Conference of Commissioners on Uniform State Laws issued model legislation on the videotaping of the interrogations of suspects.

For several years the International Association of Chiefs of Police (IACP) and the US Department of Justice's Office of Justice Programs (OJP) have been working to address the issues of wrongful convictions, culminating in 2012 with the National Summit on Wrongful Convictions. The summit came up with thirty recommendations, which were published in their report titled "Building a Systemic Approach to Prevent Wrongful Convictions."[1] In addition, the IACP's National Law Enforcement Policy Center released several model policies for law enforcement agencies, addressing false confessions and other issues.

In the summit's report, eyewitness misidentification, problems with forensic sciences, false confessions, and inaccurate informant testimony are listed as the major causes of wrongful convictions. Two of the four (false confessions and inaccurate informant testimony) can be linked directly to the way law enforcement personnel conduct interviews and interrogations and/or how confessions and statement evidence are evaluated for reliability.[2] Eyewitness evidence can also be included when you consider how the misidentification could be the result of investigator contamination or the way in which the certainty of the witness can be altered by what the investigator says after the identification is made. This again emphasizes how critical the interview skills of the investigator are when it comes to obtaining accurate and reliable evidence.

Though it recognized the roles that everyone in the criminal justice system plays when it comes to wrongful convictions, the focus of the summit quickly shifted to the "front-end leadership role of law enforcement"[3] (which is perhaps why the role of false-guilty pleas was not addressed in the report since those deals are negotiated with prosecutors, not detectives). In general, according to the summit, wrongful convictions would not happen if there were first no wrongful arrests. The participants

> saw a need to change the investigative climate to one that welcomes greater assessment and oversight; is receptive to new information regardless of its "fit" with current case information; insures that proper protocols and best practices are in place and utilized; fosters more frequent and improved training for investigators; and promotes a collective ownership approach to cases versus the current narrow model where one or two investigators may have complete responsibility for review, analysis, and case direction.[4]

The summit's recommendations, some of which I will address in conjunction with my own recommendations, call for technical, procedural, and cultural changes. Some of them seem fairly simple to implement, especially since the recommendations come from a major law enforcement organization whose members make up the leadership of a large number, if not the majority, of law enforcement agencies in the United

States. The chief, sheriff, commissioner, or director just has to say and it will be done. If it was only that easy.

DIFFICULTIES IN IMPLEMENTING REFORM

Captain Francis Healy, the special legal advisor for the Philadelphia Police Department, spoke on that very topic at the Quattrone Center for the Administration of Justice 2014 Spring Symposium, "A Systems Approach to Conviction Integrity." Assuming the role of "speak truth to power," Healy emphasized that simply putting a policy out on paper does not equal the implementation of that policy. Careful planning is required, first to ensure that the policy "can be made functional" (i.e., funding, equipment, etc., are available), and second, to obtain "buy-in" from the troops. When new policies are enacted because of legislative mandates or other pressures from outside the organization, these implementation issues are often not taken into consideration. Change is easy to order, harder to create.[5]

The "buy-in" aspect, especially among the lower ranks of a law enforcement agency, is especially critical. Healy discussed how in police culture, any change causes what he called "a grieving process." It takes time and the support of middle and lower management to "sell" the change to the officers and investigators. Without their support and their proper supervision and enforcement of the policy, total failure or a policy in name only is often the result. A good example of this is the history of the Washington, DC, Metropolitan Police Department's (MPD) path to videotaping interrogations in their entirety.

Concerned about the growing number of media accounts about false confessions and improper interrogation tactics, District of Columbia council member and chairperson of the Judiciary Committee Kathy Patterson wanted to make sure that the MPD was not having similar problems. After holding hearings and serious study, Patterson told MPD in 2002 that the Judiciary Committee wanted them to develop and implement a program requiring the videotaping of suspect interrogations in their entirety.[6]

Though police management supported the concept publically, almost everyone, from the chief of police to the most rookie investigator, hated the idea. For over a year, MPD management did everything but come up with a plan. What protocols they did develop were mostly unnecessary and intentionally burdensome, possibly in an attempt to create a self-fulfilling prophesy of a huge decrease in confessions if not absolute failure to obtain any.[7]

Patterson was pissed and took matters into her own hands. If MPD was not going to come up with a workable policy, she would. Under her guidance, the City Council passed legislation that not only established the policy and procedures under which MPD would videotape interrogations, they also included legal sanctions that could lead to the exclusion of a confession if it was not videotaped. MPD management was forced to take action, but the investigators had other plans.[8]

When it comes to rules and regulations that "got in the way," investigators can be very creative when it comes to finding loopholes or workarounds. In anticipation of the new policy, MPD investigators went into full swing. One example was that since the policy mandated videotaping when the interrogation took place in an MPD facility that had videotaping equipment (and every facility where investigators were assigned would have such equipment), they planned to take their suspects to locations that did not have investigative units, thus no videotaping equipment, and thus the requirement would not apply. Investigators who were working as part of a task force were planning to interrogate their suspects at FBI or DEA facilities in order to avoid the videotaping requirement.

Superintendent of Detectives Michael Anzallo caught wind of these workarounds and put his foot down. He let it be known that the new policy would not only be followed to the letter of the law but also the spirit. Because of his support for the new policy, he not only prevented it from becoming a paper tiger, it became entrenched into the normal course of doing business much faster than it otherwise would. In the long run (and after the grieving process), investigators admitted that videotaping was a good thing, and that they were actually getting more statements and confessions from suspects than before. They even began videotaping when they did not have to, such as when the suspect was not in custody or during interviews of witnesses.

So when making recommendations for safeguards and reform, these are some of the things that I try to keep in mind. Of course, it would have been a lot easier if MPD management had been positive about the benefits of a videotaping policy in the first place. Other agencies were already doing it. Many had been forced into it. But the overall attitude of those law enforcement agencies was that videotaping was the "best thing that was ever shoved down our throats." Using the experience of these agencies and bringing in their investigators to talk about how it leads to stronger cases and (with good interrogations, of course) leads to more convictions could have helped ease the transition by increasing buy-in.

Before moving on to discussing the actual safeguards and reforms, I need to remind you that I am not an expert in drafting policy or legislation, nor am I an attorney. My ideas come from personal observations and experience, as well as the work of others.

With that said, let's get into my ideas for safeguards and reforms.

SAFEGUARDS AND REFORMS

Videotaping

Imagine if you are a juror on a murder trial. The crime scene technician responsible for the processing of the scene and the collection of evidence is on the stand testifying. When asked by the prosecutor, the technician identifies each piece of evidence and verbally describes where he found it. When he finishes, it's the defense's turn. The defense attorney asks the technician if he had a camera available, and the technician answers yes. He is asked if he had video recording equipment available, and he answers yes. The technician is then asked why he did not bother taking pictures of the overall crime scene and specific pictures showing the location of the evidence. He responds by asking, "Why can't you just take my word for it?"

This scene happens all of the time, except that instead of a crime scene technician it is an investigator, and instead of photos or videos of evidence, it is a videotape of the interrogation in its entirety. It is not that the law enforcement agency does not have the equipment. Many will use it to capture the part of the interrogation that they want you to see, the final confession. The agency and the investigator just chose not to use the best method possible to document the recovery of all of the confession evidence. They just expect you to "take their word for it."

There is absolutely no valid excuse for any law enforcement agency in the United States not to videotape interrogations in their entirety as a routine matter of course, but several agencies continue not to, or only videotape in certain situations. They continue to justify their decision for consistently the same reasons, which I will now debunk.

Costs: Equipment and Storage

This translates into a matter of priorities. Video recording equipment, even high-quality equipment, is quite affordable. In the past, the long-term storage of videotapes might have presented a problem, but now everything is stored digitally. If finances are really a problem, agencies can get creative to obtain funding. All sorts of grants are available, and some agencies have funded their special needs by asking for contributions from the community. When I first became a police officer in 1983 we were not issued bulletproof vests. My agency obtained over two thousand bulletproof vests through donations from the business community. I am sure that Costco or Wal-Mart would be happy to donate video recording and storage equipment if asked.

Costs: Transcripts of the Recordings

As we have discussed in chapter 7, having a quality transcript of the recording of the interrogation is crucial in order for the confession evidence to be evaluated. And the cost of having a qualified person transcribing the tape can be significant. However, not all recordings need to be transcribed, especially right away, unless there is some special policy or law that mandates it, and policies and laws can be changed.

The cost of transcribing can also be spread around. Many agencies do not bear the burden alone. In many places the prosecutor's office, the courts, and/or the defense attorneys either pay for or contribute to the costs of transcribing the tapes.

Costs: Mandatory Videotaping Will Inhibit Confession

This is a concern that is especially raised in jurisdictions that do not allow a suspect to be recorded without their consent. The suspect would have to agree to being videotaped, and usually sign a waiver. Many jurisdictions don't have this requirement. They operate under what is called "one-party consent," where if only one of the people in the room (such as the investigator) says it's OK, then the other persons in the room can be recorded without their knowledge. But the general concern is that if the suspect even thinks that they are being videotaped, they are less likely to confess.

Let's address the general concern first, that videotaping inhibits confessions. Like law enforcement personnel's objections to the courts forbidding them to use the third degree and requiring that they advise a suspect of their Miranda rights, this fear has largely been unfounded. In one survey of investigations where videotaping was mandatory, 95 percent reported that the videotaping did not affect their ability to interrogate or get confessions.[9]

In my experience, many of the times when videotaping did inhibit the interrogation, it was the investigator who created the problem, not the existence of the videotape. If an investigator has enough salesmanship about them to get someone to waive their Miranda rights, talk with them, and confess to a crime, things that are definitely against a suspect's best interest, how come they can't sell them on recording the interrogation on videotape? The few times I ever had someone object to the interview being taped, they changed their mind when I explained how the tape protected both of us from false accusations and helped protect their rights in the long run.

Places that do have to obtain the suspect's consent before videotaping have addressed the issue in several ways. Some use a written consent form, similar to the form that the suspect signs when they agree to waive their Miranda rights. Others post signs in and around the interrogation room, announcing that the room/area is under video monitoring. Then, if the suspect choses to talk, their consent is inferred.

When a suspect refuses to talk with the investigator unless the video camera is turned off, that doesn't prevent the investigator from continuing to interrogate the suspect unrecorded, unless specifically prohibited by law or policy. In my old agency, the camera was on from the moment the suspect entered the room. If they did not want the interview/interrogation recorded, that was captured on the video before the camera was turned off. Supervisors have to be careful to make sure that an investigator is not using this as a workaround by creatively suggesting to the suspect that they don't want to be recorded.

Laws and policies are not etched in stone. If one or the other is found to somehow inhibit the ability of the investigator to successfully interview and interrogate suspects, they can be changed. Some states have laws that require that everyone in the room must agree to be recorded. These laws can be modified to provide an exception for law enforcement. Some agencies have adopted practices such as posting signs notifying everyone that they are subject to video recording. This removes any expectation of privacy that the subject may have, thus satisfying the law and allowing the investigator to record the interview/interrogation unimpeded.

Costs: Unable to Use Confessions Made Outside the Interrogation Room

When a law enforcement agency brings up this objection, they are usually referring to two situations. One is when a suspect makes a spontaneous statement or confession out of the blue. The other situation occurs most often in rural areas, where the investigator has to travel miles away from any police facility to conduct an interview, often at a subject's home, business, or in the investigator's car.

The proliferation of the use of dashcams (video recording cameras mounted in police cars that record the officer's movements and conversations outside the car) and bodycams (personal video recording cameras attached to the officer themselves) comes close to making this a nonissue. Portable tape recorders, carried by numerous reporters to record interviews in a subject's home or office, are cheap and readily available. Most cell phones have apps for audio recording. And I know of no law or policy that automatically renders a spontaneous statement useless because it was not electronically recorded.

Unless the investigator uses interviewing or interrogating of suspects outside the police facility to avoid the videotaping requirements, these are usually not the problematic situations that videotaping in the interrogation room is designed to address. And besides, investigators are taught to avoid interviewing or interrogating suspects outside of the interrogation room. They want the suspect to be in an isolated environment under the investigator's control, not on the suspect's turf.

Costs: Interrogation Tactics Will Become Known to the Criminals

As if anything that we do in the interrogation room now is a secret! Just turn on the television to programs such as the Biography Channel's *The Interrogators* or A&E's *The First 48*, programs that show actual investigators doing actual interrogations. Go on to YouTube and see even more. And anyone with the money can attend a Reid Institute interview and interrogation course, not just law enforcement personnel. An example is Douglass Starr, who attended Reid training in 2013 as research for his *New Yorker* article "The Interview: Do Police Interrogation Techniques Produce False Confessions?"[10] When people raise this as an issue, I always think that what they are referring to is the "not so unspoken" reason why some want to keep the interrogation process out of the public eye, which is discussed next.

Costs: The Unspoken Need to Conceal "The Truth"

In 2011, I was asked to speak to the Florida Innocence Commission about the reasons why law enforcement should be required to videotape interrogations in their entirety. The commission consisted of high-ranking law enforcement officers, prosecutors, defense attorneys, judges, and legislatures who were trying to come up with policies and best practices to prevent wrongful convictions. A local cable news channel televised the meeting and my presentation.

As part of my PowerPoint presentation, I included a slide that lists the most common objections to the idea of mandatory videotaping of interrogations that I hear from law enforcement officers. After I got through debunking each one, the Commissioner of the Florida Department of Law Enforcement (FDLE), the statewide investigative agency for the state of Florida, raised his hand. The commissioner said that there was one objection that I did not list and it was the one that he heard the most from his investigators. The commissioner said his investigators often are involved in cases in which there are multiple interviews of multiple suspects over a several week time period. The commission pointed out that:

> In the earlier interviews, they [the suspects] were denying the charges, and later those denials were used against the prosecution in court. Rather than using the last and best, they [the investigators] say the

water was muddied by the getting-started interviews. . . . The initial interrogations created a defense tool. [11]

Unfortunately, this objection did not surprise me, nor did the fact that it was made in such a public forum. In another meeting where videotaping was discussed, I listened as a St. Louis–area police chief said that her investigators told her that there were times at the beginning of an interrogation when the suspect wavered on signing away their Miranda rights. The investigators told her that based on the suspect's actions, if they were being videotaped, the defense would have pounced all over that in forthcoming motions hearings, most likely leading to the confession being declared inadmissible in court. Knowing this, they would not have been able to continue the interrogation.

The actions that these two police officials were supporting are illegal. By law, [12] the information that they and their investigators sought to keep private must be turned over to the suspect's defense attorney. It does not matter that the investigators think that the information would "muddy the waters." Many wrongful convictions have resulted from investigators and prosecutors choosing to neglect their legal, ethical, and moral responsibility and hide such evidence from defense attorneys. Additionally, many truly guilty suspects have gone free or had their convictions overturned because of such violations of the law.

In the Reid textbook, they discuss surveys of investigators regarding mandatory videotaping. In one, the objection was raised that videotaping would "open the door to defense attacks and cause *legitimate* [my emphasis] confessions to be suppressed." In another survey consisting of "Reid training investigators," 7 percent believed that the videotaping of interrogations mostly benefits the defense. [13] The reality is that the only way a videotaped interrogation can benefit the defense is if it shows the improper or questionable actions by the investigator that those 7 percent would rather hide.

The attitude exhibited by these high-ranking police officials, their obvious ignorance of the law, and their moral and ethical obligations as law enforcement officers is one of the best arguments to be made in support of mandatory videotaping.

GROWING SUPPORT FOR VIDEOTAPING

Fortunately, support for mandatory videotaping of interrogations is growing across the board. The International Association of Chiefs of Police has created model policies supporting the practice. [14] Even the Reid Institute, once one of the most adamant critics of mandatory videotaping, is now behind it. [15]

In 2013, the Department of Justice's Bureau of Justice Assistance published the results of surveys and research conducted to identify the best practices for solving homicides. One of their recommendations was that even witness interviews conducted on homicide crime scenes be videotaped. [16]

But I believe that it will be the public's outcry that will ultimately force law enforcement to make videotaping a universal practice, and for everyone, not only suspects. The obvious desire to keep questionable tactics from the public view will only backfire in this new age of transparency.

THE NEED TO VIDEOTAPE

It is not surprising that I recommend that there be mandatory videotaping of interviews and interrogations in their entirety of anyone considered to be a suspect of a crime. I also recommend that as much as possible, there be mandatory videotaping of all interviews and interrogations of witnesses, victims, and informants as well. Granted, this will not be possible in all situations, and there will be occasions where equipment failure and other unforeseen circumstances prevent it. But since law enforcement (and in many cases prosecutors) has a great deal of control over where these interviews and interrogations take place, the burden should be placed on them to explain why the interactions were not recorded.

When debating the videotaping issue, many law enforcement agencies and prosecutor's offices have agreed in principle but then said that the issue should be left up to them to decide. In general, I disagree. The same agencies and prosecutor's offices that say this are usually the ones who are resisting videotaping. And we saw what happened when the issue was left up to the Washington, DC, Metropolitan Police Department. I believe that if an agency is not currently videotaping at least interrogations in their entirety, then the local legislature must step in. And I believe that no matter who enacts the law or policy, it needs to have teeth behind it. Sanctions and punishments should be in place in the event that an investigator fails to videotape an interrogation unless they have a satisfactory explanation for why it was not done.

HOWEVER, VIDEOTAPING IS NOT THE END

Videotaping in and of itself does not solve the problem of false confessions and false witness statements, except that it prevents most investigators from using the most egregious interrogation tactics. All it does is permit others to critically examine the interrogation tactics and evaluate the quality of the confession or statement evidence. But to do that effectively, the person(s) doing the evaluation need to know what they are looking for. That leads me to my next recommendation.

ENHANCED TRAINING AND EDUCATION

Enhanced Law Enforcement Training

All the videotaping in the world will not help if no one knows what to look for. Better training is needed to fill in all of the gaps not taught during standard American interrogation training. Investigators need to be made aware of the prevalence of false confession (i.e., that the phenomenon exists), of the causes of false confessions, and that many of the techniques that they routinely use are actually not recommended by both the researchers and the leading interrogation schools. They must be made aware that these techniques cannot only lead to false confessions but also false or unreliable statements from witnesses, victims, and informants.

As in the United Kingdom and other countries that teach investigative interviewing, investigators must be taught how their own cognitive biases such as tunnel vision and lack of the proper investigative mindset contribute to the problem. The training must include instruction on how confession contamination occurs and the proper investigative steps that must be taken postconfession to help determine the reliability of the confession evidence.

The training must consist of more than classroom lecture. It needs to involve practical exercises—student investigators tasked with identifying the issues that they are taught using actual case studies and interrogation videos.

Most importantly, the training cannot stop with just one class; it must be ongoing. Investigators must be updated with the latest investigative, research, and legal updates. Evaluations on an investigator's knowledge and performance should be done on a regular basis, using videotapes of their own interviews and interrogations as a training tool.

In general, the majority of law enforcement agencies are not averse to training of this nature (except when it comes to the practical exercise and evaluation part) if it is sold to them correctly. When I and others have given presentations of this sort to law enforcement agencies across the country, the truthful pitch that we make is that we are trying to help them build better and stronger cases. However, the first time I gave such a pitch as a still-active homicide detective, I was unsure of the reception I was going to receive. It was at the annual conference of the Mid-Atlantic Cold Case Homicide Investigators Association, and the audience consisted of seasoned homicide detectives from across the country.

In the front row was a retired homicide detective who was now working as a volunteer with a national group that assists other law enforcement agencies with their cold case investigations. She had retired from the Los Angeles County Sheriff's Department after decades of experience. She had seen it all.

As I went through a case study, talking about tunnel vision and showing video clip examples of very subtle contamination occurring during an interrogation, I could feel her eyes locked on me. When I did glance over, I saw her in what the behavioral analysis folks would call a defensive stance, arms and legs tightly crossed. I just knew that she was totally unconvinced by anything that I was saying.

As soon as the presentation ended, she rushed up to the stage. I prepared myself for a confrontation as she stuck her finger in my face. Much to my surprise she said, "If any of these *&%$# in this audience say that they didn't see themselves in that video doing the same thing that investigator was doing, they're lying. I wish I had seen this twenty years ago."

Encouragingly, that has been the general reaction I receive among law enforcement personnel when I give similar presentations. Of course, I have gotten a few like the guy who told me I wasted his time. He went on to say that he never got, nor would he ever get, a false confession, because he never interrogated anyone who wasn't guilty.

In general, younger investigators seem to be more receptive than older ones. Perhaps this is because of their exposure through the media to stories about false confessions and wrongful convictions, therefore making them more open to the idea that it can occur. Ultimately, it seems the environment is ripe for training and reform and that buy-in from officers and investigators could be purchased with just a little bit of effort.

Training the Overseers

This sort of training must obviously not stop with the investigator. The investigator's supervisor, prosecutors, judges, and defense attorneys need training as well, and for obvious reasons. As we have discussed, though the investigator is the one who gets the false confession or bad statement, it has to get past a bunch of other gatekeepers before it can result in a wrongful conviction. Therefore, it's crucial that all participants in the process be exposed to the same training and be made aware of the same issues as the investigators. Prosecutors and the investigator's supervisors play an especially important role, not only in helping to identify problematic confessions but also in preventing them in the first place. Properly trained prosecutors and supervisors can work together to identify and correct any improper interrogation tactics or investigative practices being used by the investigator and help ensure that they do not continue. Trained defense attorneys will be able to critically evaluate the reliability of their client's confession, allowing them to develop a sound strategy to argue in court if issues are found.

A critically important group that has yet to be mentioned is the jury. They are the ones tasked with the ultimate determination of the reliability of the suspect's confession or the witness's testimony. Faced with such an awesome responsibility, they deserve to be able to make that determination intelligently and not based on myths, misconceptions, and old-wives' tales.

This is where expert testimony comes into play. Experts in this area come from all sorts of fields. Some are psychologists, others researchers, social scientists, or experts in police practices. They can be used to educate the jury about the fact that false confessions do occur, the reasons behind them, police training, and the causes of confession evidence contamination. What the expert cannot testify to is the actual reliability of the confession, as that is up to the jury to decide.

The courts have all sorts of rigorous requirements to determine if the testimony of an expert in any field would be appropriate to be heard by the jury. In the past, it was a relatively common occurrence for judges not to allow the testimony of experts on false confession issues, usually because the judges were operating under the same myths and misconceptions about the topic as the jury. However, more and more, defense attorneys are successfully admitting expert testimony in the area of police interrogations, investigative procedures, and false confessions. Increasing the training received by judges and defense attorneys in the areas covered above will only help increase that trend and thus provide juries with more information with which to make their decisions.

A Change in Interrogation Practices

The best reform would be to just totally junk the problematic way that law enforcement personnel in the United States interrogate and universally adopt the investigative interviewing (P.E.A.C.E.) approach. Obstacles to this suggestion were discussed in the last chapter, and the accusatory Reid Institute tactics are so embedded in our culture that I cannot see that happening in my lifetime. I do see hope though. Some law enforcement agencies, prosecutor's offices, and even public defender services have expressed an interest in investigative interviewing. When I attended the International Association of Investigative Interviewing conference in Toronto, Canada, in 2012, I was encouraged to see multidisciplinary attendees from around the world. However, it remains to be seen if law enforcement agencies in the United States will be willing to make the commitment that is needed to make a successful change.

In the meantime, there are steps that we can take to minimize the dangers and damage caused by the types of interrogation tactics taught in the United States, many of which merge with some of the other recommendations made here.

No More Lies

Of all the tactics that are currently allowed in interrogation rooms in the United States, lying or presenting false evidence is the most problematic.

Even the Reid Institute now cautions against using false evidence ploys, especially in interrogations of "a youthful suspect with low social maturity . . . a suspect with diminished mental capacity," or a suspect who says they have "no specific recollection" of having committed the crime.[17] In every single problematic confession case that I have reviewed to date, the investigator made use of false evidence ploys.

In the United Kingdom and other countries that use the investigative interviewing or P.E.A.C.E. approach, lying is forbidden. By using sound investigative practices, taking the time to gather real evidence, and knowing how to use it in the interview, they are able to obtain confessions and other valuable investigative information without the risks that lying presents.

Here in the States we justify the use of lying to suspects by saying that they are on a "lower moral plane"[18] than the rest of us. This is a dangerous mentality that has been used to justify all sorts of abuses, including but not limited to the use of third-degree tactics. Lying not only increases the risk of false or unreliable confessions and statements, it damages the reputation of law enforcement in the eyes of the public.

Justification for Interrogation

The first steps in obtaining a false confession is identifying an innocent person as a suspect and then subjecting them to a coercive interrogation. As we have seen, it often doesn't take much to lead some investigators to take that first step.

In order to prevent the abuse of many investigative tools, such as searching a suspect's home or even frisking a suspect on the street, the investigator must have sufficient justification and evidence according to the law. They have to be able to show that there is probable cause to believe that evidence may be found in the suspect's home, or that based on a suspect's actions they have reasonable suspicion to justify a frisk. I am not proposing that investigators obtain court orders before they can interrogate a suspect or witness, but if they are going to use the admittedly coercive tactics taught by the Reid Institute and others, they should be able to articulate that they are acting on more than just a hunch. The justification for interrogation should be documented and preapproved by a supervisor. Insufficient justification for an interrogation, just like insufficient justification for stopping and frisking someone on the street, could then be used in court hearings to determine if any information obtained during the interrogation should be suppressed. There could be exceptions, just as there are exceptions for when a warrant is needed to conduct a search. But by taking the extra step of making the investigator justify the use of coercive interrogation tactics to a third party, the investigator takes a step back for a minute and considers their evidence, thus helping to prevent tunnel vision from taking hold.

Require an Independent Review for Corroboration

Just as a third party should be required to review and approve the justification for the use of coercive interrogation tactics, a third party should evaluate the interrogation and confession for the proper corroboration. A supervisor, trained in proper interrogation tactics, the causes of false confessions, and the proper evaluation of confession evidence, should be assigned this task. It would be their job to play devil's advocate, poking holes not only in the interrogation and confession but also in challenging the investigator's interpretations and theories, further offering recommendations for additional follow-up. If done properly, and not just as a box to check, this would not only provide an additional safeguard to keep bad confessions from getting into the system but would also greatly improve the quality of investigations overall.

Restrict the Length of Interrogations

Though interrogations do not have to be lengthy to produce false confessions, time spent can be a contributing factor. The Reid Institute now advocates that if the interrogation has gotten nowhere in three to four hours, the investigator should "reassess and most likely" terminate the interrogation.[19] There may be circumstances in which an interrogation would take longer, but, as with the decision to interrogate, the investigator should be required to present justification to a third party before that can happen.

A good rule to follow is that if the investigator needs a break, so does the suspect. Tag-teaming the suspect by letting one investigator take a break while another goes in to take over with no corresponding break for the suspect should not be allowed.

Protection for Vulnerable Suspects

Investigators have to take their suspects as they come. That means that the group might include juveniles, people who are intellectually impaired, have substance abuse problems, or who suffer from mental health issues. It turns out that these are the very people who are overrepresented when it comes to false confessions.[20] Investigators receive very little training on how to deal with this population and often misidentify symptoms of mental illness or intellectual impairment as signs of deception or guilt. Additionally, though law enforcement has long recognized the problems created by the increased suggestibility of juvenile suspects and often uses specially trained experts to conduct juvenile witness and victim interviews, they use the same interrogation tactics on juvenile suspects as they do adults.

Additional training is needed to help investigators understand the special challenges that they face when attempting to interview and interrogate vulnerable suspects. This is where the adaptation of some British practices, as well as involving a specially trained supervisor, would be helpful. During the first step of the P.E.A.C.E. interviewing process, the preparation, the investigator must obtain as much information on the suspect as possible from as many sources as possible. If during this step or at any time the investigator comes to realize that the suspect falls into the vulnerable category, they must discuss the issue with the supervisor. During that discussion, tactics and plans are created to deal with the special issues presented by the suspect. This will help protect the suspect's rights as well as ensure that any information obtained is reliable and admissible.

In the United Kingdom, investigators are required to have an "appropriate adult" present when interviewing vulnerable subjects. That person could be the parent or guardian of the suspect or a specially trained advocate who is not employed by the law enforcement agency. According to the United Kingdom's Home Office publication *Guidance for Appropriate Adults*, their role includes:

- To support, advise and assist the detained person, particularly while they are being questioned
- To observe whether the police are acting appropriately, fairly, and with the respect for the rights of the detained person, and to tell them if [they] think they are not

- To assist with communication between the detained person and the police
- To ensure that the detained person understands their rights and that [they] have a role in protecting their rights [21]

While I am pessimistic that any law enforcement agency in the United States would rush to adopt such a policy, they should consider using a third person to assist in one problem area, especially in the case of juvenile suspects, and that is whether or not the suspect understood their Miranda warnings and waived them properly.

Studies have found that even intelligent young people do not fully understand their Miranda rights. Even if they do, they may have difficulties applying them in an interrogation situation. [22] We have discussed how investigators will sometimes, in their zeal to interrogate, manipulate the conversation about Miranda so that even seasoned criminals who know better will waive them and talk. This is where a third person, the specially trained supervisor or even another investigator not connected to the case, can help. They would advise the vulnerable suspect of their Miranda warnings, using a format like that proposed by the International Association of Chiefs of Police (IACP) in their model policy for the interrogation of juveniles. [23] Even if a third person is not used, investigators should follow the IACP policy in both letter and spirit for all vulnerable suspects.

RELIABILITY HEARINGS

One of the roles of judges in a trial is to act as the gatekeeper of the evidence. In motions hearings held before the trial begins, judges determine both whether the evidence being proposed for submission is reliable and if it has any probative value to help the jury in determining guilt or innocence. If the answer to either is no, the judge can keep it out of the trial. They do this all the time in regard to eyewitness identifications, child witnesses, and expert testimony. [24] When it comes to confession evidence, not so much.

Judges will hear arguments from the prosecutor and the defense attorney on whether or not the confession was made voluntarily. Here they dwell on things like the age and mental status of the suspect, the conditions under which they were interrogated, and whether or not they understood their Miranda warnings. In most cases they will not consider the other components of the confession, such as the level of contamination that might have taken place during the interrogation or whether or not the details that were provided by the suspect are actually factual. That they punt over for the jury to decide.

Some argue that determining the reliability of the confession should be left to a jury. If that premise is correct, then the same should apply for eyewitness identification, child witnesses, and the other types of evidence they rule on. Confession evidence is especially problematic though, as once it is before the jury, studies show that they too often accept it in blind faith, no matter how outlandish the confession or the amount or quality of evidence that disproves it. [25]

Properly trained in how false confessions and confession evidence contamination occurs and how investigators are supposed to corroborate such evidence, judges are in a much better position to weed out bad confession evidence, same as they are bad eyewitness identification and other evidence. Unlike juries, they will have probably seen more than one problematic confession or witness statement in their career. Of course, this would not prevent all false or unreliable confessions from reaching a jury, but it would add an extra level of scrutiny, making prosecutors and investigators look even closer at their work before it even gets that far. [26]

INFORMANT AND COOPERATING WITNESS REFORM

The use of informants and cooperating witnesses (CW) will continue to be an important investigative tool. This is especially true when working organized crime and other criminal conspiracy cases in which the only witnesses may be the participants themselves. But as we have seen, the ways and means by which these subjects are created and under which they operate must therefore mean that the information that they provide undergo the utmost scrutiny at every stage of the game. In order for this to work, new rules must be put in place and old ones enforced.

Taken with a Grain of Salt

The inherent danger of informant and cooperating witness information being unreliable must be in the front of the mind of any investigator and prosecutor who uses them in any investigation. The information that they provide must undergo the utmost scrutiny and be thoroughly corroborated before it is used. Interactions between the informant/CW and law enforcement must be meticulously documented, preferably by electronic recordings, and examined for evidence of contamination.

Full Disclosure

All information about the informant/CW's information and their interactions with the investigator and prosecutor should be disclosed to the defense attorney before either trial or the entering of any guilty plea, allowing enough time for the defense attorney to conduct their own review and investigation. In her book *Snitching: Criminal Informants and the Erosion of the Criminal Justice System*,[27] Alexandra Natapoff lists what she believes should be required by the prosecutors to disclose, including:

- the complete criminal history of the informant/CW
- any promises, deals, or other benefits that were made or the informant/CW has received or will receive in the future
- any threats or other inducements that were used to obtain the cooperation of the informant/CW
- all statements, including conflicting statements and recantations made by the informant/CW, dates, times, and locations that they were made, to whom, and who else was present
- any other case in which the informant/CW provided any information or testimony, and any deals or promises that were made or the informant/CW received for that information or testimony
- any other information that might impact on the credibility of the informant[28]

Reliability Hearings

Just like with confession evidence, there should be pretrial hearings held so the judge can hear arguments about the credibility of the informant/CW and the reliability of their information.

Special Jury Instructions

When an informant/CW testifies in court, the jury is supposed to be told about any deals or promises that were made and any benefits that the informant received or will receive in the future. In addition, the judge should tell the jury to be especially cautious when it comes to evaluating the reliability of testimony of someone who receives a benefit for doing so.

Guilty Pleas

The power of the prosecutor over the plea negotiation process needs to be reduced. They should not be allowed to attempt to force pleas with the use of time constraints and threats of increased punishment. All evidence upon which the prosecutor would make any charging decision should be made available to the defendant and their attorney so that they can evaluate it and make a rational decision. Independent arbitrators should be established as a go-between to help ensure that these conditions are met and the process is a fair one. An independent review of the evidence by the arbitrator could also help negate any threats by the prosecutor to seek the death penalty, bring criminal charges against the suspect's family, or seize their assets, especially if the evidence that would allow them to do so was minimal or nonexistent.

Other incentives for an innocent person to plead guilty should be minimized or eliminated. Mandatory minimum sentences should be abolished, along with holding a suspect until trial if they cannot afford bail.

Encourage Research

Research is hard to do if you don't have data, and law enforcement has had a closed-door policy to researchers for decades. When researchers turn to the laboratory to try to replicate what goes on behind those closed doors, law enforcement officials wrinkle their nose at the findings, saying they don't replicate real-life conditions. This was the case when researchers tried to understand how law enforcement eyewitness identification procedures may contribute to eyewitness misidentifications of innocent people, as well as how interrogation practices may contribute to false confessions.

Unlike in the United States, law enforcement agencies in the United Kingdom have had a long working relationship with researchers. Their hand-in-hand corroboration resulted in major reforms not only in interviews and interrogations but also in the entire investigative process. With more law enforcement agencies in the United States now videotaping interrogations in their entirety, researchers have more raw data to work with, but it is not enough. Our law enforcement agencies need to open their doors to the scientists with whom, believe it or not, they have the same goal—the development and implementation of the best investigative processes possible. Researchers not only need access to the investigative process as it is ongoing but also the ability to conduct field experiments that more accurately depict real-world situations. They, like all of us, want to make sure that we get the right guy, the right way.

Sentinel Event Reviews

Like everyone else, law enforcement agencies are much more open to outsiders looking at things that were done right. However, when things go wrong, such as a wrongful conviction, a case that goes unsolved, a near miss (such as when it is discovered before trial that the wrong person was arrested and a wrongful conviction was prevented, as in the Lex Street murders discussed in chapter 5), or a guilty person escapes conviction, law enforcement officials become defensive. This is understandable, as opening the books to scrutiny can lead to civil suits. When an internal review is done, the purpose is mostly to assign blame, usually on one or two people, punish them, and move on. Either way, little is accomplished, nothing is learned, and the root cause of the problem remains. An opportunity learned from a mistake is lost.

We have discussed earlier what it takes for a false confession to result in a wrongful conviction. Not only are there many actors involved within the entire criminal justice system, but the way the many different organizations operate and interact with each other also contributes to the mistake.

This is not a problem that is unique to law enforcement. Medicine, aviation, and other high-risk professions face the same issues. Instead of burrowing their heads in the sand, however, these professions have developed what are called "root cause analysis processes" or "sentinel event reviews."[29] The purpose of these reviews is not to assign blame to a single individual but to identify and correct hidden weaknesses within the system.

For the medical profession, a sentinel event might be a doctor operating on the wrong patient (which apparently happens more than we realize). One review of such an incident uncovered seventeen different errors, from the patient's face being draped so that it was not visible to the doctor to conflicting patient identification stickers being ignored. [30]

Go back to our discussion on the path of a false confession from its creation to its presentation to a jury, resulting in a wrongful conviction. The investigator first had to identify an innocent person as a suspect. Questionable training led them to use coercive interrogation tactics. A supervisor did not pick up on the contamination that occurred during the interrogation and assess its reliability. The prosecutor accepted the confession at face value. Tunnel vision, enhanced by pressure from the outside to bring in a quick closure and/or by overwhelming caseloads, blinded the investigator and prosecutor to alternative suspects and explanations. And a poorly trained and funded defense attorney could not provide an adequate independent investigation and defense. In both examples, there is no one single error that could account for the final outcome. Personal and organizational factors all played a part. [31]

Building on the models already in place in other professions, the criminal justice system should be holding such reviews on a regular basis. Combining the findings from such reviews with the work of researchers, the entire system would benefit, especially if the results were published so others might learn from them. The right guy would be caught and punished more often, and the number of wrongful convictions and other law enforcement sentinel events would decrease.

13

WHAT LIES IN STORE FOR THE FUTURE?

Now it is time for a confession from me, and it will be a true one. At one point or another in my career, I have committed every single sin (with the exception of using third-degree tactics) that I have been critical of in this book. I was no different from the majority of the investigators I've used as examples. All of my initial interrogation training was done on the job, picking up all of the bad habits of my predecessors. When I did receive formal training, I bought it hook, line, and sinker. That a confession would be false was the farthest thing from my mind. And, of course, I was too careful an investigator to ever contaminate a confession.

That changed in 1994 when, using the interrogation tactics I was taught and that would pass muster in any courtroom in the country, I obtained a false confession. Of course, I was not aware of it at the time, and knowing what I know now I believe that, because of the confession, the case would have ended with a conviction or a guilty plea. Fortunately, I did not commit what I have referred to as the fourth step in obtaining a false confession in that I did try to corroborate the information that the suspect provided. Not only could I not corroborate the details, I also discovered that the suspect had an ironclad alibi. I could not prove the confession to be true, so all charges were dropped.

I wanted to know why this happened, so I started reading what the experts were saying about the causes of false confessions. At that time, that was not an easy task. None of the materials that were generally available to law enforcement even mentioned the topic. I had to seek out the academics such as Saul Kassin and Richard Leo, whose work, along with others', is quoted extensively in this book. I began to read case studies of other false confessions, and I found that they paralleled my case in many ways.

I also learned about tunnel vision. To this point, the only time the term had been used in my training was in talking about how it occurs literally in police shootings, when the vision of the officer involved in a gunfight narrows onto the suspect, causing them to miss other potential threats from outside that field of view. I learned how, in the psychological sense, it could adversely impact investigations, and saw how in my case I, my supervisors, the prosecutors, and even the defense attorney fell under its spell.

Having been to and presented at numerous classes and seminars, I found that though people like to hear about success stories, what they seem to learn most from is other people's mistakes. I took the lessons I learned (and am still learning) and incorporated them into training seminars that I presented to other law enforcement officers, prosecutors, defense attorneys, and law students. And I began to advocate for reforms.

Many of my colleagues were receptive to what I had to say. Others were not so open. When, as a homicide detective, I openly advocated for my department to begin videotaping interrogations in their entirety, my nickname became Benedict Trainum. When during the course of my job I found evidence that led to the exoneration of a wrongfully convicted man, I was told by some investigators to stay away from their case files. Once, after I testified in front of the Maryland state legislature in support of videotaping, I was told that members of the Fraternal Order of Police discussed having my membership revoked.

Though they may not believe it, I understand (though do not agree with) why many of those in law enforcement feel that way. Investigations are hard work, and management does not always support the time investments necessary to conduct quality investigations. Lack of resources, high caseloads, and pressure by upper management to close cases by any means possible in order to create the desired statistics take its toll. Why would anyone welcome reform if that reform means taking away old tools that seemed to work well, or exposing the investigator to additional scrutiny that could lead to criticism of their work? All of that, and the fact that nobody likes to admit that they made a mistake.

This does not mean that investigators are bad, just human. Even the most incompetent ones I have known don't set out to arrest and convict the wrong person on purpose. They want to get it right. They want to build quality cases. They just don't have the right tools, training, and mindset when it comes to obtaining accurate, reliable, and admissible confessions and statements.

REFORM COMES BECAUSE OF THE PUBLIC

As we discussed in the last chapter, reform does not come easy, especially in the ultraconservative and paramilitaristic world of law enforcement. One thing I have learned in my career in law enforcement is that reform usually does not come from within. More often than not, change results from scandal or public embarrassment and the resulting public outcry. The advent of the use of DNA testing by law enforcement agencies, which has resulted in an ever-increasing number of exonerations of those wrongfully convicted, has focused the attention of the public and legislatures on not only problematic interrogation practices but also other serious problems within the workings of the criminal justice system.

Creation of the Innocence Project

DNA-based exonerations also helped to give birth to the Innocence Project in 1992. The project was the brainchild of Barry C. Scheck and Peter J. Neufeld, who ran it out of the Benjamin N. Cardozo School of Law at Yeshiva University. In the beginning, the Innocence Project focused on using DNA testing to exonerate the wrongfully convicted. The project expanded to become a national litigation and public policy organization focused on identifying the causes of wrongful convictions and reforming the criminal justice system.[1] Since then, other state- and university-based Innocence Projects and similar organizations have been created both in the United States and internationally. Many have gone beyond working only on cases in which DNA evidence was available. News stories of exonerations of wrongful convictions are becoming almost commonplace events.

SCANDALS ABOUND

The media has done much to contribute to the public's awareness of false confessions and wrongful convictions, and they have had no shortage of stories with which to work. In 1999, the *Chicago Tribune* published a five-part series exposing "nearly 400 cases where prosecutors obtained homicide convictions by committing the most unforgivable kinds of deception," such as hiding evidence that hurt their chances for convictions and allowing knowingly deceptive witnesses to testify.[2] Follow-ups to the original series continued over the years. In 2001, one story segment was dedicated to the questionable interrogation tactics of investigators (to include third-degree tactics) and the number of confession cases that were dismissed after arrest, resulted in acquittals, and/or were later confirmed to be false.[3]

More recently, in New York, the reputation of famed homicide detective Louis Scarcella took a fall. Scarcella and his partner were known for solving crimes and getting confessions when no one else could.[4] Years later, Scarcella's work began to undergo increased scrutiny as more and more wrongful convictions were uncovered. Among the allegations of improper interrogation tactics resulting in false confessions and manipulating witness evidence, it was discovered that Scarcella used the same crack addict informant as a witness in six of his murder cases. It turned out that the crack addict's testimony usually contradicted the testimony of other witnesses as well as the physical evidence. The result is that New York City has paid out millions of dollars in lawsuits to the victims of Scarcella's investigations, and the Brooklyn District Attorney's Office is reviewing an additional seventy cases of his.[5]

These are only two examples. Television programs such as CBS's *60 Minutes*, *48 Hours*, and others are more and more frequently featuring wrongful or questionable conviction cases. The idea that someone could falsely confess to a crime that they did not commit is gradually becoming a principle that is easier for the public to accept.

The Move to Pop Culture

The wrongful conviction movement has also entered pop culture, to where the term has become a household word. In 2010 and 2013, Barry Scheck, founder of the Innocence Project, played himself in two episodes of CBS's legal drama series *The Good Wife*.[6] The Showtime series *Rectify*, getting ready to enter its fourth season, is the fictitious story of Daniel Holden, who spent nineteen years on death row after falsely confessing to the murder of his girlfriend only to be released once new DNA testing cast doubt on his conviction.[7] The NPR podcast *Serial*,[8] which in 2014 examined the conviction of Adnan Syed for the 1999 murder of his ex-girlfriend, received national acclaim and has an almost cultlike following (full disclosure: I appeared as the featured guest on Episode Eight). The same is true for the 2015 Netflix series *Making a Murderer*, part of which highlighted the interrogation and subsequent confession of sixteen-year-old Brendon Dassey.[9] Highly popular author John Grisham broke from his norm of writing fictitious legal thrillers to write *The Innocent Man: Murder and Injustice in a Small Town*.[10] The book chronicles the wrongful convictions of Dennis Fritz and Ron Williamson for a 1982 murder in Ada, Oklahoma. And the list goes on and on.

The Backlash

As a result of the increased attention to the phenomenon of false confessions and wrongful convictions, law enforcement agencies and the criminal justice system in general have been on the receiving end of some backlash. The backlash is somewhat similar to that created by forensic science crime dramas such as CBS's *CSI: Crime Scene Investigation*. Called "The CSI Effect," the public expected law enforcement to be able to find and present definitive forensic evidence in every case.[11] As relates to interrogations, the public is becoming more skeptical of the investigator's word and expects more and more independent corroboration. This is beginning to hold true for confession evidence as well. While a large number of people still have trouble wrapping their head around the fact that someone might confess to a crime they didn't commit, the ones that do understand that it is possible are making their voices heard. An example of this occurred in the 2015 trial of Pedro Hernandez, charged with the 1979 murder of Etan Patz.

THE CONFESSION OF PEDRO HERNANDEZ

On Friday, May 27, 1979, six-year-old Etan Patz disappeared from the SoHo area of Manhattan soon after leaving his home for school. [12] The massive effort to find him by both the police and the general public ushered in a "new era in the country, marked by children's faces on milk cartons and made-for-television dramas about kidnapped children." [13] Despite an extensive investigation and many search efforts, Etan was not found.

As part of his campaign for Manhattan District Attorney in 2009, Cyrus Vance Jr. vowed to reopen the investigation into Patz's disappearance. After his election, Vance assigned a new team of prosecutors to review the case. [14]

On May 24, 2012, the New York Police Commissioner announced that Pedro Hernandez, an employee of a local bodega at the time, confessed to murdering Patz. [15] According to his attorney, Hernandez, who had a low IQ and suffered from mental illness, first confessed after a six-hour interrogation. For some reason, the investigators though it was a good idea not to videotape the entire interrogation, but only the final confession. [16]

The decision not to videotape the interrogation of an extremely vulnerable suspect in such a high-profile case is even harder to understand in light of the recommendations of the New York State Justice Task Force that all custodial interrogations be videotaped, made only four months before. [17] Of course, the investigators testified that Hernandez was not "in custody" at the time of the interrogation; however, their decision not to take the extra step came back to bite them.

The case went to trial, and the confession was presented to the jury. After one hundred hours of deliberation, the judge in the case was forced to declare a mistrial because one juror, Adam Sirois, didn't trust the confession. [18]

In an interview with Ben Feuerherd of the *New York Post*, Sirois explained that, for him, "the whole case kind of hinges on mental health, which factors into what I think are false confessions—or at least the likelihood of false confessions being made by [Hernandez]." [19] If the investigators had videotaped the entire interrogation, what Sirois would have seen might have erased any doubts about the reliability of the confession. Or it may have caused the other eleven jurors to vote not guilty.

Either way, videotaping the interrogation in its entirety would have made an analysis of the tactics possible and resulted in jurors being able to make an informed opinion as to its reliability. It is cases like this that catch the attention of policymakers and politicians, cases that are the result of the public demanding more of law enforcement than the status quo.

THE WRONGFUL-CONVICTION MOVEMENT AND INDIVIDUAL INVESTIGATORS

Cops are not immune to the influences of pop culture, and the resulting impact that I have seen, especially with younger investigators, encourages me. Above I talked about how after I found evidence that helped to exonerate an innocent man, some investigators told me to stay away from their cases. Across the board, these were the old-timers. Several of the younger investigators came up and offered their congratulations, saying that what I did actually made the department look good. I am being asked more and more frequently to present to law enforcement agencies on avoiding false confessions and the proper evaluation of confession evidence. Often I am approached afterward by younger investigators who are skeptical of the teachings of the Reid Institute and others. I believe that because of their increased exposure to the phenomena of false confessions through pop culture, they are not as willing to, as they say, drink the Kool-Aid as they were in the past. They want to do it right, to conduct quality interviews, and obtain reliable information—they just are not being given the tools. But they are open to change, and based on what you are about to read, hopefully that change is coming sooner rather than later.

THE GOVERNMENT'S RESPONSE TO WRONGFUL CONVICTIONS

Task Forces and Commissions

The federal government has responded to the increasing number of confirmed wrongful convictions, exposés, and scandals in various ways.

Task forces and commissions have been created, such the New York State Justice Task Force mentioned above and the Florida Innocence Commission mentioned in chapter 12. Though not part of the government, in 2013 the International Association of Chiefs of Police, in conjunction with the US Department of Justice, Office of Justice Programs, held their own National Summit on Wrongful Convictions.[20] These groups were formed to identify problems and best practices, some of which are implemented and others ignored.

National Institute of Justice's Sentinel Events Initiative

As discussed in the last chapter, the National Institute of Justice has an ongoing Sentinel Events Initiative. The purpose behind the initiative is to explore the feasibility of conducting sentinel events reviews of investigative failures, such as wrongful convictions. Modeled after similar reviews that are routine in the medical, aviation, and other high-risk fields, the reviews would allow the criminal justice system to learn from its mistakes. The goal is to increase the overall reliability of the criminal justice process and improve the public's confidence in the system.[21] Pilot programs are underway, and I have a great deal of hope in the impact that such reviews will have on preventing false confessions and wrongful convictions.

Conviction Integrity Units

A fairly recent development has been the creation of Conviction Integrity Units (CIU), such as the one formed in 2007 within the Dallas County District Attorney's Office by then District Attorney Craig Watkins.[22] Though run out of the prosecutor's office, the unit is headed by a defense attorney and works in cooperation with the local public defender's service and other defense attorneys.[23] It has not only successfully identified and exonerated several of the wrongfully convicted in that state but also has gone on to prosecute five defendants who they were able to identify through their work as the real perpetrators. The Dallas CIU has also worked closely with the Dallas Police Department to improve their eyewitness identification and interrogation procedures.[24]

Following the lead of Dallas, other prosecutor's offices have created their own Conviction Integrity Units. The Brooklyn Conviction Review

Unit in New York, the unit reviewing the cases of retired Detective Louis Scarcella (discussed above), has had ten exonerations in 2014.[25] But the units are not without their skeptics, who have described "particular units . . . as mere window dressing, or public relation ploys."[26]

In her article titled "Wrongful Convictions: Can Prosecutors Reform Themselves?" Hella Winston discussed problems with some units that were, unlike the Dallas model, run solely by prosecutors. They described the process of working with the units as more adversarial than truth finding. In one Manhattan case, a defense attorney identified witnesses to whom the true killer confessed. The attorney turned over the names of the witnesses to the Manhattan District Attorney's CIU, who treated them "horribly, like defendants."[27] Winston writes that in order for CIU's to be truly effective in identifying wrongful convictions and exonerating the innocent, they should be run independently of the offices that put them in jail in the first place.[28]

The North Carolina Innocence Inquiry Commission

One organization that fits that criteria is the North Carolina Innocence Inquiry Commission (NCIIC). Created in 2006, the commission is an eight-member panel consisting of a Superior Court judge, a prosecutor, a defense attorney, a victim's advocate, a member of the general public, a sheriff, and two discretionary members chosen by the Chief Justice of the North Carolina Supreme Court. The commission operates outside of the normal appeals process of the court system.[29]

Once the commission receives a claim of a wrongful conviction, the case undergoes a rigorous review and reinvestigation run by an arm of the Inquiry itself. The findings of the investigation are forwarded to the commission, which review the information. If the commission determines that there is "sufficient evidence of factual innocence to merit judicial review," the case is then heard by a three-judge panel. The judges hear the case, and if they unanimously agree that there is "clear and convincing evidence" of the subject's innocence, they are declared to be "factually innocent" and are released from prison.[30]

As with any human endeavor, there are pros and cons to both Conviction Integrity Units and the North Carolina Innocence Inquiry Commission. In general, they are both positive moves in an attempt to identify and correct wrongs in ways that had not been possible due to procedural rules that often tied the hands of the courts.

A "SCIENTIFIC" APPROACH TO INTERROGATION?

One of the darkest episodes in the history of the United States may have spurred major reform in the way interrogations will be conducted by law enforcement in the future.

During the "War on Terror," the United States ignored the lessons of history and its own moral compass and resorted to both physical and psychological torture to try to extract information from suspected terrorists. The results were that the ends did not justify the means. Not only was the use of such tactics reprehensible, the information that was secured was essentially useless.[31]

In 2006, the Intelligence Science Board[32] released a report criticizing the interrogation techniques used by American law enforcement agencies, the military, and intelligence agencies. The report said that the interrogation tactics were "mostly devoid of any scientific validity."[33] Tactics that were being used were based only on the personal "experience of investigators who train others."[34]

When President Obama took torture off the table as an acceptable means of extracting information from terrorist suspects, the intelligence community had to turn to other tactics. In 2010, the High Value Detainee Interrogation Group (HIG) was formed. The HIG has three missions: to interrogate terrorists to "assess the effectiveness of current interrogation practices and to develop novel, scientific-based methods,"[35] and to coordinate the training of those new methods across the US government,[36] much like what happened in the United Kingdom when the P.E.A.C.E. process was created (discussed in chapter 11).

Teaming up with universities around the country, the HIG research team has been studying the current research, conducting their own scientific experiments, interviewing interrogators, and reviewing videotapes of their work. As new interview and interrogation tactics are developed, the team compares them with the tactics that are currently being used by intelligence organizations, the military, and law enforcement. The team is working closely with federal and military law enforcement to evaluate the effectiveness of their new, scientifically based methods of interrogation.[37]

The response by those undergoing the new training has been positive, with many of the participants commenting on the effectiveness of the new techniques and asking why they had not been taught them before. [38]

All of the HIG team's research undergoes peer review at both the university level and by the FBI. All of their findings are available to the public on their website, www.interrogationresearch.org. [39]

In regard to the work of the HIG research group and its future impact on law enforcement interrogation practices, Tim Janowick, chief of police and advisory board member of the International Law Enforcement Educators and Trainers Association, said:

> In an era of law enforcement when jailed defendants are released amid speculation about the validity of their confessions and the interrogation techniques used to obtain them, the evidence-based research and resulting practices from the HIG will impact policing for generations to come by driving significant changes to interview and interrogation processes. [40]

This could be the death knell of current American interrogation practices as we know them.

THE SWAN SONG OF DANIAL WILLIAMS? PETITION FOR AN ABSOLUTE PARDON BASED ON INNOCENCE

On November 10, 2005, attorneys for Danial Williams and two of his three codefendants, Joe Dick and Derek Tice, filed a petition for absolute pardons based their innocence with the governor of Virginia, Tim Kaine. The attorneys also asked for a pardon for Williams's third codefendant, Eric Wilson. Wilson had only been convicted of rape, had served his sentence, and was already released from prison. The 103-page document filed by the attorneys was a detailed and overwhelming argument for the innocence of all three. Additionally, the petition was supported by a bipartisan group that included "several former Attorney Generals of the Commonwealth of Virginia; 31 former FBI Special Agents; a past president of the Virginia Bar Association, prominent state and federal law enforcement officers, former judges and prosecutors from around the country; and 13 jurors"[41] who had previously voted to convict in two of the subject's cases. Even the Reid Institute uses the Norfolk Four case as a case study highlighting how improper interrogation techniques can result in false confessions.[42]

After almost four years spent investigating and considering the petitions, on August 6, 2009, Governor Kaine denied Williams's and the others' request, instead granting them conditional pardons. This permitted Williams, Dick, and Tice to be released from prison, but they remained convicted sex offenders on parole. In response to the decision, George Kendall, the attorney who represented Joe Dick in the petition process, said:

> The Governor's decision is illogical. He agrees that there was absolutely no physical trace at the crime scene of any of the innocent sailors and that their conflicting confessions create substance doubt. His pardon statement today never asserts that the Norfolk Four were involved in this terrible crime in any way. Instead, all he has said is that our clients have failed to conclusively prove that they are innocent.[43]

They "failed conclusively to prove that they are innocent." In the eyes of Governor Kaine, confessions that fail to pass even the most basic tests of reliability and were obtained using highly coercive tactics, combined with the DNA and a corroborated confession from the real killer, are not conclusive enough. Yet another example that the power of the words "I did it" have even in light of overwhelming evidence to the contrary and especially when combined with future political aspirations and a desire not to be seen as soft on crime.

HOPE FOR THE FUTURE?

Danial Williams is home, but still a prisoner. As a convicted murderer and registered sex offender on parole, his movements are severely restricted and job possibilities limited. Any violation of the conditions of his release, no matter how slight, could result in his immediate reimprisonment. Williams's nightmare is far from over, but neither is the battle.

On September 14, 2009, just one month after Governor Kaine's refusal to declare Williams and the others innocent, the case against Derek Tice was overturned by the US District Court for the Eastern District of Virginia. The decision was based on two failures of Tice's original attorney: first, the failure to introduce a letter in which Omar Ballard admitted to killing Michelle Bosko, and second, the failure to introduce expert testimony to show that the crime was committed by only one person.[44] The case went back to the Virginia prosecutors to determine if they were going to retry Tice.

On August 4, 2010, almost a year to the day of Governor Kaine's decision, all charges against Tice were dismissed after the prosecutor determined that they did not have sufficient evidence against Tice to proceed. Tice was no longer a convicted murderer and sex offender, and he is no longer under the restrictions placed on him by Governor Kaine's conditional pardon.[45]

On May 10, 2010, following a federal grand jury investigation, Robert Glenn Ford, the detective who was ultimately responsible for obtaining the confessions from Williams and the others, was indicted for extortion. During his career as a detective, Ford would accept money from inmates and in return tell judges and prosecutors that they had provided valuable information in homicide investigations. The inmate would then get a reduced sentence for his nonexistent cooperation.[46] Ford was convicted and sentenced to twelve-and-a-half years in prison.[47]

EPILOGUE

Despite his release from prison, Williams's court battles are not over. In April 2015, he and Joe Dick had a hearing in federal court in Richmond, Virginia, in their ongoing quest to overturn their wrongful convictions. The judge's decision has yet to be announced at the time this book went to press. But the main takeaway from Williams's story, actually from this entire book, is that what happened to Williams and his codefendants can happen to you or ones close to you. It doesn't have to be a murder case, such as the scenario that I laid out in the first part of the introduction involving the fictitious murder of one of your neighbors. It could be any kind of criminal wrongdoing in which law enforcement mistakenly latches onto you as a suspect. And you don't have to necessarily confess yourself. As you have seen, the investigators will be using the same interrogation tactics to induce others to get them to say what the investigators believe to be true about you. Even if you are not convicted (or convinced to plead guilty), time and money is lost, and your reputation damaged.

Change and reform begins with you. As evidenced in the 2015 public responses to police shootings of unarmed African American men, the criminal justice system (and law enforcement agencies in particular) will respond to adverse public opinion. One good thing remains: As resistant as law enforcement agencies are to change, deep down, most individual investigators want to get it right. They need the right tools, the right training, and the right mindset. With your voice, and the reforms suggested in chapter 12, they can get it. Then we can all sleep better.

NOTES

INTRODUCTION

1. Peter Brooks, *Troubling Confessions: Speaking Guilt in Law and Literature* (Chicago: The University of Chicago Press, 2000), 4.

2. Tom Wells and Richard A. Leo, *The Wrong Guys: Murder, False Confessions, and the Norfolk Four* (New York: The New Press, 2008).

3. http://www.norfolk4.com.

1. HISTORY

1. Neil Hanson, *The Great Fire of London: In That Apocalyptic Year, 1666* (Hoboken: John Wiley & Sons, 2002).

2. John H. Langbein, *Torture and the Law of Proof: Europe and England in the Ancien Régime* (Chicago: University of Chicago Press, 2006), 3.

3. Aaron Kirschenbaum, *Self-Incrimination in Jewish Law* (New York: The Burning Bush Press, 1970), 19.

4. George C. Thomas III and Richard A. Leo, *Confessions of Guilt: From Torture to Miranda and Beyond* (Oxford: Oxford University Press, 2012), 20.

5. Ibid.

6. Ibid.

7. James Q. Whitman, *The Origins of Reasonable Doubt: Theological Roots of the Criminal Trial* (New Haven: Yale University Press, 2008), 59–66.

8. Ibid., 56–60.

9. Ibid., 61.

10. Ibid., 61–62.

11. Sadakat Kadri, *The Trial: A History from Socrates to O. J. Simpson* (London: Harper Perennial, 2006), 30.

12. Whitman, *The Origins of Reasonable Doubt*, 65.

13. Ibid., 3–4.

14. Ibid., 100.

15. Ibid.

16. Langbein, *Torture and the Law of Proof*, 12–14.

17. Kelly D. Harrison, *Forensic Interviewing for Law Enforcement* (Xlibris Corporation, 2013), 18.

18. Robert Jones, "A Brief History of the Inquisition," 12, accessed December 17, 2015, http://www.ironmaidencommentary.com/?url=album10_xfactor/inquisition&lang=eng&link=albums.

19. Langbein, *Torture and the Law of Proof*, 9.

20. Thomas and Leo, *Confessions of Guilt*, 22–23.

21. Langbein, *Torture and the Law of Proof*, 74–75.

22. Ibid., 75–76.

23. Ibid., 134.

24. Thomas and Leo, *Confessions of Guilt*, 40.

25. Ibid., 47.

26. Ibid., 48.

27. Ibid., 56–66.

28. Ibid., 76.

29. Gary Potter, *The History of Policing in the United States* (Richmond, EKU Police Studies), accessed December 2, 2015, http://plsonline.eku.edu/insidelook/history-policing-united-states-part-1.

30. Ibid., 5.

31. Thomas and Leo, *Confessions of Guilt*, 124.

32. Ibid., 110.

33. Ibid., 77.

34. Ibid., 122.

35. G. Daniel Lassiter, ed., *Interrogations, Confessions, and Entrapment* (New York: Springer, 2006), 52–53.

36. Emanuel H. Lavine, *The Third Degree* (Garden City: The Vanguard Press, Inc., 1930).

37. William Goldman, *Marathon Man*, director John Schlesinger (1976, Paramount Pictures).

38. Ibid., 61–65.

39. Jerome H. Skolnick and James J. Fyfe, *Above the Law: Police and the Excessive Use of Force* (New York: The Free Press, 1993), 47.

40. Lassiter, *Interrogations, Confessions, and Entrapment*, 52–53.

41. Cornelius W. Willemse, *Behind the Green Lights* (New York: Alfred A. Knopf, 1931).

42. Ibid., 354.

43. James Gruen, *Behind the Green Lights*, director Christy Cabanne (1935, Mascot Pictures).

44. Scott Darling and Charles G. Booth, *Behind Green Lights*, director, Otto Brower (1946, Twentieth Century Fox Studios).

45. Skolnick and Fyfe, *Above the Law*, 46.

46. *Brown v. Mississippi*, 297 U.S. 278 (1936).

47. Thomas and Leo, *Confessions of Guilt*, 133.

48. Ibid., 134.

49. Charles E. Silberman, *Criminal Violence, Criminal Justice* (New York: Vintage Books, Random House, 1980), 231.

50. Amina A. Memon, Aldert Vrij, and Ray Bull, *Psychology and Law: Truthfulness, Accuracy, and Credibility, Second Edition* (Chichester: John Wiley & Sons, 2003), 72.

51. Richard A. Leo, *Police Interrogation and American Justice* (Cambridge: Harvard University Press, 2008), 60.

52. Ibid., 59.

53. Skolnick and Fyfe, *Above the Law*, 45.

54. Lassiter, *Interrogations, Confessions, and Entrapment*, 53.

55. Skolnick and Fyfe, *Above the Law*, 44.

56. Leo, *Police Interrogation and American Justice*, 59.

57. Edwin Montefiore Borchard, *Convicting the Innocent: Sixty-Five Actual Errors of Criminal Justice* (Garden City: Garden City Publishing Co., 1932).

58. Harry Soderman and John J. O'Connell, *Modern Criminal Investigation* (New York: Funk & Wagnall Co., 1935).

59. Ibid., 5.

60. Ibid., 6.

61. W. R. Kidd, *Police Interrogation* (New York: R. V. Basuino, 1940), 6–7.

62. August Vollmer, foreword to *Police Interrogation*, v.

63. Kidd, *Police Interrogation*, 45–46.

64. Ibid., 100.

65. Ibid., 103–33.

66. Ibid., 125.

67. Ibid., 169.

68. Ibid., 92–97.

69. Ibid., 64–65.

70. Ken Alder, *The Lie Detectors: The History of an American Obsession* (Lincoln: University of Nebraska Press, 2007), 250.

71. Ibid.

72. Ibid., 125.

73. Robert McG. Thomas, Jr., "Fred Inbau, 89, Criminologist Who Perfected Interrogation," *New York Times*, May 28, 1998, accessed December 17, 2015, http://www.nytimes.com/1998/05/28/us/fred-inbau-89-criminologist-who-per-fected-interrogation.html.

74. Fred E. Inbau, *Lie Detection and Criminal Investigation, Second Edition* (Baltimore: Williams & Willkins Company, 1948), 96.

75. Ibid., 148–49.

76. Peter Maas, *Serpico* (New York: HarperCollins Publishers, Inc., 2005), 93–94.

77. *Miranda v. Arizona*, 384 U.S. 436.

78. Ibid.

79. Ibid.

80. Ibid.

81. Ibid.

82. Ibid.

83. Leo, *Police Interrogation and American Justice*, 5.

84. Joseph Wambauch, *The Blooding* (New York: Perigord Press, 1989).

85. Ibid.

86. *North Carolina v. Alford*, 400 U.S. 25 (1970).

87. Fred E. Inbau, John E. Reid, and Joseph P. Buckley, *Criminal Interrogation and Confessions, Third Edition* (Baltimore: Williams & Wilkins, 1986).

2. DO WE EVEN HAVE A PROBLEM?

1. Biography of Paul Cassell, last accessed December 14, 2015, https://faculty.utah.edu/u0031056-PAUL_G._CASSELL/biography/index.hml.

2. Paul G. Cassell, "Protecting the Innocent from False Confessions and Lost Confessions—And from Miranda," *Journal of Criminal Law and Criminology* 88, no. 2 (1998): 497–556.

3. Ibid., 507.

4. Paul G. Cassell and Bret S. Hayman, "Police Interrogation in the 1990's: An Empirical Study of the Effects of *Miranda*," *UCLA Law Review* 839 (1996): 868.

5. Cassell, "Protecting the Innocent," 532.

6. Ibid., 519–20.

7. Ibid., 518.

8. Ibid., 524–38.

9. Ibid., 531.

10. Ibid.

11. Ibid., 524.

12. US Department of Justice Office of Legal Policy, "Report to the Attorney General on the Law of Pre-Trial Interrogation: Truth in Criminal Justice Report No. 1," 1986, 57–58.

13. Debbie Cenziper, "Prosecutors Build Murder Cases on Disputed Shaken Baby Syndrome Diagnosis," *Washington Post*, March 20, 2015, accessed June 27, 2015, http://www.washingtonpost.com/graphics/investigations/shaken-baby-syndrome.

14. Edwin Montefiore Borchard, *Convicting the Innocent: Sixty-Five Actual Errors of Criminal Justice* (Garden City: Garden City Publishing Co., 1932).

15. Ibid.

16. "Bernard Ward," The National Registry of Exonerations, accessed June 27, 2015, https://www.law.umich.edu/special/exoneration/Pages/casedetail.aspx?caseid=4206.

17. Antonne M. Jones, *Equal Verdicts* (Chester, VA: Clear Vision Publishing, 2011).

18. Ibid., 9–16.

19. Ibid., 23–24.

20. Ibid., 24–25.

21. Ibid., 33–40.

22. Ibid., 91.

23. Ibid., 124–25.

24. Jacqueline Soteropoulos, "Lex St. Survivor Apologizes for Earlier Account. She Said Drugs Made Her Misidentify the Original Four Defendants as the Shooters Who Killed 7 People," Philly.com, March 2, 2004, http://articles.philly.com/2004-03-02/news/25385456_1_gunmen-star-witness-gunman.

25. "% Exonerations by Contributing Factor," The National Registry of Exonerations, accessed December 15, 2015, http://www.law.umich.edu/special/exoneration/Pages/ExonerationsContribFactorsByCrime.aspx.

26. Saul M. Kassin, Steven A. Drizin, Thomas Grisso, Gisli H. Gudjonsson, Richard A. Leo, and Allison D. Redlich, "Police-Induced Confessions: Risk Factors and Recommendations," *Law and Human Behavior* 34 (2010): 3–38, http://web.williams.edu/Psychology/Faculty/Kassin/files/White Paper online (09).pdf.

27. Ibid., 9.

28. Michael A. Fletcher and Steven Mufson, "GM's Culture Is Blamed in Safety Crisis," *Washington Post*, March 31, 2014.

29. *Colorado v. Connelly*, 479 U.S. 157 (1986), 182.

30. Lindsey Devers, "Plea and Charge Bargaining: Research Summary," US Department of Justice Bureau of Justice Assistance, 2011, 1.

31. Saul M. Kassin, Sara C. Appleby, and Jennifer Torkildson-Perillo, "Interviewing Suspects: Practice, Science, and Future Directions," *Legal and Criminological Psychology* 15 (2010): 42.

32. Edwin Montefiore Borchard, *Convicting the Innocent; Sixty-Five Actual Errors of Criminal Justice* (Garden City: Garden City Publishing Co., 1932).

33. Fred E. Inbau, John E. Reid, Joseph P. Buckley, and Brian C. Jayne, *Criminal Interrogation and Confessions, Fifth Edition* (Burlington: Jones and Bartlett Learning, 2013), 337.

3. TYPES OF CONFESSIONS AND STATEMENTS

1. Saul M. Kassin, Steven A. Drizin, Thomas Grisso, Gisli H. Gudjonsson, Richard A. Leo, and Allison D. Redlich, "Police-Induced Confessions: Risk Factors and Recommendations," *Law and Human Behavior* 34 (2009): 12–13, http://web.williams.edu/Psychology/Faculty/Kassin/files/ White%20Paper%20online%20(09).pdf.

2. Sari Horwitz and Michael Ruane, *Sniper: Inside the Hunt for the Killers Who Terrorized the Nation* (New York: Ballantine Books, 2004).

3. Ibid.

4. Julia Shaw and Stephen Porter, "Constructing Rich False Memories of Committing Crime," *Association for Psychological Science* 1, no. 11 (2015), https://people.ok.ubc.ca/stporter/Welcome_files/Psychological%20Science-2015-Shaw-0956797614562862.pdf.

5. Tom Wells and Richard A. Leo, *The Wrong Guys: Murder, False Confessions, and the Norfolk Four* (New York: The New Press, 2008), 62.

6. Wells and Leo, *The Wrong Guys*, 68.

4. TAKING THE FIRST STEPS

1. Tom Wells and Richard A. Leo, *The Wrong Guys: Murder, False Confessions, and the Norfolk Four* (New York: The New Press, 2008).

2. Edward Connors, Thomas Lundregan, Neal Miller, and Tom McEwen, "Convicted by Juries, Exonerated by Science: Case Studies in the Use of DNA Evidence to Establish Innocence After Trial," US Department of Justice Office of Justice Programs, National Institute of Justice, June 1996.

3. Ibid., 20–21.

4. Jack G. Handler, *Ballentine's Law Dictionary* (Albany: Delmar, 1994), 431.

5. Wells and Leo, *The Wrong Guys*, 14.

6. Ibid.

7. Fred E. Inbau, John E. Reid, Joseph P. Buckley, and Brian C. Jayne, *Criminal Interrogation and Confessions, Fifth Edition* (Burlington: Jones and Bartlett Learning, 2013), 35.

8. Warren D. Holmes, *Criminal Interrogation: A Modern Format for Interrogating Criminal Suspects Based on the Intellectual Approach* (Springfield, Charles C. Thomas, Ltd., 2002), 4.

9. Ibid.

10. National Centre for Policing Excellence, *Practice Advice on Core Investigative Doctrine* (Centrix, 2005).

11. D. Kim Rossmo, *Criminal Investigative Failures* (Boca Raton: CRC Press, Taylor & Francis Group, 2009), 4.

12. Ibid.

13. Gregg O. McCrary, "Review and Analysis of the Norfolk 4 Investigation," *Behavioral Criminology International*, March 1, 2015, 13.

14. FPT Heads of Prosecutions Committee Working Group, "Report on the Prevention of Miscarriages of Justice," Department of Justice, Canada, September 2004, 3.

15. John A. Eterno and Eli B. Silverman, *The Crime Numbers Game: Management by Manipulation* (Boca Raton: CRC Press, Taylor & Francis Group, 2012), 57–80.

16. Terrence McCoy, "*The First 48* Makes Millions Off Imprisoning Innocents," *Miami New Times*, January 16, 2014, http://www.miaminewtimes.com/news/the-first-48-makes-millions-off-imprisoning-innocents-6394571.

17. C. Ronald Huff, Arye Rattner, and Edward Sagarin, *Convicted But Innocent: Wrongful Conviction and Public Policy* (Thousand Oaks: SAGE Publications, 1996), 137.

18. Inbau, Reid, Buckley, and Jayne, *Criminal Interrogation and Confessions, Fifth Edition*.

19. Nathan J. Gordon and William L. Fleisher, *Effective Interviewing & Interrogation Techniques, Second Edition* (Amsterdam: Academic Press, 2006).

20. Inbau, Reid, Buckley, and Jayne, *Criminal Interrogation, Fifth Edition*, 105.

21. Ibid., 111–17.

22. Ibid., 119.

23. Gerald I. Nierenberg and Henry H. Calero, *How to Read a Person Like a Book* (New York: Simon & Schuster, 1973).

24. Timothy Roland Levine, David Daniel Clare, J. Peter Blair, Steve McCornack, Kelly Morrison, and Hee Sun Park, "Expertise in Deception Detection

Involves Actively Prompting Diagnostic Information Rather Than Passive Behavioral Observation," *Human Communication Research* 40 (2014): 422–62.

25. Aldert Vrij, Christian A. Meissner, and Saul M. Kassin, "Problems in
Expert Deception Detection and the Risk of False Confessions: No Proof to the
Contrary," *Psychology, Crime & Law* 21 (2015): 901.

26. Alan Hirsch, "Going to the Source: The 'New' Reid Method and False
Confessions," *Ohio State Journal of Criminal Law* 11 (2013): 819.

27. Inbau, Reid, Buckley, and Jayne, *Criminal Interrogation, Fifth Edition*,
144–52.

28. Ibid., 149–50.

29. IACP National Law Enforcement Policy Center, "Interviewing and Interrogating Juveniles: Concepts and Issues Paper," International Association of
Chiefs of Police, 2013.

30. David Simon, *Homicide: A Year on the Killing Streets* (New York: Henry
Holt and Co., 2001), 215.

31. Wells and Leo, *The Wrong Guys*, 15.

32. Ibid., 16.

5. GOOD POLICE WORK OR COERCION?

1. *Oregon v. Mathiason*, 429 U.S. 492 (1977).

2. Fred E. Inbau, John E. Reid, Joseph P. Buckley, and Brian C. Jayne,
Criminal Interrogation and Confessions, Fifth Edition (Burlington: Jones and
Bartlett Learning, 2013), xiv.

3. *The Wire*, "More with Less," directed by Joe Chappelle, written by David
Simon, HBO, January 6, 2008.

4. Inbau, Reid, Buckley, and Jayne, *Criminal Interrogation, Fifth Edition*.

5. Ibid., 300.

6. Ibid., 319.

7. *The Reid Technique of Interviewing and Interrogation (workbook)* (Chicago: John E. Reid & Associates, Inc., 2007), 5.

8. Telephone interview with Reid student Gary David.

9. "99% of Reid Technique Confessions Admitted," John E. Reid & Associates, Inc., accessed October 30, 2015, https://www.reid.com/r_about.html.

10. David L. Strauss, *Barbarous Souls* (Evanston, IL: Northwestern University Press, 2010), 37.

11. Ibid.

12. "Darrel Parker," The National Registry of Exonerations, accessed October
24, 2015, https://www.law.umich.edu/special/exoneration/Pages/casedetail.
aspx?caseid=4015.

13. *The Central Park Five*, Film by Ken Burns, David McMahon, and Sarah Burns, PBS, 2013.

14. Fred E. Inbau, John E. Reid, and Joseph P. Buckley, *Criminal Interrogation and Confessions, Third Edition* (Baltimore: Williams & Wilkins, 1986).

15. www.reid.com.

16. Strauss, *Barbarous Souls*, 242.

17. Inbau, Reid, Buckley, and Jayne, *Criminal Interrogation, Fifth Edition*, 103.

18. Aldert Vrij, Christian A. Meissner, and Saul M. Kassin, "Problems in Expert Deception Detection and the Risk of False Confessions: No Proof to the Contrary," *Psychology, Crime & Law* 21 (2015): 901.

19. Ruben Castaneda, "Mistaken Arrests Leave Prince George's Murder Unsolved," *Washington Post*, June 22, 2003.

20. Ibid.

21. Ibid.

22. Ibid.

23. Ibid.

24. Inbau, Reid, Buckley, and Jayne, *Criminal Interrogation, Fifth Edition*, 5.

25. US Department of Justice Office of Legal Policy, "Report to the Attorney General on the Law of Pre-Trial Interrogation: Truth in Criminal Justice Report No. 1," 1986, 57–58.

26. Saul M. Kassin, Sara C. Appleby, and Jennifer Torkildson-Perillo, "Interviewing Suspects: Practice, Science, and Future Directions," *Legal and Criminological Psychology* 15 (2010): 42.

27. Inbau, Reid, Buckley, and Jayne, *Criminal Interrogation, Fifth Edition*, 273.

28. Ken Wallertine, *Street Legal: A Guide to Pre-Trial Criminal Procedures for Police, Prosecutors, and Defenders* (Chicago: American Bar Association, 2007), 115.

29. *Brewer v. Williams*, 430 U.S. 387 (1977).

30. Inbau, Reid, Buckley, and Jayne, *Criminal Interrogation, Fifth Edition*, 344.

31. Saul M. Kassin and Karlyn McNall, "Police Interrogations and Confessions: Communicating Promises and Threats by Pragmatic Implication," *Law and Human Behavior* 15 (1991): 233.

32. Ibid.

33. Rob Warden, "How and Why Illinois Abolished the Death Penalty," *Minnesota Journal of Law & Inequality* (2012), accessed October 26, 2015, https://www.law.northwestern.edu/legalclinic/wrongfulconvictions/documents/How-and-Why-Illinois-Abolished-the-Death-Penalty.pdf.

34. Richard J. Ofshe and Richard A. Leo, "The Decision to Confess Falsely: Rational Choice and Irrational Action," *Denver University Law Review* 74 (1997): 1014.

35. Ibid.

36. Kassin and McNall, "Police Interrogations and Confessions," 233.

37. Inbau, Reid, Buckley, and Jayne, *Criminal Interrogation, Fifth Edition*, 203.

38. Louis C. Senese, *Anatomy of Interrogation Themes: The Reid Technique of Interviewing and Interrogation* (Chicago: John E. Reid and Associates, 2012),

39. Ibid,, 117.

40. Ibid., 100.

41. Ibid., 124.

42. Ibid., 160.

43. Ibid., 226.

44. "Critic's Corner–Research," John E. Reid & Associates, Inc., accessed December 31, 2015, http://www.reid.com/educational_info/criticresearch.html.

45. Saul M. Kassin and Katherine L. Kiechel, "The Social Psychology of False Confessions: Compliance, Internalization, and Confabulation," *Physical Science, American Psychological Society* 7, no. 3 (1996): 125–28.

46. "Critic's Corner–Research."

47. Melissa B. Russano, Christian A. Meissner, Fadia M. Narchet, and Saul M. Kassin, "Investigating True and False Confessions within a Novel Experimental Paradigm," *Physical Science, American Psychological Society* 16 (2005).

48. Conversation with Reid student Gary David.

49. Inbau, Reid, Buckley, and Jayne, *Criminal Interrogation, Fifth Edition*, 5.

50. Ibid., 344.

51. Saul M. Kassin and Gisli H. Gudjonsson, "True Crimes, False Confessions," *Scientific American Mind*, June 1, 2005, 26.

52. David E. Zulawski and Doublas E. Wicklander, *Practical Aspects of Interview and Interrogation, Second Edition* (Boca Raton: CRC Press, Taylor & Francis Group, 2002), 4–5.

53. Zulawski and Wicklander, *Practical Aspects of Interview and Interrogation, Second Edition*, 34–35.

54. Inbau, Reid, Buckley, and Jayne, *Criminal Interrogation, Fifth Edition*, 347.

55. *The Reid Technique of Interviewing and Interrogation (workbook).*

56. Brian C. Jayne and Joseph P. Buckley, *The Investigator Anthology: A Compilation of Articles and Essays about the Reid Technique of Interviewing and Interrogation* (Chicago: John E. Reid and Associates, 2010), 426.

57. Ibid.

58. Ibid., 427.

59. Inbau, Reid, Buckley, and Jayne, *Criminal Interrogation, Fifth Edition*, xi.

60. Ibid., 353.

61. Ibid., 352.

62. Ibid.

63. Multiple conversations with Prof. David Gary.

6. CONTAMINATION

1. Brandon L. Garrett, "The Substance of False Confessions," *Stanford Law Review* 62, no. 4 (2010): 1051–19.

2. Ibid.

3. Elizabeth F. Loftus, "Leading Questions and Eyewitness Report," *Cognitive Psychology* 7 (1975).

4. Ibid.

5. John E. B. Myers, Karen J. Saywitz, and Gail S. Goodman, "Psychological Research on Children as Witnesses: Practical Implications for Forensic Interviews and Courtroom Testimony," *Pacific McGeorge Scholarly Commons* 28 (1996): 6–91.

6. Fred E. Inbau, John E. Reid, Joseph P. Buckley, and Brian C. Jayne, *The Essentials of the Reid Technique* (Sudbury: Jones and Bartlett Publishers, 2005), 101.

7. Louis C. Senese, *Anatomy of Interrogation Themes: The Reid Technique of Interviewing and Interrogation* (Chicago: John E. Reid and Associates, 2012).

8. Ibid., 45.

9. Ibid., 67.

10. Ibid., 93.

11. Fred E. Inbau, John E. Reid, Joseph P. Buckley, and Brian C. Jayne, *Criminal Interrogation and Confessions, Fifth Edition* (Burlington: Jones and Bartlett Learning, 2013), 307.

12. Dantalion Jones, *The Handbook of Psychic Cold Reading* (Dantalion Jones, 2010), 9.

13. Ibid., 27.

14. Ibid., 25.

15. Steven Green, "Alleged Murder Witness Won't Aid Prosecutors," *Washington Post*, November 4, 1975.

16. Case file and investigator interviews with family members.

17. *48 Hours*, "Death on the Hudson," produced by Patti Aronofsky, Elena Difiore, and Lourdes Aguiar, CBS, September 12, 2015.

18. Susan Berk-Seligson, *Coerced Confessions: The Discourse of Bilingual Police Interrogations* (Berlin: Mouton de Gruyer, 2009), 100–9.

7. STATEMENT EVALUATION

1. Debbie Cenziper, "Prosecutors Build Murder Cases on Disputed Shaken Baby Syndrome Diagnosis," *Washington Post*, March 20, 2015, accessed June 27, 2015, http://www.washingtonpost.com/graphics/investigations/shaken-baby-syndrome.

2. Mark Costanzo, Netta Shaked-Schroer, and Katherine Vinson, "Juror Beliefs about Police Interrogations, False Confessions, and Expert Testimony," *Journal of Empirical Legal Studies* 7, no. 2 (2010): 231.

3. National Centre for Policing Excellence, *Practice Advice on Core Investigative Doctrine* (Centrix, 2005), 62.

4. Eric Shepherd and Andy Griffiths, *Investigative Interviewing: The Conversational Management Approach* (Oxford: Oxford University Press, 2007), 3.

5. Ibid.

6. Ibid., 3–4.

7. Ibid., 4.

8. Personal experience and interview with Reid student Gary David.

9. Tom Bevel and Ross M. Gardner, *Bloodstain Pattern Analysis: With an Introduction to Crime Scene Reconstruction, Third Edition* (Boca Raton: CRC Press, Taylor & Francis Group, 2008), 319.

10. *Serial* (podcast), "Episode One," hosted by Sarah Koenig, National Public Radio, October 3, 2014.

11. Ibid.

12. Susan Berk-Seligson, *Coerced Confessions: The Discourse of Bilingual Police Interrogations* (Berlin: Mouton de Gruyer, 2009), 100–9.

13. "Investigation Management—Record Keeping," College of Policing, Authorized Professional Practice, accessed March 1, 2015, https://www.app.college.police.uk/app-content/investigations/managing-investigations/#auditable-decision-making.

8. WITNESSES

1. Hugo Munsterberg, *On the Witness Stand: Essays on Psychology and Crime* (Greentop: Greentop Academic Press, 2009), 33–35.

2. Ibid., 35.

3. Ibid.

4. Ibid., 41.

5. *Strickler v. Green*, 527 U.S. 263 (1999).

6. Bennett L. Gershman, "Witness Coaching by Prosecutors," *Cardoza Law Review* 23 (2001): 840–42.

7. Jennifer Thompson-Cannino, *Picking Cotton: Our Memoir of Injustice and Redemption* (New York: St. Martin's Griffin, 2010), 32–33.

8. Carl Sagan, *The Demon-Haunted World: Science as a Candle in the Dark* (New York: Random House, 1996), 153–68.

9. Saul M. Kassin, Itiel E. Dror, and Jeff Kukucka, "The Forensic Confirmation Bias: Problems, Perspectives, and Proposed Solutions," *Journal of Applied Research in Memory and Cognition* 2, no. 1 (2013).

10. Itiel E. Dror and David Charlton, "Why Experts Make Errors," *Journal of Forensic Identification* 56, no. 4 (2006).

11. Ibid.

12. Ibid.

13. David Simon, *Homicide: A Year on the Killing Streets* (New York: Henry Holt and Co., 2001), 35.

14. Timothy E. Moore, Brian L. Cutler, and David Shulman, "Shaping Eyewitness and Alibi Testimony with Coercive Interview Practices," *Champion Magazine* (October 2014).

15. Fred E. Inbau, John E. Reid, Joseph P. Buckley, and Brian C. Jayne, *Criminal Interrogations and Confessions, Fifth Edition* (Burlington: Jones and Bartlett Learning, 2013), 337.

16. Gershman, "Witness Coaching by Prosecutors," 842.

17. *Brady v. Maryland*, 373 U.S. 83 (1963).

18. Paul Shechtman, "How a Man Named Brady Made History 50 Years Ago," *New York Law Journal* 249 (2013).

19. Ibid.

9. COOPERATORS AND INFORMANTS

1. Dennis G. Fitzgerald, *Informants, Cooperating Witnesses, and Undercover Investigations: A Practical Guide to Law, Policy, and Procedure* (Boca Raton: CRC Press, Taylor & Francis Group, 2015), 5.

2. http://www.vidocq.org.

3. Fitzgerald, *Informants, Cooperating Witnesses, and Undercover Investigations*, 48.

4. Alexandra Natapoff, *Snitching: Criminal Informants and the Erosion of American Justice* (New York: New York University Press, 2009), 138.

5. Ibid., 27.

6. Donald Eugene Gates, The Innocence Project, accessed November 9, 2015, http://www.innocenceproject.org/cases-false-imprisonment/donald-eugene-gates.

7. Ibid.

8. Ibid.

9. Ibid.

10. Ibid.

11. Personal interview with detective (now judge) William Hennessy.

12. Donald Eugene Gates, The Innocence Project, and personal knowledge of the case.

13. Vincent Bugliosi and Curt Gentry, *Helter Skelter: The True Story of the Manson Murders* (New York: W. W. Norton, 1974).

14. Fitzgerald, *Informants, Cooperating Witnesses, and Undercover Investigations*, 49.

15. Ibid.

16. Tom Lowenstein, "Innocent Man on Death Row?" and "Snitch Work" (a two-part article), *Philadelphia City Paper*, June 2004.

17. Ibid.

18. Ibid., and personal interviews with Tom Lowenstein and Hall's associate, who prefers to remain nameless.

19. Ibid.

20. Ibid.

21. "Report of the 1989–90 Los Angeles County Grand Jury," County of Los Angeles, California, http://www.ccfaj.org/documents/reports/jailhouse/expert/1989-1990%20LA%20County%20Grand%20Jury%20Report.pdf.

22. Ibid.

23. Fitzgerald, *Informants, Cooperating Witnesses, and Undercover Investigations*, 49.

24. "Information on MPD Rewards," Metropolitan Police Department, Washington, DC, accessed December 19, 2015, http://mpdc.dc.gov/node/1106586.

25. Fitzgerald, *Informants, Cooperating Witnesses, and Undercover Investigations*, 452.

10. PLEA BARGAINING

1. Jed S. Rakoff, "Why Innocent People Plead Guilty," *New York Review of Books*, November 20, 2014, accessed November 11, 2015, http://www.nybooks.com/articles/2014/11/20/why-innocent-people-plead-guilty.

2. Lindsey Devers, "Plea and Charge Bargaining: Research Summary," US Department of Justice Bureau of Justice Assistance, 2011, 3.

3. C. Ronald Huff and Martin Killias, eds., *Wrongful Convictions and Miscarriages of Justice: Causes and Remedies in North American and European Criminal Justice Systems* (New York: Routledge, Taylor & Francis Group, 2013), 251.

4. Alexandra Natapoff, *Snitching: Criminal Informants and the Erosion of American Justice* (New York: New York University Press, 2009), 79.

5. Ibid.

6. Steve Bogira, *Courtroom 302: A Year Behind the Scenes in an American Criminal Courthouse* (New York: Vintage Books, Random House, Inc., 2005), 38.

7. Transcript of Michael Hetrick's interrogation.

8. Ibid.

9. Ibid.

10. Transcript of Reco Coates interrogation.

11. Ibid.

12. *North Carolina v. Alford*, 400 U.S. 25 (1970).

13. "Detail List of Exonerations," National Registry of Exonerations, accessed November 11, 2015, http://www.law.umich.edu/special/exoneration/Pages/detaillist.aspx.

14. Ibid.

I I. IS THERE A BETTER WAY?

1. "The Marcus-Nelson Murders," *Kojak*, CBS, March 8, 1973.

2. Selwyn Raab, *Justice in the Back Room: The Explosive Story of Forced Confessions* (Cleveland: The World Publishing Company, 1967).

3. Fred E. Inbau, John E. Reid, Joseph P. Buckley, and Brian C. Jayne, *Criminal Interrogation and Confessions, Fourth Edition* (Burlington: Jones and Bartlett Learning, 2004).

4. "Ad Hoc Committee: Findings and Recommendations," Report to District of Columbia Superior Court Judge Lee Satterfield, February 12, 2013, 1.

5. Personal interviews with committee members.

6. *Jalonte Little v. United States* (Nos 10-CF-765 and 13-CO-481), District of Columbia Court of Appeals, 2015.

7. G. Daniel Lassiter, ed., *Interrogations, Confessions, and Entrapment* (New York: Springer, 2006), 181–95.

8. Ibid.

9. Ibid., 184–85.

10. Ibid., 183.

11. Fred E. Inbau, John E. Reid, Joseph P. Buckley, and Brian C. Jayne, *Criminal Interrogation and Confessions, Fifth Edition* (Burlington: Jones and Bartlett Learning, 2013), xiv.

12. Eric Shepherd, and Andy Griffiths, *Investigative Interviewing: The Conversational Management Approach*, 2nd ed. (Oxford: Oxford University Press, 2013), 17–18.

13. Ibid.

14. Tom Williamson, Becky Milne, and Stephen P. Savage, eds., *International Developments in Investigative Interviewing* (Abingdon: Routledge, 2012), 156–70.

15. "Guidance for Appropriate Adults," UK Home Office, 2003, accessed December 20, 2015, https://www.gov.uk/government/publications/guidance-for-appropriate-adults.

16. Adam Mason, *Scenes of a Crime*, 2011. Digital rental, directors Blue Hadaegh and Grover Babcock.

17. Raymond F. Toliver, *The Interrogator: The Story of Hanns Joachim Scharff, Master Interrogator of the Luftwaffle* (Atglen: Schiffer Publishing Company, 1997).

18. Brent Snook, Joseph Eastwood, John C. House, and Todd Barron, "Dispelling Myths and Moving Forward with PEACE," *Blue Line Magazine*, November 2010.

19. Ibid.

20. "Critics Corner, The Reid Technique," John E. Reid & Associates, accessed December 17, 2015, http://www.reid.com/educational_info/critictechnique.html.

21. Inbau, Reid, Buckley, and Jayne, *Criminal Interrogation and Confessions, Fifth Edition*, xiv.

22. Snook, Eastwood, House, and Barron, "Dispelling Myths and Moving Forward with PEACE."

12. SAFEGUARDS AND REFORM

1. "National Summit on Wrongful Convictions: Building a Systematic Approach to Prevent Wrongful Convictions," International Association of Chiefs of Police, US Department of Justice, Office of Justice Programs Wrongful Conviction Summit, August 2013.

2. Ibid., 5,

3. Ibid., 2.

4. Ibid., xiv.

5. Notes taken by author during conference.

6. Kathy Patterson, "Bill 14-3, 'Electronic Recording Procedures Act of 2002,'" Council of the District of Columbia Report, November 26, 2002.

7. Kathy Patterson, "Bill 15-1073, 'Electronic Recording Procedures Act of 2004,'" Council of the District of Columbia Report, November 26, 2002.

8. Ibid.

9. Fred E. Inbau, John E. Reid, Joseph P. Buckley, and Brian C. Jayne, *Criminal Interrogation and Confessions, Fifth Edition* (Burlington: Jones and Bartlett Learning, 2013), 50.

10. Douglas Starr, "The Interview: Do Police Interrogation Techniques Produce False Confessions?" *The New Yorker*, December 9, 2013.

11. Jan Pudlow, "The Truth about False Confessons," *The Florida Bar News*, November 1, 2011, accessed November 16, 2015, https://www.floridabar.org/DIVCOM/JN/jnnews01.nsf/8c9f13012b96736985256aa900624829/03431989320f0ce3852579330045dbe6!OpenDocument.

12. *Brady v. Maryland*, 373 U.S. 83 (1963).

13. Inbau, Reid, Buckley, and Jayne, *Criminal Interrogation*, 50.

14. IACP National Law Enforcement Policy Center, "Electronic Recording of Interrogations and Confessions: Concepts and Issues Paper," International Association of Chiefs of Police, February 2007.

15. Inbau, Reid, Buckley, and Jayne, *Criminal Interrogation*, 50–51.

16. David L. Carter, "Homicide Process Mapping: Best Practices for Increasing Homicide Clearances," US Department of Justice, Bureau of Justice Assistance, 2013, 28.

17. Inbau, Reid, Buckley, and Jayne, *Criminal Interrogation*, 352.

18. Ibid., xiv.

19. "The Reid Technique: A Position Paper," John E. Reid & Associates, Inc., 2015, accessed December 10, 2015, http://www.reid.com/educational_info/r_tips.html.

20. Saul M. Kassin, Sara C. Appleby, and Jennifer Torkildson-Perillo, "Interviewing Suspects: Practices, Science, and Future Directions," *Legal and Criminological Psychology* 15 (2010): 44.

21. "Guidance for Appropriate Adults," UK Home Office, 2003, accessed December 20, 2015, https://www.gov.uk/government/publications/guidance-for-appropriate-adults.

22. IACP National Law Enforcement Policy Center, "Interviewing and Interrogating Juveniles: Concepts and Issues Paper," International Association of Chiefs of Police, 2013.

23. Ibid.

24. Richard A. Leo, Peter J. Neufeld, Steven A. Drizin, and Andrew E. Taslitz, "Promoting Accuracy in the Use of Confession Evidence: An Argument for

Pretrial Reliability Assessments to Prevent Wrongful Convictions," University of San Francisco School of Law, Research Paper No. 2012-12, 2012, 72–82, accessed December 10, 2015, http://ssrn.com/abstract=2215885.

25. Ibid., 21.

26. Ibid., 98–99.

27. Alexandra Natapoff, *Snitching: Criminal Informants and the Erosion of American Justice* (New York: New York University Press, 2009).

28. Ibid., 192–93.

29. James M. Doyle, "NIJ's Sentinel Events Initiative: Looking Back to Look Forward," *National Institute of Justice Journal* 273 (2014): 10–14, accessed December 20, 2015, https://www.ncjrs.gov/pdffiles1/nij/244144.pdf.

30. Ibid.

31. Ibid.

13. WHAT LIES IN STORE FOR THE FUTURE?

1. "What Is the Innocence Project? How Did It Get Started?" Innocence Project, accessed December 31, 2015, http://www.innocenceproject.org/faqs/ what-is-the-innocence-project-how-did-it-get-started.

2. Steve Weinberg, "A Short History of Exposing Misconduct," Center for Public Integrity, June 26, 2003, accessed December 29, 2015, http://www. publicintegrity.org/2003/06/26/5528/short-history-exposing-misconduct.

3. Maurice Possley, Steve Mills, and Ken Armstrong, "Veteran Detective's Murder Cases Unravel," *Chicago Tribune*, December 19, 2001, accessed December 31, 2015, http://www.chicagotribune.com/news/watchdog/chi-011217confession-story.html.

4. Sean Flynn, "Brooklyn's Baddest," *GQ Magazine*, August 4, 2014, accessed January 1, 2016, http://www.gq.com/story/brooklyns-baddest.

5. Noel Brinkerhoff and Danny Biederman, "Was Louis Scarcella the Worst Detective in the Nation?" AllGov, January 13, 2015, accessed January 1, 2016, http://www.allgov.com/news/controversies/was-louis-scarcella-the-worst-homicide-detective-in-the-nation-150113?news=855357.

6. *The Good Wife*, "Nine Hours," directed by Julie Hebert, written by Robert King and Michelle King, December 12, 2010, and *The Good Wife*, "Everything Is Ending," directed by Robert King, written by Robert King and Michelle King, CBS, September 29, 2013.

7. *Rectify*, created by Ray McKinnon, Sundance TV, first season premiered April 22, 2013.

8. *Serial* (podcast), "Episode One," Hosted by Sarah Koenig, National Public Radio, October 3, 2014.

9. *Making a Murdered*, directed and written by Laura Ricciardi and Moria Demon, Netflix, December 18, 2015.

10. John Grisham, *The Innocent Man: Murder and Injustice in a Small Town* (New York: Doubleday, 2006).

11. Donald E. Shelton, "'The CSI Effect': Does It Really Exist?" *NIJ Journal* 259 (2008), accessed January 1, 2016, http://www.nij.gov/journals/259/pages/csi-effect.aspx.

12. "Police and Neighbors Join in a SoHo Search for Missing Schoolboy," *New York Times*, May 27, 1979.

13. Joseph Goldstein and William K. Rashbaum, "After 33 Years, Police Make Arrest in Case of Etan Patz," *New York Times*, May 24, 2012, accessed January 1, 2016, http://www.nytimes.com/2012/05/25/nyregion/man-claims-he-strangled-etan-patz-police-say.html.

14. Richard Esposito, "Elan Patz: Officials Discuss How the Case Was Reopened in ABC News Exclusive," ABC News, April 21, 2012, accessed January 1, 2016, http://abcnews.go.com/US/etan-patz-officials-discuss-case-reopened-abc-news/story?id=16187114.

15. Goldstein and Rashbaum, "After 33 Years, Police Make Arrest."

16. James C. McKinley Jr., "Confession to Etan Patz's Killing Came Hours into Interview, Detective Testifies," *New York Times*, September 18, 2014, accessed January 1, 2016, http://www.nytimes.com/2014/09/19/nyregion/in-etan-patz-case-detective-says-lengthy-interview-preceded-a-confession.html.

17. "Recommendations Regarding Electronic Recording of Custodial Interrogations," New York State Justice Task Force, January 2012.

18. Adam Sirois, as told to Ben Feuerherd, "Why I Said Not Guilty: Etan Patz Jury's Lone Holdout Speaks," *New York Post*, May 10, 2015, accessed January 1, 2016, http://nypost.com/2015/05/10/etan-patz-jurys-lone-pro-acquittal-holdout-speaks.

19. Ibid.

20. "National Summit on Wrongful Convictions: Building a Systematic Approach to Prevent Wrongful Convictions," International Association of Chiefs of Police, US Department of Justice, Office of Justice Programs Wrongful Conviction Summit, August 2013.

21. "NIJ's Sentinel Events Initiative," National Institute of Justice, accessed November 20, 2015, http://nij.gov/topics/justice-system/pages/sentinel-events.aspx.

22. "Exonerations in 2014," 7, National Registry of Exonerations, January 27, 2015, accessed January 1, 2016, http://www.law.umich.edu/special/exoneration/Documents/Exonerations_in_2014_report.pdf.

23. Ibid., 11.

24. Ibid., 7.

25. Ibid., 10.

26. Ibid., 11.

27. Hella Winston, "Wrongful Convictions: Can Prosecutors Reform Themselves?" Crime Report, March 27, 2014, accessed January 1, 2016, http://www.thecrimereport.org/news/inside-criminal-justice/2014-03-wrongful-convictions-can-prosecutors-reform-themselv.

28. Ibid.

29. The North Carolina Innocence Inquiry Commission: A State Agency, accessed January 1, 2016, http://www.innocencecommission-nc.gov.

30. Ibid.

31. Andrea Mitchell, Robert Windrem, and Erin McClam, "Senate Report Finds CIA Interrogation Tactics Were Ineffective," NBC News, December 9, 2014, accessed January 1, 2016, http://www.nbcnews.com/storyline/cia-torture-report/senate-report-finds-cia-interrogation-tactics-were-ineffective-n264621.

32. Robert Fein, et al. *Educing Information, Interrogation: Science and Art: Foundations for the Future* (Washington, DC: National Defense Intelligence Council, 2006), accessed December 24, 2015, https://fas.org/irp/dni/educing.pdf.

33. Christian A. Meissner and Mark Fallon, "Using Science to Improve the Practice of Interviewing and Interrogation," *Police Chief Magazine*, September 2015, accessed December 21, 2015, http://www.policechiefmagazine.org/magazine/issues/92015/pdfs/Meissner-Fallon_PoliceChief_September2015.pdf.

34. Ibid.

35. Ibid.

36. Telephone conversation with Christian Meissner, PhD, March 10, 2016

37. Meissner and Fallon, "Using Science to Improve.".

38. Conversation with Meissner.

39. Ibid.

40. "Interrogation: Expanding the Frontiers of Research and Practice," High-Value Detainee Interrogation Group, UTEP Research Communications, 2015, accessed December 12, 2015, http://fliphtml5.com/xaga/cwpt.

41. "Four Innocent Navy Men Granted Conditional Pardons by Virginia Governor: After More Than 11 years, Justice Still Eludes the Norfolk Four," Press Release, Norfolk Four, August 6, 2009, accessed January 1, 2016, http://www.norfolkfour.com/images/uploads/pdf_files/N4_Clemency_Press_Release.pdf.

42. "Investigator Tips," John E. Reid & Associates, Inc., March/April 2011, accessed January 1, 2016, http://www.reid.com/educational_info/r_tips.html?serial=1299080308558447.

43. "Four Innocent Navy Men Granted Conditional Pardons by Virginia Governor."

44. *Tice v. Johnson*, US District Court for the Eastern District of Virginia, 3:08CV69, Norfolk Four, accessed January 1, 2016, http://www.norfolkfour. com/images/uploads/pdf_files/Tice_Opinion.pdf.

45. "Case Update," Norfolk Four, accessed January 1, 2016, http://norfolk4. com/.

46. Tim McGlone, "Norfolk Ex-Detective Accused of Taking Money from Suspects," *Virginian-Pilot*, May 11, 2010, accessed January 1, 2016, http://www. pilotonline.com/news/local/crime/norfolk-ex-detective-accused-of-taking-money-from-suspects/article_1810bc23-7e33-5ae3-8634-4b2b7cad5139.html.

47. Tim McGlone, "Ex-Norfolk Detective Gets 12½ Years for Corruption," *Virginia-Pilot*, February 26, 2011, accessed January 1, 2016, http://www. pilotonline.com/news/local/crime/ex-norfolk-detective-gets-years-for-corruption/article_5980848c-0e03-5025-b7fa-a554b631a9c5.html.

BIBLIOGRAPHY

Ackley, Craig N., Shannon M. Mack, Kristen Beyer, and Philip Erdberg. *Investigative and Forensic Interviewing: A Personality-Focused Approach,* Boca Raton: CRC Press, Taylor & Francis Group, 2011.

Alder, Ken. *The Lie Detectors: The History of an American Obsession.* Lincoln: University of Nebraska Press, 2007.

Ariely, Dan. *Predictably Irrational: The Hidden Forces That Shape Our Decisions.* New York: Harper Perennial, 2009.

Aubry, Jr., Arthur S., and Rudolph R. Caputo. *Criminal Interrogation, Third Edition.* Springfield: Charles C. Thomas, 1980.

Beck, Richard. *We Believe the Children: A Moral Panic in the 1980s.* Philadelphia: Public Affairs, Perseus Books Group, 2015.

Benforado, Adam. *Unfair: The New Science of the Criminal Justice System.* New York: Crown Publishers, 2015.

Berk-Seligson, Susan. *Coerced Confessions: The Discourse of Bilingual Police Interrogations.* Berlin: Mouton de Gruyer, 2009.

Bevel, Tom, and Ross M. Gardner. *Bloodstain Pattern Analysis: With an Introduction to Crime Scene Reconstruction, Third Edition.* Boca Raton: CRC Press, Taylor & Francis Group, 2008.

Bogira, Steve. *Courtroom 302: A Year Behind the Scenes in an American Criminal Courthouse.* New York: Vintage Books, Random House, Inc., 2005.

Borchard, Edwin Montefiore. *Convicting the Innocent: Sixty-Five Actual Errors of Criminal Justice.* Garden City: Garden City Publishing Co., 1932.

Brooks, Peter. *Troubling Confessions: Speaking Guilt in Law and Literature.* Chicago: The University of Chicago Press, 2000.

Buckley, David M., and Brian C. Jayne. *Electronic Recording of Interrogations.* Chicago: John E. Reid & Associates, Inc., 2005.

Bull, Ray, Tim Valentine, and Tom Williamson, eds. *Handbook of Psychology of Investigative Interviewing: Current Developments and Future Directions.* Chichester: Wiley-Blackwell, 2009.

Carter, David L. "Homicide Process Mapping: Best Practices for Increasing Homicide Clearances." US Department of Justice, Bureau of Justice Assistance, 2013.

Carter, Elisabeth. *Analyzing Police Interviews: Laughter, Confessions, and the Tape.* London: Bloomsbury Publishing, 2011.

The Central Park Five. Film by Ken Burns, David McMahon, and Sarah Burns. PBS, 2013.

Cialdini, Robert B. *Influence: The Psychology of Persuasion.* New York: Collins Business, 2007.

Connors, Edward, Thomas Lundregan, Neal Miller, and Tom McEwen. "Convicted by Juries, Exonerated by Science: Case Studies in the Use of DNA Evidence to Establish Innocence After Trial." U.S. Department of Justice Office of Justice Programs, National Institute of Justice, June 1996.

Costanzo, Mark, Netta Shaked-Schroer, and Katherine Vinson. "Juror Beliefs about Police Interrogations, False Confessions, and Expert Testimony." *Journal of Empirical Legal Studies* 7, no. 2 (2010): 231–47.

Curtis, Timothy E. "Investigative Interviewing in England Part 1: Models for Interviewing Witnesses and Suspects." Visiting expert's paper for the 155th International Training Course of the United Nations Asia and Far East Institute for the Prevention of Crime and Treatment of Offenders.

DeClue, Gregory. *Interrogations and Disputed Confessions: A Manual for Forensic Psychological Practice*. Sarasota: Professional Resource Press, 2005.

Department of the Army. *US Intelligence and Interrogation Handbook*. Guilford: The Lyons Press, 2005.

Doyle, James M. "NIJ's Sentinel Events Initiative: Looking Back to Look Forward." *National Institute of Justice Journal* 273 (2014): 10–14. Accessed December 20, 2015. https://www.ncjrs.gov/pdffiles1/nij/244144.pdf.

Dror, Itiel E., and David Charlton. "Why Experts Make Errors." *Journal of Forensic Identification* 56, no. 4 (2006): 600–16.

Ekman, Paul. *Telling Lies: Clues to Deceit in the Marketplace, Politics, and Marriage*. New York: W. W. Norton, 2009.

Eterno, John A., and Eli B. Silverman. *The Crime Numbers Game: Management by Manipulation*. Boca Raton: CRC Press, Taylor & Francis Group, 2012.

Fein, Robert, et al. *Educing Information, Interrogation: Science and Art: Foundations for the Future*. Washington, DC: National Defense Intelligence Council, 2006. Accessed December 24, 2015. https://fas.org/irp/dni/educing.pdf.

Feld, Barry C. *Kids, Cops, and Confessions: Inside the Interrogation Room*. New York: New York University Press, 2013.

Fisher, Ronald P., and R. Edward Geiselman. *Memory-Enhancing Techniques for Investigative Interviewing: The Cognitive Interview*. Springfield: Charles C. Thomas, 1992.

Fitzgerald, Dennis G. *Informants, Cooperating Witnesses, and Undercover Investigations: A Practical Guide to Law, Policy, and Procedure*. Boca Raton: CRC Press, Taylor & Francis Group, 2015.

Garrett, Brandon L. "Contaminated Confessions Revisited." *Virginia Law Review* 101 (2015): 395–454.

Garrett, Brandon L. *Convicting the Innocent: Where Criminal Prosecutions Go Wrong*. Cambridge: Harvard University Press, 2011.

Garrett, Brandon L. "The Substance of False Confessions." *Stanford Law Review* 62, no. 4 (2010): 1051–19.

Geberth, Vernon J. *Practical Homicide Investigation: Tactics, Procedures, and Forensic Techniques, Fourth Edition*. Boca Raton: CRC Press, Taylor & Francis Group, 2006.

Gershman, Bennett L. "Witness Coaching by Prosecutors." *Cardoza Law Review* 23 (2001): 829–63.

Gordon, Nathan J., and William L. Fleisher. *Effective Interviewing & Interrogation Techniques, Second Edition*. Amsterdam: Academic Press, 2006.

Gould, Jon B. *The Innocence Commission: Preventing Wrongful Convictions and Restoring the Criminal Justice System*. New York: New York University Press, 2008.

Grisham, John. *The Innocent Man: Murder and Injustice in a Small Town*. New York: Doubleday, 2006.

Gudjonson, Gisli H. *The Psychology of Interrogations and Confessions: A Handbook*. Chichester, John Wiley & Sons, Ltd., 2003.

"Guidance for Appropriate Adults." UK Home Office, 2003. Accessed December 20, 2015. https://www.gov.uk/government/publications/guidance-for-appropriate-adults.

Hanson, Neil. *The Great Fire of London: In That Apocalyptic Year, 1666*. Hoboken: John Wiley & Sons, 2002.

Harrison, Kelly D. *Forensic Interviewing for Law Enforcement*. Xlibris Corporation, 2013.

Holmes, Warren D. *Criminal Interrogation: A Modern Format for Interrogating Criminal Suspects Based on the Intellectual Approach*. Springfield, Charles C. Thomas, Ltd., 2002.

Hroch, Miroslav, and Anna Skybova. *Ecclesia Militans: The Inquisition*. New York: Dorset Press, 1990.

Huff, C. Ronald, and Martin Killias, eds. *Wrongful Convictions and Miscarriages of Justice: Causes and Remedies in North American and European Criminal Justice Systems*. New York: Routledge, Taylor & Francis Group, 2013.

Huff, C. Ronald, Arye Rattner, and Edward Sagarin. *Convicted But Innocent: Wrongful Conviction and Public Policy*. Thousand Oaks: SAGE Publications, 1996.

IACP National Law Enforcement Policy Center. "Electronic Recording of Interrogations and Confessions: Concepts and Issues Paper." International Association of Chiefs of Police, February 2007.

IACP National Law Enforcement Policy Center. "Interviewing and Interrogating Juveniles: Concepts and Issues Paper." International Association of Chiefs of Police, 2013.

Inbau, Fred E. *Lie Detection and Criminal Interrogation, Second Edition*. Baltimore: Williams & Willkins, 1948.

Inbau, Fred E., John E. Reid, and Joseph P. Buckley. *Criminal Interrogation and Confessions, Third Edition*. Baltimore: Williams & Wilkins, 1986.

Inbau, Fred E., John E. Reid, Joseph P. Buckley, and Brian C. Jayne. *Criminal Interrogation and Confessions, Fourth Edition*. Burlington: Jones and Bartlett Learning, 2004.

Inbau, Fred E., John E. Reid, Joseph P. Buckley, and Brian C. Jayne. *Criminal Interrogation and Confessions, Fifth Edition*. Burlington: Jones and Bartlett Learning, 2013.

Inbau, Fred E., John E. Reid, Joseph P. Buckley, and Brian C. Jayne. *The Essentials of the Reid Technique: Criminal Interrogation and Confessions*. Sudbury: Jones and Bartlett Publishers, 2005.

"Interrogation: Expanding the Frontiers of Research and Practice." High-Value Detainee Interrogation Group, UTEP Research Communications, 2015. Accessed December 12, 2015. http://fliphtml5.com/xaga/cwpt.

Jayne, Brian C., and Joseph P. Buckley. *The Investigator Anthology: A Compilation of Articles and Essays about the Reid Technique of Interviewing and Interrogation*. Chicago: John E. Reid and Associates, 2010.

Jones, Antonne M. *Equal Verdicts*. Maple Shade: Clear Vision Publishing, 2011.

Jones, Dantalion. *The Handbook of Psychic Cold Reading*. Dantalion Jones, 2010.

Kadri, Sadakat. *The Trial: A History, from Socrates to O. J. Simpson*. London: Harper Perennial, 2006.

Kassin, Saul M. "Why Confessions Trump Innocence." *American Psychologist* 67, no. 6 (2012): 431–45.

Kassin, Saul M., Sara C. Appleby, and Jennifer Torkildson Perillo. "Interviewing Suspects: Practices, Science, and Future Directions." *Legal and Criminological Psychology* 15 (2010): 39–55.

Kassin, Saul M., Itiel E. Dror, and Jeff Kukucka. "The Forensic Confirmation Bias: Problems, Perspectives, and Proposed Solutions." *Journal of Applied Research in Memory and Cognition* 2, no. 1 (2013): 42–52.

Kassin, Saul M., and Gisli H. Gudjonsson. "True Crimes, False Confessions." *Scientific American Mind*, June 1, 2005.

Kassin, Saul M., and Katherine L. Kiechel. "The Social Psychology of False Confessions: Compliance, Internalization, and Confabulation." *Physical Science, American Psychological Society* 7, no. 3 (1996): 125–28.

Kassin, Saul M., and Karlyn McNall. "Police Interrogations and Confessions: Communicating Promises and Threats by Pragmatic Implication." *Law and Human Behavior* 15 (1991).

Kenrick, Douglas T., Steven L. Neuberg, and Robert B. Cialdini. *Social Psychology: Goals in Interaction, Fifth Edition*. Boston: Allyn & Bacon, 2005.

Kidd, W. R. *Police Interrogation*. New York: R. V. Basuino, 1940.

Kirschenbaum, Aaron. *Self-Incrimination in Jewish Law*. New York: Burning Bush Press, 1970.

Lane, Roger. *Murder in America: A History*. Columbus: Ohio State University Press, 1997.

Langbein, John H. *Torture and the Law of Proof: Europe and England in the Ancien Régime*. Chicago: The University of Chicago Press, 2006.

Lassiter, G. Daniel, ed. *Interrogations, Confessions, and Entrapment*. New York: Springer, 2006.

Lassiter, G. Daniel, and Christian A. Meissner, eds. *Police Interrogations and False Confessions: Current Research, Practice, and Policy Recommendations*. Washington, DC: American Psychological Association, 2010.

Lavine, Emanuel H. *Secrets of the Metropolitan Police*. Garden City: The Vanguard Press, Inc., 1936.

Lavine, Emanuel H. *The Third Degree*. Garden City: The Vanguard Press, Inc., 1930.

Leo, Richard A. *Police Interrogation and American Justice*. Cambridge: Harvard University Press, 2008.

Leo, Richard A., Peter J. Neufeld, Steven A. Drizin, and Andrew E. Taslitz. "Promoting Accuracy in the Use of Confession Evidence: An Argument for Pretrial Reliability Assessments to Prevent Wrongful Convictions." University of San Francisco School of Law, Research Paper No. 2012-12, 2012. Accessed December 10, 2015. http://ssrn.com/abstract= 2215885.

Levinson, Sanford, ed. *Torture: A Collection*. Oxford: Oxford University Press, 2004.

Loftus, Elizabeth F. "Leading Questions and Eyewitness Report." *Cognitive Psychology* 7 (1975): 550–72.

Loftus, Elizabeth F., and Katherine Ketcham. *The Myth of Repressed Memory: False Memories and Allegations of Sexual Abuse*. New York: St. Martin's Press, 1994.

Lord, Vivian B., and Allen D. Cowan. *Interviewing in Criminal Justice: Victims, Witnesses, Clients, and Suspects*. Sudbury: Jones and Bartlett Publishers, 2011.

Lowenstein, Tom. "Innocent Man on Death Row?" and "Snitch Work" (a two-part article). *Philadelphia City Paper*, June 2004.

Macdonald, John M., and David L. Michaud. *Criminal Interrogation*. Denver: Apache Press, 1992.

Maidment, MaDonna. *When Justice Is a Game: Unravelling Wrongful Convictions in Canada*. Black Point: Fernwood Publishing, 2009.

Maas, Peter. *Serpico*. New York: HarperCollins Publishers, Inc., 2005.

Meissner, Christian A., Allison D. Redlich, Sujeeta Bhatt, and Susan Brandon. "Interview and Interrogation Methods and Their Effects on True and False Confessions." *Campbell Collaboration*, June 25, 2012.

Meissner, Christian A., Allison D. Redlich, Stephen W. Michael, Jacqueline R. Evans, Catherine R. Camilletti, Sujeeta Bhatt, and Susan Brandon. "Accusatorial and Information-Gathering Interrogation Methods and Their Effects on True and False Confessions: A Meta-Analytic Review." *Journal of Experimental Criminology* 10 (December 2014): 459–86.

Memon, Amina A., Aldert Vrij, and Ray Bull. *Psychology and Law: Truthfulness, Accuracy, and Credibility, Second Edition*. Chichester: John Wiley & Sons, 2003.

Milne, Rebecca, and Ray Bull. *Investigative Interviewing: Psychology and Practice*. Chichester: John Wiley & Sons, Ltd., 1999.

Moore, Timothy E., Brian L. Cutler, and David Shulman. "Shaping Eyewitness and Alibi Testimony with Coercive Interview Practices." *Champion Magazine* (October 2014): 35–42.

Morton, James. *The First Detective: The Life and Revolutionary Times of Eugene-Francois Vidocq, Criminal, Spy and Private Eye*. London: Ebury Press, Random House, 2004.

Munsterberg, Hugo. *On the Witness Stand: Essays on Psychology and Crime*. Greentop: Greentop Academic Press, 2009.

Myers, John E. B., Karen J. Saywitz, and Gail S. Goodman. "Psychological Research on Children as Witnesses: Practical Implications for Forensic Interviews and Courtroom Testimony." *Pacific McGeorge Scholarly Commons* 28 (1996): 6–91.

Napier, Michael R. *Behavior, Truth and Deception: Applying Profiling and Analysis to the Interview Process*. Boca Raton: CRC Press, Taylor & Francis Group, 2010.

Natapoff, Alexandra. *Snitching: Criminal Informants and the Erosion of American Justice*. New York: New York University Press, 2009.

National Centre for Policing Excellence. *Practice Advice on Core Investigative Doctrine*. Centrix, 2005.

"National Summit on Wrongful Convictions: Building a Systematic Approach to Prevent Wrongful Convictions." International Association of Chiefs of Police, US Department of Justice, Office of Justice Programs Wrongful Conviction Summit, August 2013.

Nierenerg, Gerald I., and Henry H. Calero. *How to Read a Person Like a Book*. New York: Simon & Schuster, 1973.

"An Offer You Can't Refuse: How U.S. Federal Prosecutors Force Drug Defendants to Plead Guilty." Human Rights Watch, 2013.

Ofshe, Richard J., and Richard A. Leo. "The Decision to Confess Falsely: Rational Choice and Irrational Action." *Denver University Law Review* 74 (1997): 979–1122.

Oxburgh, Gavin, Trond Myklebust, Tim Grant, and Rebecca Milne, eds. *Communication in Investigative and Legal Contexts*. Malden: John Wiley & Sons, Ltd., 2016.

Potter, Gary. *The History of Policing in the United States*. Richmond, EKU Police Studies. Accessed December 2, 2015, http://plsonline.eku.edu/insidelook/history-policing-united-states-part-1.

Raab, Selwyn. *Justice in the Back Room: The Explosive Story of Forced Confessions*. Cleveland: The World Publishing Company, 1967.

Rabon, Don. *Investigative Discourse Analysis*. Durham: Carolina Academic Press, 1994.

Rabon, Don, and Tanya Chapman. *Interviewing and Interrogation, Second Edition*. Durham: Carolina Academic Press, 2009.

Rabon, Don, and Tanya Chapman. *Persuasive Interviewing: A Forensic Case Analysis*. Durham: Carolina Academic Press, 2007.

Radelet, Michael L., Hugo Adam Bedau, and Constance E. Putnam. *In Spite of Innocence: The Ordeals of 400 Americans Wrongly Convicted of Crimes Punishable by Death*. Boston: Northeastern University Press, 1992.

Rakoff, Jed S. "Why Innocent People Plead Guilty." *New York Review of Books*, November 20, 2014. Accessed November 11, 2015. http://www.nybooks.com/articles/2014/11/20/why-innocent-people-plead-guilty.

"The Reid Technique: A Position Paper." John E. Reid & Associates, Inc., 2015. Accessed December 10, 2015. http://www.reid.com/educational_info/r_tips.html.

The Reid Technique of Interviewing and Interrogation (workbook). Chicago: John E. Reid & Associates, Inc., 2007.

"Report of the 1989–90 Los Angeles County Grand Jury." County of Los Angeles, California. http://www.ccfaj.org/documents/reports/jailhouse/expert/1989-1990%20LA%20County%20Grand%20Jury%20Report.pdf.

Roberson, Cliff, and Scott Mire. *Ethics for Criminal Justice Professionals*. Boca Raton: CRC, Taylor & Francis Group, 2010.

Rossmo, D. Kim. *Criminal Investigative Failures*. Boca Raton: CRC Press, Taylor & Francis Group, 2009.

Rowland, Ian. *The Full Facts Book of Cold Reading, Sixth Edition*. Ian Rowland Limited, 2014.

Russano, Melissa B., Christian A. Meissner, Fadia M. Narchet, and Saul M. Kassin. "Investigating True and False Confessions within a Novel Experimental Paradigm." *Physical Science, American Psychological Society* 16 (2005).

Sagan, Carl. *The Demon-Haunted World: Science as a Candle in the Dark*. New York: Random House, 1996.

Scheck, Barry, Peter Neufeld, and Jim Dwyer. *Actual Innocence: When Justice Goes Wrong and How to Make It Right*. New York: Penguin Group, Ltd., 2003.

Senese, Louis C. *Anatomy of Interrogation Themes: The Reid Technique of Interviewing and Interrogation*. Chicago: John E. Reid and Associates, 2012.

Shechtman, Paul. "How a Man Named Brady Made History 50 Years Ago." *New York Law Journal* 249 (2013).

Shepherd, Eric, and Andy Griffiths. *Investigative Interviewing: The Conversational Management Approach*, 2nd ed.. Oxford: Oxford University Press, 2013.

Silberman, Charles E. *Criminal Violence, Criminal Justice*. New York: Vintage Books, Random House, 1980.

Simon, Dan. *In Doubt: The Psychology of the Criminal Justice Process*. Cambridge, MA: Harvard University Press, 2012.

Simon, David. *Homicide: A Year on the Killing Streets*. New York: Henry Holt and Co., 2001.

Skerker, Michael. *An Ethics of Interrogation*. Chicago: University of Chicago Press, 2010.

Skolnick, Jerome H., and James J. Fyfe. *Above the Law: Police and the Excessive Use of Force*. New York: The Free Press, 1993.

Snook, Brent, Joseph Eastwood, John C. House, and Todd Barron. "Dispelling Myths and Moving Forward with PEACE." *Blue Line Magazine*, November 2010.

Soderman, Harry, and John J. O'Connell. *Modern Criminal Investigation*. New York: Funk & Wagnall Co., 1935.

Softley, Paul, David Brown, Bob Forde, George Mair, and David Moxon. *Police Interrogation: An Observational Study in Four Police Stations, Home Office Research Study No. 61*. London: Her Majesty's Stationery Office, 1980.

Starr, Douglas. "The Interview: Do Police Interrogation Techniques Produce False Confessions?" *The New Yorker*, December 9, 2013.

Strauss, David L. *Barbarous Souls*. Evanston, IL: Northwestern University Press, 2010.

Thomas III, George C., and Richard A. Leo. *Confessions of Guilt: From Torture to Miranda and Beyond*. Oxford: Oxford University Press, 2012.

Toliver, Raymond F. *The Interrogator: The Story of Hanns Joachim Scharff, Master Interrogator of the Luftwaffe*. Atglen: Schiffer Publishing Company, 1997.

US Department of Justice Office of Legal Policy. "Report to the Attorney General on the Law of Pre-Trial Interrogation: Truth in Criminal Justice Report No. 1," 1986.

Vrij, Aldert. *Detecting Lies and Deceit: Pitfalls and Opportunities, Second Edition*. West Sussex: John Wiley & Sons, Ltd., 2008.

Wagenaar, Willem Albert, and Hans Crombag. *The Popular Policeman and Other Cases: Psychological Perspectives on Legal Evidence*. Amsterdam: Amsterdam University Press, 2005.

Wagenaar, W. A., P. J. van Koppen, and H. F. M. Crombag. *Anchored Narratives: The Psychology of Criminal Evidence*. Hertfordshire: Harvester Weatsheaf, 1993.

Wallertine, Ken. *Street Legal: A Guide to Pre-Trial Criminal Procedure for Police, Prosecutors, and Defenders*. Chicago: American Bar Association, 2007.

Walsh, David, Gavin E. Oxburgh, Allison D. Redlich, and Trond Myklebust, eds. *International Developments and Practices in Investigative Interviewing and Interrogation, Volume 2: Suspects*. London: Routledge, Taylor & Francis Group, 2015.

Walters, Stan B. *Principles of Kinesic Interview and Interrogation, Second Edition*. Boca Raton: CRC Press, 2003.

Wambaugh, Joseph. *The Blooding*. New York: Perigord Press, 1989.

Warden, Rob, and Steven Drizin, eds. *True Stories of False Confessions*. Evanston: Northwestern University Press, 2009.

Wells, Tom, and Richard A. Leo. *The Wrong Guys: Murder, False Confessions, and the Norfolk Four*. New York: The New Press, 2008.

Whitman, James Q. *The Origins of Reasonable Doubt: Theological Roots of the Criminal Trial*. New Haven: Yale University Press, 2008.

Willemse, Cornelius W. *Behind the Green Lights*. New York: Alfred A. Knopf, 1931.

Williamson, Tom, Becky Milne, and Stephen P. Savage, eds. *International Developments in Investigative Interviewing*. Abingdon: Routledge, 2012.

Wilson, Christopher P. *Cop Knowledge: Police Power and Cultural Narrative in Twentieth-Century America*. Chicago: The University of Chicago Press, 2000.

Wilson, Derek. *The Tower: The Tumultuous History of the Tower of London from 1078*. New York: Charles Scriber's Sons, 1978.

Woods, Jr., DeVere D. *O'Hara's Fundamentals of Criminal Investigation, Eighth Edition*. Springfield: Charles C. Thomas Publisher, Ltd., 2013.

Wright, Lawrence. *Remembering Satan*. New York: Alfred A. Knopf, Inc., 1994.

Wrightsman, Lawrence S., and Saul M. Kassin. *Confessions in the Courtroom*. Newbury Park: Sage Publications, 1993.

Yeschke, Charles L. *The Art of Investigative Interviewing: A Human Approach to Testimonial Evidence.* Boston: Butterworth-Heinemann, 1997.

Zalman, Marvin, and Julia Carrano. *Wrongful Conviction and Criminal Justice Reform: Making Justice.* New York: Routledge, Taylor and Francis Group, 2014.

Zulawski, David E., and Doublas E. Wicklander. *Practical Aspects of Interview and Interrogation, Second Edition.* Boca Raton: CRC Press, Taylor & Francis Group, 2002.

INDEX

ABOUT THE AUTHOR

Jim Trainum was with the Washington, DC, Metropolitan Police Department for a total of twenty-seven years—the last nineteen of which he was assigned to the homicide branch. During his career, Trainum worked on numerous local and federal task forces and joint projects. He created and was the director of his department's Violent Crime Case Review Project, which oversaw the review of old homicide cases. Trainum is a member of the International Homicide Investigators Association, the Homicide Research Working Group, the International Investigative Interviewing Research Group, and the Vidocq Society. He is also a member of the board of the Mid-Atlantic Cold Case Homicide Investigators Association. Trainum has presented at universities, police academies, prosecutor's offices, legislative bodies, and conferences on various topics ranging from cold case investigative techniques, criminal profiling, avoiding investigative pitfalls, videotaping of interrogations, police reform issues, and false confessions. He is the recipient of the Ethics in Law Enforcement Award, an honorary Professional Associate Professorship from Marymount University, and the 2009 Champion of Justice Award from the Innocence Project. Trainum is the coauthor of a chapter in the book *Criminal Investigative Failures*, in which he details the circumstances surrounding a false confession that he obtained in 1994. He is the author of the article "'I Did It'—Confession Contamination and Evaluation," that was published in the June 2014 web edition of *The Police Chief* magazine. In 2010, Trainum completed an assessment of the interrogation practices of the New Orleans Police Department at the request of the US Department of Justice. In 2014, he appeared on the NPR podcast *Serial*, where he discussed the investigation of the 1993 murder of Hae Lee by the Baltimore, Maryland, Police Department. Trainum also reviews cases as a volunteer with the National Center for Missing & Exploited Children as well as the Parents of Murdered Children's Second Opinion Services program.

EAST ¹/₁₇